LANGUAGE AND SCOTTISH LITERATURE

SCOTTISH LANGUAGE AND LITERATURE

General Editor
Douglas Gifford
University of Glasgow

ASSISTANT EDITOR AND PROJECT CONVENOR
Dr Beth Dickson
University of Glasgow

ADVISORY TEAM
James N. Alison
Her Majesty's Inspectorate
Dr John Corbett
University of Glasgow
Ann Donovan
Hillhead Academy
David Drever
Kirkwall Academy
Morna Fleming
Beath Academy
Gordon Gibson
University of Paisley: Craigie Campus
John Hodgart
Dalry Academy
Alan MacGillivray
University of Strathclyde
Dr James McGonigle
St Andrews College, Bearsden
Jan Mathieson
Ardrossan Academy
Dr Elaine Petrie
Falkirk College of Technology
Ronald Renton
St Aloysius College
George Sutherland
Scottish Examinations Board

Other volumes in the series:
Scottish Literature: A Study Guide
Edited by Douglas Gifford and Beth Dickson
Teaching Scottish Literature: Curriculum and Classroom Applications
Edited by Alan MacGillivray

Thanks are due to Professor R. J. Lyall whose vision and hard work developed the postgraduate courses from which this project grew. Thanks are also due to Jackie Jones and the staff of Edinburgh University Press who were consistently encouraging and saw the proposal through to publication.

Language and Scottish Literature

SCOTTISH LANGUAGE AND LITERATURE

———— • ————

JOHN CORBETT

EDINBURGH UNIVERSITY PRESS

© John Corbett, 1997

Edinburgh University Press
22 George Square, Edinburgh EH8 9LF

Typeset in Linotype Jansen
by Koinonia Ltd, Bury
and printed and bound in Great Britain

A CIP record for this book is available from the
British Library

ISBN 0 7486 0826 5

Marco Polo describes a bridge, stone by stone.
'But which is the stone that supports the bridge?' Kublai Khan asks.
'The bridge is not supported by one stone or another,' Marco
answers, 'but by the line of the arch that they form.'
Kublai Khan remains silent, reflecting. Then he adds: 'Why do you
speak of the stones? It is only the arch that matters to me.'
Polo answers: 'Without the stones there is no arch.'

Italo Calvino, *Invisible Cities*
(trans. William Weaver)

CONTENTS

SCOTTISH LANGUAGE
AND LITERATURE

In 1987 the Department of Scottish Literature in the University of Glasgow launched its ambitious three-year distance-taught M.Phil. programme in Scottish Literature and Language, covering the entire range of Lowland Scottish writing from its beginnings to the present day. The eighteen volumes which comprise the course form the largest coherent body of materials and criticism available on the subject. By 1994, interest in these materials, fuelled by developments in Scottish Examination Board examinations at Standard Grade, Higher and Sixth Year levels, had led the Department to consider making some of these materials more widely available to teachers and students. Aided by a generous New Initiative grant from the University of Glasgow, and the appointment of Dr Beth Dickson as Development Officer, work on the feasibility of such adaptation began in 1994. An Advisory Team was established, with a view to taking advice from interested colleagues in schools and colleges regarding suitable forms of adaptation, exemplars and complementary relationships with cognate projects such as *The Kist/A' Chiste* (1996), that splendid anthology of materials for the earlier school from the Scottish Consultative Council on the Curriculum.

In the light of the increased recognition of Scottish literature and language as an important part of Scottish culture generally, and the new emphasis given to it in Higher and CSYS courses (presently restructuring as *Higher Still*), the volumes were planned to give essential guidance in three separate but linked areas: in literature, in language and in practical exploitation of these in classrooms and seminars. Recognising that many teachers and students are unfamiliar with Scottish literature, and considering the wide range of genres and approaches within its traditions of nearly 700 years, the volumes seek to supply essential guidance to older periods as well as modern (though understandably the emphasis is biased towards the modern), to supply generous examples and to indicate where helpful materials may be found. That said, the volumes also hope to engage and satisfy the reader whose interest is more general.

The three volumes can each stand alone, but can also be linked to each other. The Advisory Team and the volume editors and authors gave careful consideration to establishing a shared context for their specific contributions. The volumes thus share a tolerant and wide-ranging view of what constitutes Scottish writing and language, and encourage both an awareness of the plurality of Scottish identity and culture and a respect for the ways in which those identities and cultures are constantly developing and changing.

The first volume, *Scottish Literature: A Study Guide*, gives basic intro-ductions to the great periods of Scottish literature: the medieval, the eighteenth century, the neglected nineteenth century, the 'Scottish Renaissance' of the twentieth century, and the contemporary and prolific revival of fiction, poetry and drama today. It gives in-depth treatment of major texts from authors such as Henryson and Scott to MacDiarmid, Gunn and Gibbon, contemporary poets like MacCaig, Morgan and Lochhead, as well as many others. Throughout, the aim is to present Scottish writing and writers in accessible and stimulating discussion which asks the reader questions as well as suggesting further authors, texts and possible comparisons. The second volume, *Language and Scottish Literature*, explores varieties of Scots and links them with literary studies; investigating questions of vocabulary and metaphor, it looks at language in use, examining sounds and structures, narrative and issues going beyond the text. In keeping with the aim of the series to look at Scottish culture of older periods, the volume ends with a discussion of the language of older Scottish texts. The third volume, *Teaching Scottish Literature: Curriculum and Classroom Applications*, en-gages with current debates concerning what constitutes a Scottish text, the place of Scottish texts in an English course, the theoretical issues in teaching such texts, and the use of varieties of Scots in courses and writing. The volume gives extensive and varied exemplars while suggesting exemplars for interdisciplinary use and how to use writing workshops.

Douglas Gifford
Series General Editor

COPYRIGHT

Where appropriate, every effort has been made to trace the copyright holders of the literary material quoted. The author apologises for any omissions. The poems quoted include: Kate Armstrong, 'This is the Laund', and Sheena Blackhall, 'Bairn Sang', from *The New Makars* (Mercat Press); John Graham, 'Jakobsen'; Alan Jackson, 'Young Politician'; Tom Leonard, 'Hercules Unzipped', 'Right inuff', 'Paroakial', 'Unrelated Incidents (2)' from *Intimate Voices* (Galloping Dog); Liz Lochhead, 'The Inventory', from *Dreaming Frankenstein* (Polygon); Edwin Morgan, 'A View of Things' and 'Glasgow Sonnets' from *Selected Poems* (Carcanet); Edwin Muir, 'Scotland's Winter' and 'The Late Wasp', from *Selected Poems* (Faber and Faber). I am also most grateful to Bill Findlay and Martin Bowman for making available the text of their unpublished translation of Michel Tremblay's *The House among the Stars*.

ACKNOWLEDGEMENTS

Thanks are due to numerous people who contributed, directly and indirectly, to this book, and space permits me to name only a few. Douglas Gifford, of the University of Glasgow's Scottish Literature Department, and Jackie Jones, of Edinburgh University Press, provided the opportunity to write the book, and Beth Dickson helped to coordinate the Scottish Language and Literature project as a whole. Their supervision combined the necessary enthusiasm with a light touch. Catherine Macafee's as yet unpublished coursework for the Scottish Literature distance-taught M.Phil. degree was a source of inspiration and a standard to aspire to. Undergraduate students in the 'Stylistics and Scottish Literature' course at the University of Glasgow survived earlier versions of the present material, and their responses informed later improvements. Beth Dickson, Catherine Macafee, Chrystine Ray and Christian Kay read and commented on drafts of the manuscript; Professor Kay's notes and queries were especially detailed and valuable. The faults which remain, despite best advice, are naturally my own. Finally, special thanks are due to Chrys Ray for her support, encouragement and patience throughout the writing of this book.

John Corbett

1

———— • ————

VARIETIES OF SCOTS

AIMS

For almost as long as linguistics and literature have been independent academic disciplines, aspects of linguistic theory have been applied to literary studies. Known variously as poetics, stylistics or, more recently, literary linguistics, the application of linguistic theory has resulted in a powerful set of analytical techniques which help us to account for the various ways in which literary texts might be interpreted. These techniques have also been extended to include the interpretation of such non-literary texts as journalistic articles, advertisements and even scientific papers.

To date, however, there has been little systematic attempt to apply linguistic theory to the interpretation of Scottish texts, literary and non-literary. Some extremely useful discussions exist in journals, books and university courses (e.g. Aitken 1977; Aitken and McArthur 1979; Agutter 1988; Macafee 1981, 1983, c. 1988, c. 1989; McClure 1995; and Murison 1977). Nevertheless, in all but a few cases (notably McClure 1979, 1995; and Macafee c. 1988, c. 1989), these discussions focus on very specific aspects of Scots and Scottish Literature – for example, the literary language of Older Scots (e.g. Agutter 1988), or a single author, like John Galt's use of Scots in a text such as *The Entail* (McClure 1981a). Most book-length studies tend to consider the language from a fairly general point of view (e.g. Letley 1988a, 1988b). The purpose of the present book, then, is to provide an accessible overview of current linguistic theories, and to suggest ways in which they might be applied to the interpretation of a range of mainly modern Scottish texts, literary and non-literary. A considerable omission in this project is, of course, literature in Gaelic. The omission is reluctant; but, since I have neither the space nor the competence to deal with Gaelic stylistics, that task must be left to another hand. I hope, however, that many of the analytical techniques and theoretical principles found in these pages can be transferred to the reading of Gaelic texts. The focus here, however, will be on varieties of lowland Scots and Scottish English.

1

WHAT IS SCOTS?

Since the linguistic situation in modern Scotland is extremely complex, it is necessary at the outset to define our terms. What do we mean by 'Scots' when we use it to denote a variety or varieties of language?

This simple activity (based on Macafee c. 1989) is designed to encourage you to reflect upon your own awareness of some Scots/English items, and to consider your attitude to them. In the following list, categorise the words and phrases as 'Scots' or 'English'. Then say whether or not you would use the word/phrase, and, if your answer is yes, in what context you might use it. Finally, say whether or not you think the form is stigmatised (i.e. whether or not it is 'bad' usage).

Form	Scots or English?	Would you use it (when)?	Stigmatised?
1. Whit dae ye cry it?			
2. Who's first?			
3. gallus			
4. Listen to thae loons and quines.			
5. I'll be there by the back of nine.			
6. Yir patter's like watter.			
7. I ken that!			
8. She lives up the close.			
9. Are ye feart?			
10. a gigot chop			
11. aiblins			
12. a scunner			
13. procurator fiscal			
14. barrie			
15. Is he back with the messages?			
16. culpable homicide			
17 a sore head			
18 rone pipes			
19 wee			
20 bramble			

In fact, all these words and phrases could arguably be termed 'Scots' – although Scots of different kinds. 'Patter' (meaning 'fluency') is urban Scots, often associated with Glasgow; 'loons and quines' (young men and women) is current in the rural north-east; 'aiblins' (perhaps) is literary Scots, now confined to written texts; 'culpable homicide' is a term in Scots law equivalent to English 'manslaughter'; 'procurator fiscal' has no English equivalent, but is close to 'district attorney' in the USA; 'wee' is a widely-used Scots term which even finds its way into the speech of non-Scots, usually in such phrases as 'a wee dram' (a little whisky).

As you go through your own answers in the second and third columns, you'll probably find – if you're resident in Scotland – that you use some terms but not others, and that some terms (e.g. 'gallus', 'barrie', meaning 'bold' and 'good') are stigmatised while others (e.g. 'culpable homicide', 'rone pipes') are not. Indeed, it might come as a surprise to some Scots that items like 'a sore head' (headache), 'who's first' (who's next) and 'rones' (the horizontal gutters along the eaves of a roof) are in fact peculiar to Scotland. Such terms are referred to as 'covert Scotticisms' (Aitken 1979: 106–7).

The point of this brief activity is to demonstrate that there are varieties of Scots, which may be categorised in different ways: geographically, socially, in terms of the urban–rural split, in terms of register (that is, the language of different situations, such as the law, fishing, house-construction, etc.), or in terms of being literary or non-literary. This book will deal only briefly with the description and development of these varieties – for more extensive discussions, see, for example, Templeton (1973); Murison (1977); Aitken and McArthur (1979); or Kay (1986) – but the fact that there is not one variety but several different varieties of Scots is important for literary linguistics.

Although this activity focuses on the vocabulary of Scots, it is also important to recognise that a variety can be distinguished by other linguistic features. Varieties have distinctive grammatical features – for example, grammatical inflexions indicating tense, or particular pre-positions, or idiosyncratic word-orders. Scots has a distinctive '-it' or '-t' past inflexion, which occurs in Scots 'tellt' ('told'). Varieties also have distinctive discourse features, such as the Scots use of *see* to intro-duce a new topic (as in Margaret Hamilton's 'Lament for a Lost Dinner Ticket', which begins: 'See ma mammy/see ma dinner ticket …').

To these dialectal features may be added features of accent – the pronunciation associated with a particular variety. This is not a neces-sary association – Standard English texts can be pronounced in a Scot-tish accent, and rich Scots texts could be pronounced in an American or Australian accent – but normally varieties will have an associated accent or accents. There is a great range of Scottish accents, most containing short vowel sounds in words like *greed, bath, pool* and a strongly-pronounced /r/ before the consonant in words like *girl, heard, spurt*. All these features – vocabulary, grammar, discourse organisation and accents – make up the Scots language system (or systems).

Stylistics in general is concerned with showing how the selection of options from the language system can result in a particular interpretation. The Scots language system is not, as we have seen, monolithic. Stylistic effects can therefore be achieved by choosing from the different varieties of Scots – urban Scots might produce one type of effect, rural Scots another, legal or technical Scots another again. The fact that some of these forms might be stigmatised can be useful in a variety of ways too: for example, as part of character development, or to promote identification with or rejection of members of a particular so-cial group (stigmatised Scots is largely associated with the urban work-ing classes). How did these varieties come into being?

A BRIEF HISTORICAL SURVEY

Older Scots is conventionally dated from AD 1100–1700. These six centuries take the development of lowland Scots from just after the Norman Conquest to just before the Union of Parliaments and the effective creation of Great Britain.

The linguistic ancestor of Scots was a blend of Old English (OE) and Old Norse (ON), as spoken by the inhabitants of northern England between the time of the first Viking invasions of around AD 800 and the Norman Conquest of 1066. Relatively few people in Scotland would have spoken this Anglo-Norse variety, although in some places, like the northern islands, Viking influence was strong – indeed a Norwegian variety, Norn, was spoken in Shetland until the end of the nineteenth century. However, the dominant language in Scotland between AD 800 and 1066 was a variety of Gaelic, sometimes called 'Ersche' (Irish) because it had arrived in Scotland with an invading tribe from Ireland, back in the sixth century AD. This was the language of the Scottish court by the time of the arrival of William the Conqueror in England.

The Norman Conquest had an indirect but decisive role in the history of Scots. The deposed English monarchy sought refuge in Scot-land, the princess Margaret eventually marrying the Scottish king, Malcolm III (c. 1031–93). Many English refugees followed their past rulers, swelling the ranks of northern English speakers in southern Scotland. Relationships with the new regime in the south were later established, however, to the extent that David I, Malcolm's successor, was educated at the court of Henry I of England. On his return to Scotland, David introduced the feudal system to Scotland, granting lands to Norman barons, and he also established burghs, which drew further waves of northern English speakers to the south of Scotland. By this time, the Anglo-Norse variety of these settlers was beginning to show signs of the Norman French language of their feudal masters.

Traces of the earlier linguistic situation can still be found in Scotland today. Gaelic is spoken and written in daily life in the north-west of Scotland and the islands. It has a regular media presence on BBC Radio Scotland, and a recent revival in the fortunes of the language has been marked by an upsurge in films and television programmes, partly funded by the UK government's Gaelic Film Fund.

OE and ON traces can still be found in common usage, both in northern England and also in Scotland. The kind of pronunciation which we hear in the Scots nonsense-sentence 'There's a moose loose aboot this hoose' is very close to the Old English pronunciation of 'mūs' ('mouse') and 'hūs' ('house'), for example. The vowel is shorter but the quality is similar to that of Old English. Moreover, common Scots words like 'kirk' and 'brig' are Norse-influenced equivalents of Saxon English 'church' and 'bridge'. Indeed, the Norse influence is one of the major features which differentiates Scots, and much northern English, from southern English (Murison 1977; Smith 1994): even the current Norwegian and Danish words for 'vacuum cleaner' ('støvsuger') is almost a compound of two cognate Scots words still heard today: 'stour' (dust) and 'souk' (suck).

Nevertheless, the Scots tongue has obviously changed dramatically since 1100. As we have seen, the Norman influence had as deep an effect on the speech of the lowland Scottish kingdom as it had on the language of the kingdom over the border. In Scotland, the local variety, which became the dominant language of the Lothian area and the Scottish court, was called, simply, 'Inglis'. By the seventeenth century, Inglis had spread throughout lowland Scotland, displacing Gaelic in the south-west. Gaelic was still dominant in the northern Highlands until the failed Jacobite risings of the eighteenth century, after which the Celtic language was driven underground for a while, hanging on only in the geographical peripheries of the north-west mainland and the Hebridean islands (Withers 1992).

Scots, then, has always been a hybrid language – a mixture of Old English, Old Norse and French, with lesser borrowings from other languages such as Gaelic. It shares a common core of vocabulary and grammar with English, particularly northern English – and the political border of Scotland does not necessarily correspond to a marked linguistic boundary. As Aitken (1979: 86) observes, there are certain vocabulary items which are distinctively Scots, such as 'gowpen' ('double handful') or 'tummle wulkies' ('turn somersaults'). Then there are other items where the vocabulary items are related, but there is a long-established difference in pronunciation, for instance, 'heid' and 'head', or 'truith' and 'truth'. But there is a large part of the vocabulary – as well as the general principles of pronunciation and grammar –

which are 'core' features, common to both Scots and English. Such items would include words like 'some' or 'winter'. Some might argue that Scots has a distinct pronunciation and a distinctive grammar – and it is true that the Scottish accent is recognisable, and that Scots has certain grammatical realisations which are are also different from southern English – for example, the '-it' past inflexion mentioned above. Nevertheless, the phonological system from which the Scottish accent is realised, and the general grammatical system which governs the particular realisations, are little different from their English counterparts. What we are dealing with, when considering Scots and English, are not two monolithic and distinct systems, but a range of varieties which sometimes diverge but nevertheless have much in common.

Let us pause and consider an example of Older Scots verse, from the court of James IV (1473–1513). A peculiarly Scottish verse tradition is the 'flyting', which may derive from a Celtic tradition whereby rival poets indulged in a competition to see who could insult the other in the most extravagant terms. Flyting-like dialogues resurface in Scots poetry up to the time of Burns, and even occasionally today, but the most famous and the foulest is the flyting of the east-coast poet, William Dunbar, and the west-coast poet, Gavin Kennedy, in the early sixteenth century. Dunbar's contribution contains a reference to what is presumably the westerner's mother tongue, Gaelic, also known as Irish or 'Erse'. The name is evidently also a pun in sixteenth-century Scotland, as the sly final line of this stanza indicates:

> Iersch brybour baird, vyle beggar with thy brattis,
>   Cuntbitten crawdon Kennedy, coward of kynd,
> Evill farit and dryit, as Denseman on the rattis,
>   Lyke as the gleddis had on thy gule snowt dynd;
>   Mismaid monstour, ilk mone owt of thy mynd,
> Renunce, rebald, thy rymyng, thow bot royis,
>   Thy trechour tung hes tane ane heland strynd;
> Ane lawland ers wald make a better nois.

> [Gaelic robber poet, vile beggar with your brats
>   Cunt-bitten coward Kennedy, natural coward,
> Ill-fared and excreted, like a Dane on the wheels,
>   It's as if the hawks had dined on your yellow snout;
>   Poorly-made monster, each moan from your mind,
> Renounce, rogue, your rhyming, you only rave,
>   Your traitorous tongue has taken a highland strain;
> A lowland arse (= Erse/Gaelic) would make a better noise.]

There are many Scots features here: native terms of abuse such as 'crawdon', 'rebald'; grammatical items such as 'ilk' meaning 'each'; grammatical features such as the '-it' past inflexion, as in 'dryit'. But Dunbar probably would not have considered his own Scots as qualitatively different from English: indeed, elsewhere he praises Chaucer's use of 'oure tong', 'our Inglisch', suggesting a common language (cf. McClure 1981b). Rather, Dunbar attacks the language of his compatriot Kennedy, an act which illustrates traditional highland versus lowland rivalries and prejudices. In medieval and Renaissance Scotland, then, the linguistic divide between 'Inglis' and 'Erse' marks one long-established cultural divide: between lowlander and highlander. If the flyting of Dunbar and Kennedy is anything to go by, the linguistic divide might also have marked a metropolitan–rural, or court–parochial snobbery.

In Dunbar's time, as we have seen, the Scots–English distinction probably did not mean as much as it does now, but the distinct qualities of 'Inglis' in Scotland were to become much more of a cultural focus as the sixteenth century progressed. Scotland was transformed as the Reformation in Europe reached its shores. Scottish Reformers like John Knox always had one eye on the influence of the English throne: his anglicised Scots was designed to reach English readers, and his *First Blast of the Trumpet Against the Monstrous Regiment* [i.e. 'Rule'] *of Women* is said to have infuriated the young Elizabeth of England, later to become Elizabeth I. The rise of printing in England, much more prevalent than in Scotland, was beginning to have an effect: Scottish texts might be printed in England and have their language anglicised; and English texts could be more widely distributed in the north. But the body-blow to the richly distinct Scots variety was the removal of the Scottish court to England in 1603. James VI of Scotland, himself a poet and essayist who had spearheaded a modest Scottish literary renais-sance in Edinburgh, became James I of the new United Kingdom, commissioner of an influential authorised version of the Bible (in English) and patron of a group of dramatic players who had clustered around a successful playwright called William Shakespeare. It is hardly surprising that the language of religious and literary prestige became associated with southern English; and, with the great standardising pressures of the seventeenth and eighteenth centuries, Scots as well as Gaelic became widely associated with the vulgar, the barbaric, the parochial. This attitude is evident quite early in Scottish literature. William Drummond of Hawthornden (1585–1649) is the last Scottish poet of the Renaissance: although he lived all his life in Scotland, spoke Scots and wrote his early poetry in Scots, he consciously edited all obvious Scotticisms from his published work. Compare this satirical poem with Dunbar's Scots of just over a hundred years earlier:

Would ye know these royal knaves
Of free Men would turne us slaves;
Who our Union doe defame
  With Rebellions Wicked Name?
Read these Verses, and yee il spring them,
Then on Gibbetes straight cause hing them.
They complain of sinne and follye,
In these tymes so passing hollye
They their substance will not give,
Libertines that we may live ...

The language of this poem is much more intelligible to those familiar with modern standard English, though the rhymes suggest a Scottish pronunciation of 'hing' and 'follye'. Accent apart, there is little to distinguish this variety from the literate variety found in the London court, and from the Union of the Crowns we can date the view, held by Drummond and still held by some today, that the English of the south is somehow inherently better than its Scottish cousin.

Even so, as late as 1718 in parts of Scotland, little or no distinction seems to have been made between Scots and English. Aitken (in T. McArthur 1992: 894) notes that the Stirling Burgh Records of 23 August 1718 state that 'They decided not to disjoin, but to continue the Scots or English classe in the gramer school as formerly'. If this example is representative of wider usage, then, for many people of the period, the terms 'Scots' and 'English' appear to be synonymous. The next major change in attitude (at least among the literate classes) follows the failure of the final Jacobite uprising in 1745. The crushing of the ambitions of French-born Charles Edward Stuart was followed in Scotland by an astonishing cultural revival, climaxing in the Scottish Enlightenment. It may well be that the political defeat for Scotland encouraged a cultural counter-reaction. Whatever the reason for the enormous upsurge of intellectual and creative energies in the Scotland of the later eighteenth century, part of the movement was a rekindling of interest in Scots, now widely seen as a variety of speech and writing which was markedly different from English. The movement was largely literary, sparked by the anthologies and original poetry of Allan Ramsay, then Robert Fergusson, and then, most famously, Robert Burns. Burns was followed by Walter Scott, who not only wrote and collected Scots poetry but also extended the use of the vernacular to the dialogue in his novels, a practice which was taken up by John Galt and Robert Louis Stevenson among others. The mid-eighteenth century, then, saw a revival in the fortunes of Scots, but there was a new factor: writers in Scots were beginning to stress the differences from English;

in the writing of the time, it is the very nativeness of Scots that is often being emphasised and celebrated. The linguistic code of the nation has become an icon of Scottishness.

To some extent, however, the eighteenth-century Scots revival reinforced attitudes which had begun to be evident two centuries earlier: that Scots was parochial and vulgar. The new development of these attitudes was not simply to reject them as false, but to reassess the parochial and vulgar in the light of the first stirrings of romanticism. Scotland seemed a prime location for noble savagery, so the Scots language seemed more 'authentic' or 'purer' than its southern counterpart. Scotland has never quite recovered from its success in these years: the supposed translations of the Gaelic poet Ossian captivated Europe before being found to be the elaborate hoax of the poet James Macpherson; the poetry of Burns and the prose of Walter Scott better deserved their international fame.

Robert Burns is probably Scotland's best-known poet, and his language can be regarded as a standardising model for much modern Scots. A present-day advertising campaign in Scots for Grant's whisky (which used slogans such as 'Unco sonsie' and 'Gars your weason fissle') refers inquirers to specific sources in Burns's poems. But even Burns switches back and forth from English to Scots, sometimes with embarrassing effect, but often imperceptibly and powerfully (cf. Smith 1996). Consider the following verses of 'To a Mouse':

> I'm truly sorry Man's dominion
> Has broken Nature's social union,
> An' justifies that ill opinion
>   Which makes thee startle
> At me, thy poor, earth-born companion
>   An' fellow-mortal.

Apart from the typically Scottish stanza form, there is little which is Scots about the language here. In the fourth line, the English word 'makes' is even preferred to the Scottish synonym 'gars'. The elision of the /d/ in 'and' might reflect a spoken mode, but that is not especially Scottish. But the poem moves easily into a denser idiom:

> But Mousie thou art no thy lane
> In proving foresight may be vain:
> The best laid schemes o' Mice and Men
>   Gang aft a-gley
> An' lea'e us nought but grief and pain,
>   For promis'd joy.

This stanza is markedly Scots: the vocabulary ('gang a-gley', or 'go astray'), the pronunciation ('lea'e', or 'leave') and the grammar ('art no thy lane', or 'are not alone') all signal the Scottishness of the poem.

Much Scots writing after Burns tends to tread the more popular of the paths which he laid down: love lyrics, comic narratives and conventional moral observations (often to do with pinpricking pretensions). Scottish literature is henceforth often rural in setting, nationalist in sentiment, sentimental in its nationalism and saturated in nostalgia. But post-Burnsian, traditional Scots is not the only option available to modern writers.

PRESENT-DAY SCOTS

Scots today is a patchwork of varieties, geographical and social. The kind of Scots that we have been considering, the traditional variety whose roots lie in the Anglo-Norse language of lowland Scotland, has splintered into a range of distinctive dialects. It is a point of some dispute how far Scots ever achieved a distinct standard of its own. Preliminary work on the Helsinki Corpus of Older Scots suggests that the language of the sixteenth-century Scottish court was indeed moving towards a consistency of spelling and grammar that marks a standard variety (Meurman-Solin 1993), and there is some evidence from educational pamphlets and books that a polite Scottish variety was promoted in competition with southern English as late as the eighteenth century (Jones 1995); nevertheless, the removal of the political and artistic centre of the emerging standard to London in the early seventeenth century predated the great standardising impulses of the Augustan era. Only in the seventeenth and eighteenth centuries was polite English codified and 'fixed' in dictionaries and grammar books, and only in the nineteenth century was the concept of a 'standard English' explicitly developed, by analogy with the standard weights and measures which had evolved with the Industrial Revolution (T. McArthur 1992: 979). The standard variety in Scotland became Scottish Standard English: a variety of English which is a close cousin to the non-standard varieties of Scots, but which is even closer to English Standard English.

The result is that non-standard Scots varieties today have to defend themselves against the prejudices which accompany most if not all non-standard varieties which mark the political, economic and artistic 'peripheries'. Moreover, the different varieties compete for the distinction of being labelled 'authentic' Scots. For what is the mark of 'authenticity'? Let us consider some of the varieties and some of the claims.

RURAL SCOTS

The types of Scots which most retain features of Older Scots, and Burnsian Scots, are the varieties which are found in rural Scotland. The north-east in particular has a proud and vigorous tradition of speaking, writing and performing a variety of Scots. Indeed, the name Doric, which can sometimes refer to all varieties of traditional Scots, has become increasingly identified with the rural Scots of the countryside around Aberdeen. Doric is often used as a vehicle for literature with themes involving farming or fishing – traditional north-east industries – and for humour and nostalgia. This recent example is the opening of 'Lady's Choice', a short story by Sheena Blackhall:

Jist merriet, Janet McHardie wis bein led roon the guests like a prize heifer, bi her faither, Jeems Cochrane. The guests hid pyed guid siller for the presents – hidna mockit her – and war entitled tae gie her the aince-ower. She wis wearin a wee fite hat, clapt abune her lugs like a booed ashet. She passed Kirsty's table wi nae devaul – a sharged scrat o' a bride: it nocht merriege tae beef her oot a bittie.

'Fancy wearin' a hat like yon!' observed a weel-wisher.

'Mebbe she's bauld,' quo anither.

'Bauld or no, he'll nae be carin, the nicht,' snichered a third.

Jeems Cochrane plunkit himsel doon aside Kirsty, pechin like a scrapit soo. She cudna suffer him – he mind't her on a traction engine – the mair whisky ye poored doon him, the mair he loot aff steam, puffin oot twa chikks as reid's a bubbly jock's gobblers. She hodged awa, as he socht her leg wi his orra ham o' a haun. There wisna a decent bit aboot him; his spik wis as rank as dung, and the reek o' sharn clung till him despite some sma attention wi carbolic saip. She wis obleeged tae the chiel for the eese o' his cottar hoose, bit cannie niver tae let him in ower the door. A widow-wummin couldna be ower carefu in a sma place, wi the likes o Jeems Cochrane as a landlord.

'Dis it nae mak ye jealous, noo, thinkin foo Janet'll spend the nicht?' he speired.

She didna heed him or his orra spik, far mair taen up wi surveyin the guests. Waddins and funerals; human calendars. Fowk ye'd kent in Spring mid-ben a short simmer; flaxen barley weiren nearer the hairst. Ithers, wha'd been stracht's a blade whan ye wis a bairn, were stookit sheaves noo – the ault fowk, huddlit thegither, wytin o' the last shak o' the win. It wisna mowse – it feared ye tae think on't.

> There wis John Dow, careerin roon a jug as fu's a puggie,
> oxterin up a wee punk quine wi hair as spikey's a hedgehog, as
> skyrie's a rainbow. John, wha'd haen a thatch like Samson's, near
> as bald as a pickit hen.

The spellings ('noo', 'doon', 'braid', 'ault', etc.) suggest Scottish pronunciations of common core vocabulary items, that is, those items shared
with varieties of English. In addition, there are also specifically Scots
words ('bubbly-jock', 'lugs', 'oxterin', 'skyrie', etc.). The '-it' grammatical inflexion makes an appearance ('stookit' and 'pickit', etc.),
alongside grammatical features such as the negative particle '-na' in
'couldna'. Some of the Scots markers are specifically north-east: the /f/
sound, or 'phoneme', corresponds to <wh> or <h> spellings elsewhere,
in 'fite' (white) and 'foo' (how). Furthermore, we find here the /i/ phoneme where, elsewhere in Scotland, there would be /ø/ or /ʊ/, as in
'eese' (use).

Doric is of course only one of the rural varieties of present-day Scots.
Ayrshire and Galloway retain distinctive features (see Macaulay 1991
for a recent description of the Ayrshire variety), and the most exotic
bloom in the Scots garden is probably Insular Scots, which thrives in
Orkney and Shetland. More strongly Norse-influenced than its mainland counterparts, Insular Scots is strongly represented in regional
literature. The excerpt from the poem below, by John Graham,
celebrates the centenary of the arrival in Shetland of the Faroese
linguist Jakob Jakobsen, who did much to record the older tongue of
the Shetlanders, Norn:

> A hunder year sin syne
> Shetland men sailed der smacks
> Nort ta da Faroe Bank.
> Dere dey shot der lang-lines
> Deep i da green dyoob,
> Doon amang da steedin cod.
> Da mirl an da yark on da line
> Liftet der herts as dey haeled –
> 'Licht i da lum'
> 'White upo white'
> Owre da heildin gunnel
> Dey cam sprikklin.

In this extract, we see some of the characteristic features of Insular
Scots: the /d/ and /t/ phonemes where in other varieties of Scots, and in
Scottish English, there would be /ð/ and /θ/; and distinctive vocabulary
items, such as 'mirl' (quiver, tremble), 'yark' (tug), 'heildin' (tilting) and

'sprikklin' (wriggling). Other vocabulary items, such as 'sin syne' (ago) and 'lum' (chimney) are shared with other varieties of Scots.

The problem with championing a single present-day rural or insular variety, such as Doric or Shetlandic, as *the* representative of Scots is largely to do with the fact that they are peripheral: the relative geographical isolation that has resulted in continuity of form and use also means that communication in these varieties, for all its vigour, is a minority pursuit. The major part of the population of Scotland lies in the industrial central belt. National economic activity and artistic prestige (if not political power) gravitate towards Edinburgh and Glasgow.

URBAN SCOTS

Most Scots speakers in the industrial central belt switch from a Standard Scottish English to an urban variety of Scots, *patois*, or 'the patter'. This is regarded simply as broken English by some advocates of traditional Scots (notoriously Grant, in his Introduction to the *Scottish National Dictionary*). Rural varieties of a language, however, are often regarded by urban dwellers as the language of country bumpkins. On the other hand, the problem with holding urban Scots up to be representative of contemporary Scots is that it is often highly stigmatised: it is associated with the working class, or further, the uneducated, disenfranchised, powerless underclass. Thus it is given little social value, and was even excluded from the pages of the *Scottish National Dictionary*, which defines Scots words and their uses from 1700 to the present day. This attitude is lamented by Tom Leonard in his poem 'Right inuff', which begins:

> right inuff
> ma language is disgraceful
>
> ma maw tellt mi
> ma teacher tellt mi
> thi doactor tellt mi
> thi priest tellt mi

The most obviously Scottish feature of this poem is the pronunciation, accentuated by the idiosyncratic 'phonetic spelling'. There is evidence, here and elsewhere, of some particularly Scots vocabulary items 'wainz' (children), 'smout' (person of no significance) and grammar ('tellt' is a weak verb with a reduced '-it' inflexion). Urban Scots, accent apart, is not very different from Scottish Standard English, although there are distinguishing features of vocabulary and grammar as well as pronunciation (see Macafee 1983, 1994 on Glasgow speech). However, many of the differences which do exist are stigmatised, and the social processes which underlie the stigma are a fertile area for examination by writers such as Tom Leonard and James Kelman.

In fact, in his short story 'Mr Endrews speaks', Tom Leonard needs to change only one orthographic feature, <a> to <e> , in order to represent the pronunciation of the middle-class urban Scot: the infamous 'Kelvinside' accent (whose Edinburgh counterpart is 'Morningside'):

> Of course, none of you listening to me here this morning will ever go to Glasgow University, I'm aware of thet. Most of you will be in the hends of the Glasgow constabulary before very long, end some of you will no doubt make your appearance in the High Court on a cherge of murder. Now I want you to hev the honour of St Kevin Berry's in mind when you plead guilty, end under no circumstances should you use the glottal stop. I want you all to say, 'Guilty,' in a clear, well-mennered voice, with no trace of slovenly speech.

The prejudices here explored and satirised are more of a class nature than a nationalist nature – it would be difficult for middle-class Scots to rally around a working-class variety, and working-class pride also has a certain amount of contempt, economically expressed in 'Right inuff', for middle-class opinion.

LALLANS

There is always the possibility of inventing a standard where none was before. Lallans, a form of 'plastic Scots' based on the traditional varieties of Older Scots, has been proposed by Scots language 'activists'. The Scots Language Society promotes the use of Lallans in everyday life, and advocates the teaching of Lallans in schools throughout Scotland: it would not be restricted to any one area, and it would not be associated with any particular social class – although Tom Leonard has argued that it smells to him of cultural elitism (e.g. 1984: 97ff.). It is fair to say that, thus far, Lallans has not been widely adopted, although efforts continue to be made to give it wider currency, as for example in the 1993 message from the SNP convener Alex Salmond to the party faithful, printed in English, Gaelic and Lallans:

> 'A Message frae the National Convener'
> The 1993 yeirlie Convene staunds at the hinner end o a spell o eftir election stievemakkin for the SNP an the oncome o twa vital walin campaigns for Scotland.

I the time sin the walin the SNP haes throcht a fair pairt o the rebiggin wi regaird til organisation an siller needfu ti allou us ti bear the gree agin our Unionist faes.

Wi hae, forby, cairriet on betterin our poleetical staundin as gaugit baith i pow counts an the outcome o Council walins, an aaready we hae, stellit an yokit til the campaign, maist o our foreseen Candidates for neist yeir's walin til the Paurliament o Europe.

The daeins o the Convene sall tak tent til the poleetical maitters that will be at the hert o that campaign, wi the wecht siccar on Unthirldom as the gait ti pittan richt aa the hairm an wrangs that Government frae Westminster haes gart Scotland dree.

The bygaen yeir haes brocht ti licht monie neu examples o the puirtith o London pouer gaen agley i Scotland – the Braer mishanter, the ongaun threit til Scotland's watter, the swick at Rosyth an the ettle tae fause-bounder our Councils.

The key maitter i the incomin yeir will be the forrit-luikin leet o cheynges that anerlie Unthirldom ben Europe can bring hame til the folk o Scotland.

Alex Salmond MP
National Convener
Scottis National Pairtie

This is an interesting text from different points of view. First, it is an attempt to honour a commitment to extend the use of Lallans from a minority, literary function towards political discourse. The spellings partly reflect Scottish pronunciation ('staunds', 'watter', 'maist') and partly the desire to be different from English ('yeir', 'yeirlie', 'neu'). There is the revival of some archaisms ('puirtith', or 'poverty', is now confined to literature, according to the *Concise Scots Dictionary*), and an echo of the Burns poem considered earlier ('gaen agley'). The vocabulary of this letter is discussed further in Chapter 4.

This use of the word 'unthirldom' in the message caused some adverse press comment at the time of the convention: some observers wondered what was wrong with the good Scots word 'freedom', as used by John Barbour in his fourteenth-century poem, *Brus*. 'Unthirldom' is a coinage based on the existing verb participle 'unthirled' (eighteenth-century) which means 'unsubjugated', particularly 'freed from thirlage to a mill'. Its cognate English term, ironically perhaps, given the press reaction, is 'unenthralled'.

The Lallans passage illustrates some of the strategies and some of the problems of recreating a distinct standard Scots: words must be invented, revived and extended, and then one must hope that the Scottish people understand them, let alone use them. The publicity campaign for Grant's whisky, already referred to, elicited similar ambivalences in 1995. On prominent display, there were posters extolling the virtues of Grant's whisky in a series of slogans in Scots that many Scottish people found unfamiliar, or, at least, that they seldom, if ever, used. The accompanying television campaign utilised this ambivalence: one commercial featured a young man in a telephone booth, phoning his grandmother to ask what 'Unco sonsie' actually means.

The problem for Lallans is largely one of acceptance. In the process of becoming a standard language, a language variety usually goes through various processes (cf. Cooper 1989): it is codified, used in education, widely used in written discourse, and generally accepted as the educated, prestige form by the society that adopts it. The nineteenth and twentieth centuries have seen accelerated codifications of Scots – particularly in the two great dictionary projects, *The Dictionary of the Older Scottish Tongue* and *The Scottish National Dictionary* – and recently there has been an increasing emphasis on the presence of Scots in the schools curriculum. Scots in various forms is used in literature, and, more sporadically, in other written texts. However, so far at least, the use of Lallans as a prestige form, in preference to Standard Scottish English, has not pervaded Scottish society to any significant extent. The one regular outlet for literature largely in Lallans remains *Lallans*, the long-running magazine of the Scots Language Society. An anthology of creative and critical writing culled from the twenty-one years of the magazine's existence, *Mak it New*, has recently been published (MacCallum and Purves 1995).

STANDARD SCOTTISH ENGLISH

The relationship between Standard Scottish English (SSE) and the varieties of Scots discussed above is a sensitive one. Those who would champion the use of Scots as a marker of a distinctive culture tend to emphasise the differences, and claim that Scots and English are two separate languages. Others see the varieties as close linguistic cousins (cf. Aitken 1979, and in McArthur 1992: 903–5). Aitken defines SSE as 'the mother tongue of a large minority of native-educated Scots (mainly the middle classes and those who have received a higher education) and the public language of most of the remainder (mainly the working class of the Lowlands)' (in McArthur 1992: 903).

Although Standard Scottish English shares most of its features with the Standard Englishes found elsewhere, it is also influenced by traditional Scots in its pronunciation, vocabulary and grammar. Like the Scots varieties mentioned above, it is rhotic, that is, the /r/ is pronouned before the consonant in words like 'born', 'fern', 'world', and 'farm', and also word-finally in items like 'sir', 'bar', 'fur'. It retains distinctive vocabulary items, some of which are overt, like 'canny' (careful with money), 'dreich' (miserable), 'douce' (respectable) and 'wabbit' (exhausted), and some of which may be covert, like 'pinkie' (little finger), 'burn' (stream) and 'tablet' (a type of sweet). And it retains various distinctive grammatical features, such as the use of the definite article in phrases like 'the school', 'the cold', and the use of the past participle after 'need', as in 'My hair needs washed'. It is important to stress that covert Scotticisms are widely-accepted forms – often not considered to be Scottish at all by the people who use them.

Examples of SSE can often be found in the Scottish press (e.g. in Bob Campbell's articles 'Class of 93 Steps Out' and 'Calling the Tune' in *The Scotsman Weekend*, 18 December 1993, p. 9). The Scotticisms are italicised:

> Outside Bruntsfield Primary School in Edinburgh's south side, it's a *dreich* December Wednesday night. Inside, in a smallish gym, a group of 16 people arranged in a circle are dancing to a tape of fiddle music. So far, so unsurprising, but this is not a circle dance as such. The people are learning a Cape Breton solo step dance which has died out in Scotland but had been transported there by the 12,000 Scots who fetched up in that part of Nova Scotia in the latter part of the 18th century and the early part of the 19th century.
>
> Once in, the action is fast and furious: 'We tend to get on the floor and *gie it laldie*,' smiles Mary, 'and as long as we get round the floor without kicking anybody it doesn't matter if the Pas de Basque isn't correct. What I like about this place is folk'll come in and they'*ll maybe* want to do a Dashing White Sergeant and there's only four at the table; they grab folk at the next table. "Oh we *cannae* do it" and they go "No it's *awright*" and everybody pulls each other round the floor.'

The Scottish Standard English narrative allows for the use of a non-stigmatised overt Scotticism, 'dreich'. The use of a Scotticism here is further licensed by the fact that the content is markedly Scottish: traditional Scottish dancing. A slightly denser variety of Urban Scots, however, is confined to the direct speech of the dancers themselves – one grammatical feature here is the typical Scots use of 'will/-'ll maybe' instead of the modal auxiliary verb 'might'.

A book about language and Scottish Literature might conceivably elect to ignore literature written in Standard Scottish English, on the grounds that such writing is, perforce, English Literature. I have chosen not to do this, for reasons which will be discussed in more detail later in this chapter. There is also a practical reason for not excluding SSE from a typology of Scots: writers seldom confine themselves to one area in the long continuum from dense rural Scots to SSE.

THE DENSITY OF SCOTS

McClure (1979) suggests a model for defining the Scots used in any particular text. He proposes two axes on which a text might be plotted: the first axis corresponds to the continuum between 'literary' and 'colloquial' Scots; and the second axis corresponds to the continuum between 'thin' Scots (which would be close to Scottish Standard English) and 'dense' Scots (which would contain a high proportion of distinctively Scottish vocabulary items, grammatical features and/or pronunciations). On such a model, the SNP letter printed above would correspond to 'dense literary', since it contains many distinctively Scots items, few of which would actually be spoken, and the *Scotsman Weekend* articles above would represent 'thin colloquial', being written in a language variety which contains Scottish items, such as 'dreich', but which would be largely understandable in all parts of the English-speaking world.

The model is a useful way of initially classifying Scots texts, although, as McClure acknowledges, it is an oversimplification, partly because it does not take into consideration the chronological dimension: what is 'colloquial' Scots in one century might well be an anachronistic 'literary' item in another, given the change in language. More worryingly, the 'literary–colloquial' continuum does not itself distinguish between urban and rural colloquial Scots, a distinction which is often vital in establishing a speaker's specific identity and background. Neither does it account easily for more complex texts, where the varieties of Scots used are deliberately mixed.

SCOTS MIXED

As we have seen, defining Scots is not easy, and describing attitudes to Scots depends very much on who you are talking to and which variety of Scots you are talking about. There can be little doubt, however, that Scots still exerts a powerful influence over Scottish writers. If poetry was the medium of choice at the start of the twentieth century, then drama seems to have overtaken it as the century draws to a close. A range of Scots is represented by these texts. Some employ daring examples of code-mixing, that is, the employment of more than one variety of Scots (or English) for dramatic effect. An example of the ingenious use of code-mixing occurs in the translation of Michel Tremblay's *The House among the Stars*. In this play, three generations of a family appear on stage simultaneously, in one place (the family home) but at three different periods of time. The oldest generation speaks rural Scots: a family scandal threatens to send them in shame to the city. The middle generation are city-dwellers and they speak urban Scots – they're returning to the family home for a break in the country. The youngest generation speaks Standard Scottish English – having established themselves in the city, they've moved up the social ladder to become middle-class academics. The following excerpt gives a brief taste:

EDOUARD: Ah think we'd better go intae the hoose …

THE FAT WOMAN: The mosquitoes arenae oot yit, ah'm gaunnae sit oan the verandah.

EDOUARD: Yir right. It's owre early fur bed yit. Ah'll go'n see if ah kin coax Bartine tae jine us.

THE FAT WOMAN: Light mair lamps when yir in…This hoose is sad-like right enough when thurs nae lights in it at night-time …

EDOUARD (*In a falsetto voice*): Bartine? It's me, your sister-in-law back again … You and me's going to have a wee chinwag … You know how much you enjoy that!

Silence.
Josaphat lights his pipe.

THE FAT WOMAN: Ye kin smell the water fae up here.

MATTHIEU: It's funny, isn't it? I can't smell the trees and the water anymore. When we arrived it was fresh and strong. Two hours later it's gone. It makes you want to go away so's you can come back and smell it again.

The Fat Woman and Mathieu take a deep breath.

JOSAPHAT: The smell ae ma pipe tobaccie'll bring Victoire oot … (*He turns towards the house.*) Ah need tae hiv a talk wi you.

THE FAT WOMAN: (*Rather loud.*) Are yese comin oot?

MATTHIEU: It gives me a funny feeling listening to you tell your family's stories …

A closer analysis of the translation shows that Josaphat and Victoire's speech is a variety of conservative, literary Scots, rather than a technically-accurate representation of twentieth-century north-east Doric

(Corbett 1996). Yet the contrast of the lyrical, archaic language of the oldest generation with the lively vernacular of the middle generation and the lightly-Scottish English of the youngest generation adds to the sense of poignancy and loss, a sense that is dramatically powerful in the context of the play. The history of one family is dramatised by the range of Scots on display – a dramatic strategy which would be lost if only one variety of the language had been used for the translation.

Given the diversity of Scottish linguistic varieties and the heterogeneity of Scotland's social, geographical and ethnic communities, it is perhaps inevitable that there is a certain amount of rivalry and disagreement about the nature of Scots, and which variety 'best' reflects it. One educational strategy is to teach ourselves and our children how to cope with diversity – an approach advocated, for example, by Stuart McHardy of the Scots Language Resource Centre, and Liz Niven, an educationist working on Scots language resources for the 5–14 schools curriculum. Their approach has been criticised by some. For example, Neil MacCallum, a poet, editor and past Preses of the Scots Language Society, writes in a letter to *The Herald* (20 March 1995):

Teaching Dialect

I regret having to take issue with much of what Stuart McHardy, director of the Scots Language Resource Centre, has to say about teaching dialect as opposed to something approaching standard Scots (*Education Herald*, March 7).

When he quotes the view of Liz Niven, of Dumfries and Galloway Education Department, that the vast majority of bairns already speak Scots, both would seem to have their head in the clouds.

I suspect that outwith the Gaidhealtachd the current linguistic practice of most school children veers more towards that identified by the late A. D. Mackie when introducing *Poems in the Two Tongues*: 'Scots, as you have it here, was not his mother tongue, but neither for the matter of that was English. What he spoke from earliest infancy was a bastard lingo compounded of rudimentary Scots on the one hand and mispronounced English on the other.'

The Scots element will have been diluted over the passing years.

Although it may be fashionable to give primacy to dialects over a standard or literary Scots, how on earth will these be taught? There is hardly any significant body of published literary work in specific Scottish dialects, with the exception of the rather special case of Shetlandic and to a lesser extent that of Buchan or Northeast Scots.

While I am no educationist, I would suggest you cannot teach a language without adequate texts.

Such material does exist within the canon of Scots literature over the past three centuries and despite all the pressures brought to bear against it this literary language remains remarkably consistent.

When posing the question about how modern we must be, Stuart McHardy claims Irvine Welsh and James Kelman as writers in the Scots language. I too want Scots work to deal with contemporary concerns yet would never suggest that those two operate in that medium.

Only someone with little or no appreciation of the distinctive lexis and syntax pertaining to the Scots language could make such an inaccurate claim.

As a letter to a newspaper, this claim may well be intended as a controversial contribution to a long-running debate. Even so, it is disingenuous in its assumption that an institutionalised Standard Scots existed and exists. The point has been made, and will be made again (particularly in Chapter 11), that there never has been a Standard Scots as we presently understand Standard English, and the very concept of a standard variety is a relatively recent one. The letter is also more exclusive in its definition of Scots than I intend to be: James Kelman and Irvine Welsh are accomplished exponents of their chosen medium, and it seems unnecessarily disparaging to insinuate that it is a 'bastard lingo'. The very idea of linguistic 'purity' is indeed suspect (see Cameron 1995 for a discussion of 'verbal hygiene' in English).

Possibly the letter is prompted mainly by a desire that Lallans, which arguably has the potential to be a fully standard variety of Scots, should not be neglected in the current revival of interest in local varieties of Scots. And indeed it would be wrong to ignore a movement which is and has been of considerable cultural and political significance, even if its practitioners are a vocal minority. Even so, the narrow view, that the only Scots worth discussing is a nebulous 'standard Scots', is not the one adopted in this book.

As suggested earlier, few speakers of Scots now confine themselves to one variety of language. It is more likely that individuals move between available varieties according to the social context and desired effect. For that reason, if no other, the texts considered in this book will range among different varieties of Scots, whether anglicised, rural, urban or literary.

2

———————— • ————————

LANGUAGE AND LITERARY STUDIES

Modern linguistics, which is usually traced back to Ferdinand de Saussure's *Course in General Linguistics*, published posthumously in 1916, emerged around the same time as modern literary criticism; and, in Europe, linguistic theory was being applied to literary texts by the 1920s. The intellectual ancestors of the present book are therefore distanced from us by time, and also by language, culture and politics. In 1920s post-revolutionary Moscow, and also in Prague through the 1930s, influential groups of scholars were considering, devising and adapting theories of linguistic form, and relating them to linguistic function. (For a brief and helpful summary of the main ideas of the Moscow and Prague schools, see Cook 1994.) Given the turbulent history of the twentieth century, the influence of the Moscow School and the Prague School has been fragmented: some books took a long time to be translated and so to gain a wider following in the west, while certain scholars went into exile, influencing the direction of linguistics in their new place of residence. One such scholar and exile was Roman Jakobson (1896–1982).

Roman Jakobson is an influential figure in the development of stylistics, or, as he termed it, with Aristotle, 'poetics'. Jakobson is a useful starting point for us because he was a Russian, active in the Moscow School before moving to the (now) Czech Republic in 1920 to co-found the Prague Linguistic Circle. In 1941 he emigrated to the USA, and between 1946 and 1967 he held professorial posts at Columbia and Harvard Universities. In 1958 he delivered a famous 'closing statement' to a conference at Indiana University on *Style in Language*, the proceedings of which became an influential book edited by Thomas Sebeok. The importance of this conference and Jakobson's contribution to it is discussed, for example, in Traugott and Pratt (1980: 22) and in the proceedings of a subsequent conference held at the University of Strathclyde (Fabb et al. 1987). On the other hand, Graham Hough in

Style and Stylistics (1969: 113) describes the published proceedings of
the Indiana conference as 'on the whole profoundly depressing [con-
taining] more nauseous jargon than any similar work known to me'.
The attitude of mainstream literary studies to the contribution of
linguists will be discussed shortly.

Jakobson is nevertheless interesting, not least because he represents
diverse schools, east and west. Much later work in stylistics is influenced by his thoughts on how language works, and on the relationship
between language and literature, specifically poetry. Here I wish to
pick out some of Jakobson's ideas which will echo in different ways
throughout this book.

First, language is considered in the context of a complete communicative situation. Jakobson (1960) formulates this situation as follows:

CONTEXT

MESSAGE

ADDRESSER..ADDRESSEE

CONTACT

CODE

This simple diagram can be seen as the precursor to Mills' more detailed
model of text production and reception, to be discussed shortly.
Jakobson depicts the communicative situation as one involving an
addresser and an addressee. The communication occurs within a
particular context (e.g. reading a book in bed, or listening to an audio-
book while jogging), and a particular code (e.g. Standard English or a
variety of Scots). The communication will also involve a message and/
or social contact: some communications are more to do with establishing and maintaining social roles than transferring information.

The communicative situation is then mapped onto six functions of
language. Jakobson's argument is that in communication the functions
of language are oriented mainly towards one of these components of
the communicative situation (i.e. the dominant), although other
functions will also be present. So the functions of language which correspond to the communicative situation are:

REFERENTIAL

POETIC

EMOTIVE..CONATIVE

PHATIC

METALINGUAL

In other words, that aspect of language which is most concerned with
the context, i.e. language which mainly functions to give information

about the world, is classed as having a referential function. Language which is concerned with expressing the attitudes of the addresser has an emotive function. The conative function of language is oriented towards the addressee and is realised, for example, by commands, direct addresses. Language which is primarily concerned with maintaining human contact has a phatic function, and language which is concerned with clarifying or referring to language is metalingual in function. The poetic function, according to Jakobson, is oriented towards the message for its own sake. We shall return to this function shortly.

Before focusing on the poetic function, consider the following text types. For each type, the communicative orientation and the dominant function are suggested:

Text type	Communicative orientation	Dominant function
1. gossip in a bar	contact	phatic (social)
2. a short story by Irvine Welsh	message	poetic (literary)
3. a newspaper report in *The Herald*	context	referential (about the world)
4. a recipe in the *Taste of Scotland* cookery book	addressee	conative (concerned with the reader's behaviour)
5. a definition in the *Concise Scots Dictionary*	code	metalingual (concerned with language)
6. a student's phone call home, complaining about his/her flatmates	addresser	emotive (concerned with the speaker's emotions)

It is important to note here that orientation towards one aspect of the communicative situation does not exclude the other aspects, and that the dominant linguistic function therefore might be accompanied by secondary linguistic functions. For example, a newspaper report is primarily oriented towards events in the 'real world', that is, the context. Its dominant function would therefore be referential. However, it might also be pleasing as an elegant or witty piece of writing: its secondary orientation would therefore be towards the message and it would have a secondary poetic function. A recipe, on the other hand, would be conative insofar as its main purpose is to direct the reader's behaviour as the reader cooks the meal. A secondary function would be referential, as the ingredients, for example, would refer to items in the 'real' world.

ORIENTATION TOWARDS THE MESSAGE

Having outlined, in general, the communicative situation and related it to different language functions, let us consider the poetic function in greater detail. What is Jakobson offering us here? The promise seems to be a scientific way of defining and identifying poetry, without reference to readers or even poets. All we have to do is determine whether, for a specific text, its dominant orientation is towards the message itself. In other words, a poem or story is produced for its own sake: it is a verbal artefact.

The fact that a poem is a verbal artefact was important to many early stylisticians: an intricately-designed poem is easier to categorise *as* a poem than one which is not. It is also easier to talk about. For Jakobson, patterning is the key issue: he expresses this concern in terms which refer to concepts established by Saussure (1916), namely paradigm and syntagm. For Saussure, syntagm and paradigm are terms which show how elements of the language are selected from the vocabulary stock and combined according to grammatical rules.

syntagmatic relations (axis of combination)

paradigmatic	what I	*love*	about	*dormice*	is	*their size*
relations		*hate*		*rain*		*its sneer*
(axis of						
selection)						

The two axes represent two different kinds of grammatical relation: along the horizontal axis (the axis of combination), words are combined into larger syntactic units. These relations are signalled by such markers as subject–verb concord. Down the vertical axis (the axis of selection) we see those linguistic items which can be interchanged with each other: for example, *hate* can be substituted for *love*, and therefore each has a paradigmatic relation with the other. However, *what* cannot be substituted for *love*, and in such a case no paradigmatic relation exists.

Jakobson is keen to avail himself of linguistic theory when defining poetry. He therefore refers to Saussure's two axes in his famous, but rather opaque, formula (1960):

> The poetic function projects the principle of equivalence from the axis of selection into the axis of combination.

This explanation is less complicated than it may first appear. Jakobson's argument is that in poetry, the choices made down one axis are somehow equivalent to the combinations realised along the other. How does this work in practice?

Let's begin with the kind of poem that Jakobson's definition favours: a sonnet by one of the most linguistically accomplished of Scots poets, John Stewart of Baldynneis:

> Dull dolor dalie dois delyt destroy,
> Will wantith wit waist worn with wickit wo,
> Cair cankirt causith confortles convoy,   convoy *companion*
> Seveir sad sorrow scharplie schoris so,   schoris *threatens*
> My myrthles mynd may mervell monie mo;
> Promp peirles proper plesand perll preclair,   promp *assist*
> Fair fremmit freind, firm fellest frownyng fo,   fremmit *distant*
> Rych rubie rycht renownit royall rair,
> Send succor soone so suadge sall sourest sair,
> Grant grivous gronyng gratious guerdon guid,
> For favor flowing from fresche faces fair
> Restoris rychtlie restles rancor ruid,
> Bot beutie breding bittir boudin baill   boudin baill
>   *deep remorse*
> Dois dalie deedlie dwynyng dartis daill.   daill *distribute*

How does this poem conform to Jakobson's linguistic definition of poetry? We can point to at least three ways: two phonological and one syntactic. On the axis of combination, we find a *tour de force* of alliteration, in the first line on /d/:

> |x   /| x /|x   / | x / | x /|
> Dull dolor dalie dois delyt destroy.

If we were to switch axes and consider replacing one word in this line with another, the substitute word would also have to begin with the alliterating consonant /d/. The axis of selection is projected into the axis of combination; there are equivalent constraints in both directions:

> syntagmatic relations (axis of combination)

> paradigmatic   d--- d--- d--- d--- etc
> relations   d---
> (axis of   d---
> combination)   etc.

In short, if alliteration decrees that words on the syntagmatic axis must begin with a particular consonant, then the corresponding items on the paradigmatic axis must also begin with that sound. The same point holds true for stress patterns. As in most traditional verse, there is a metrical pattern, and in sonnets that pattern is conventionally iambic pentameter (see Chapter 7 for a fuller discussion). One foot is combined with another four feet to make up the pentameter line. Equally, if that foot were replaced, the substitute foot should (in principle) have the same stress pattern.

	syntagmatic relations (axis of combination)
paradigmatic	x / x / x / x / x /
relations	x /
(axis of	x /
combination)	x /

Finally, if we look at the grammatical patterns, we see that many lines correspond to a main clause. The sonnet is a combination of clauses, most corresponding to the line unit. If we were to select a unit to replace a line, then it would not only have to alliterate and conform to the metrical pattern, but it is likely that it would also have to be a syntactically well-formed clause.

These constraints do not apply to everyday language. When we have conversations, we are not careful to begin every word in an utterance with the same consonant, nor do we make sure that our utterances have a recurrent rhythmic pattern. The presence of such constraints in poetry is part of what makes (some) poems highly patterned, and it is this linguistic feature that Jakobson seizes upon. He is careful not to mark off poetry totally from other types of language (one of the functions might dominate, but language is essentially multifunctional). Poems, therefore, might also persuade, or even inform, but their dominant function is to be highly-patterned verbal artefacts.

Even so, Jakobson does not argue that this necessary poetic patterning is purely playful (or 'ludic'). The repetitions and parallelisms that we find in poetry prompt us to seek some meaningful associations between repeated features. So, in the sonnet under consideration, we might ask such questions as:

1. is there some connection in meaning between alliterating words?
2. is there some connection in meaning between rhyming words?

Here, the alliterating words support the metre in defining each poetic line, and the opening and closing lines share the alliteration on the plosive /d/: the poem, about a daily recurrence of woe, appropriately comes full circle. The rhymes in the poem fall into interlocking quatrains: *abab bcbc cdcd ee*. The three quatrains interlock the related themes of the lover's complaint, his adoration of the lady and his plea for 'succor'. The concluding couplet, separated in rhyme while echoing the opening line in alliteration, returns the lover anew to his familiar misery. Rhyme and alliteration, then, while not determining the meaning of the poem, can be related to it in this way.

TRADITIONAL AND MODERN VERSE

Not all poems are as intricately structured as those of John Stewart of Baldynneis. Much twentieth-century poetry, in particular, avoids the extreme patterning of earlier centuries. Jakobson was born in the last decade of the nineteenth century, and, accordingly, his notion of poetry was shaped by the tradition in pre-revolutionary Russia. How does his definition stand up to modern verse? Consider a short poem by Tom Leonard:

> Hercules Unzipped
>
> slingit owryir shoodir then
> go izza petrol pump

What price the axes of selection and combination here? There is still patterning: the alliteration on /p/ in 'petrol pump' might (arguably) be discounted as corresponding to everyday usage and therefore accidental, but the lines as a whole still correspond to syntactic units and both are imperative in form: each line is a suggestion. If we were to add to these lines, or to replace either of them with another, the 'poetic quality' of the language would presumably demand that the new line also be a suggestion.

Or would it? The sonnet, which conforms to a long tradition of European poetry, exhibits a much higher degree of conventional patterning than the Tom Leonard poem. Does that mean that the sonnet is 'more' of a poem? Does it mean that it is a better poem? How much patterning can you strip away before a text ceases to function as a poem? In the end, is 'poem' a linguistic category at all, or is it rather a socially-constructed genre?

These are questions which will recur throughout this book. Jakobson's linguistic definition of poetry comes at a time when stylisticians were establishing their field in the west, and its disciplinary function is to demonstrate – or to attempt to demonstrate – that fundamental linguistic concepts can be applied to descriptions of literature. This book shares that assumption, although we shall return, more sceptically, to the question of whether linguistic concepts can be used to define literature.

MORE RECENT DEVELOPMENTS

We have dwelt so far on Jakobson because he is an influential figure, and because he serves as a link between various schools (Russian, Czech and American). We will not be dwelling solely on his model of the communicative situation, nor on his particular range of linguistic functions; but it is useful to consider them because they operate as a backdrop to other attempts to marry linguistics and literature. We will hear echoes of Jakobson, for example, if we read the stylistic manuals of Widdowson (1975, 1992), or if we explore the functional linguistics of Michael Halliday (1971, 1985).

Halliday in particular is a primary influence on the methods presented in this book. Much influenced by the Prague School, Halliday has developed a grammar of English which views the organisation of the clause as a set of three functions which reformulate Jakobson's six:

ideational: clauses represent the world (real or fictional)

interpersonal: clauses express attitudes about their propositions and signal social relations between interlocutors

textual: clauses are organised in such a way as to distribute salient information at certain points in the clause structure.

The first two of these functions (ideational and interpersonal) are clearly related to Jakobson's referential and emotive/conative functions. We shall be exploring them in more depth, particularly in Chapter 3. The point here is that as we consider the history of stylistics, we see recurring concerns and evolving categories in a quest to make our interpretative strategies explicit. The practical value of Halliday's functions as opposed to Jakobson's is that the former's categories are explicitly tied to units of language, namely constituents of the clause. Each utterance, spoken or written, can therefore be analysed to reveal its array of linguistic functions. As we shall soon see, significant patterns can then be established across the sequence of utterances which make up a text.

CRITICISMS OF STYLISTICS

Literary studies has not always been sympathetic to the import of ideas and analytical techniques from linguistics. Traditionally, literary studies favours complex and elegant responses to canonical texts, and a shift in focus towards the process of interpretation can at times seem reductive, even trivial. A critic of Widdowson once objected that his own students' remarks about Robert Frost's 'Stopping by Woods on a Snowy Evening' had been more revealing and insightful than Widdowson's stylistic analysis (Widdowson 1975: 121ff.). Widdowson defends himself by arguing that stylistics offers a 'strategy for interpretation' which may guide weaker students towards fuller interpretation. In effect, he implies that traditional literary criticism assumes that all readers have highly-developed intuitive abilities which guide them in interpreting literature, and that their main goal is to develop the ability to *express* their interpretations. By focusing attention on the interpretative process, however, stylistics and its related disciplines might give support for various readings of literary texts.

Widdowson is careful not to claim objective status for any interpretation arrived at by stylistic analysis; rather, he limits the power of stylistics to the process of accounting for different individual interpretations. Yet the apparent rigour of linguistic theory and its often arcane terminology have sometimes suggested that a 'scientific' basis has been discovered for a particular reading of a text. The appeal to objectivity is strongly attacked by Fish (1980): he observes that the fact that stylisticians proceed by invoking linguistic theories to account for any one interpretation itself confers value on that interpretation. The stylistician is simply involved in *post hoc* justification of an intuition; he or she is actually no closer to the process of interpretation than a 'traditional' literary critic.

Another defence of linguistic analysis is offered by Simpson (1993: 113), who argues that

> avoiding linguistic positivism often requires no more than a modicum of caution. First of all, linguistic analysis, whether literary-stylistic or not, still remains an important, if not essential, means of explaining how texts mean. The question really is how far one goes in the interpretation which accompanies linguistic analysis.

In effect, Simpson is following Widdowson in limiting the claims made for stylistics and literary linguistics. Linguistics can provide an account of how one or more interpretations come about; it cannot itself evaluate which interpretation is preferable. The right to subjectivity of the individual reader is maintained. As noted earlier, Chapter 10 of this book will provide some pointers to ways in which literary linguistics might investigate the subjectivity of individual readers by switching attention from textual products to interpretative processes.

Stylistics has also been attacked from another flank: in a discussion of 'style', Hodge and Kress (1988: 80) claim that 'A hybrid discipline, "stylistics", developed from a mixture of literary criticism and linguistics, but it was never a vigorous or productive discipline, in spite of a small number of distinguished proponents (e.g. Spitzer, Auerbach, Halliday)'. The criticism levelled at stylistics is that it is too restricted insofar as it fails to offer a social critique. Hodge and Kress argue that stylistics places emphasis on the words on the page and their textual interrelationship; it fails to relate the text to the wider set of social processes and (questionable) conventions, processes that themselves can be 'read' in a similar way to a text. In offering a wider role for 'linguistic criticism' or 'social semiotics', Hodge and Kress do not question the value of such methodologies as are presented in this book; rather, they advocate their critical application to a whole range of communicative media, including the visual construction of comic strips, paintings and advertisements. Their challenge to stylistics is taken up, for example, by Fairclough (1989), who analyses the language of power, and Mills (1995), who promotes a 'feminist stylistics'.

The above summary of trends in stylistics shows some of the main points of debate within the field. For some, stylistics is attractive because, by adopting the established methods of the linguistic sciences, it offers an apparently 'objective' means of interpreting and evaluating literary texts. To others, however, the claim to objectivity seems more facile, and the appeal to linguistics is seen as simply a way of dressing up traditional, 'subjective' interpretations in persuasive jargon. To others still, the focus on linguistic description neglects to engage with political questions about how different forms of communication, verbal and visual, establish and maintain relationships of power in our society. Common to all these differing approaches is a concern with the text: what it might mean to different readers, and how it communicates certain social values and assumptions. The present book will attempt, like Traugott and Pratt (1980) and Montgomery et al. (1992), to introduce readers to some of the skills necessary to apply linguistic theory to the interpretation of texts. I do not intend to be exclusive in my approach to literary linguistics, nor do I expect or hope to supplant more traditional, or intuitive, types of response to literature. However, I do believe that there is a strong call for a stylistic approach to Scottish literature, especially since the social assumptions about Scotland's distinctive identity, and its status as a nation or region within the United Kingdom, find their expression in language. The choice of linguistic medium for a Scottish writer is always a political one, and a close examination of the language used by Scots is a powerful means of casting light upon questions of personal, regional, social and national identity.

WHY A SCOTTISH LITERARY LINGUISTICS?

Scottish journalists often talk about 'putting a kilt on a story', by which they mean finding a Scottish angle to British or international stories. Is this what Scottish Literature does – 'tartan up' a common heritage? Or is Scottish Literature qualitatively different from English, or, for that matter, Irish, American, Australian or Indian Literature? A further pertinent question to be raised here is whether there is a need for a book on Scottish literary linguistics – is a guide to general stylistics not sufficient?

Nations, it has recently been argued by Anderson (1983) and McCrone (1992) among others, are not different from each other in absolute, essential terms. Even so, they are powerful concepts in the public imagination. A trivial but evocative example of this power was the outcry in the Scottish press in the summer of 1994 when the Scottish Rugby Union legislated that anyone who had been resident in Scotland for twelve months would be eligible to play for the national side. The message was clear: if you stay in Scotland for a year, then you are, in effect, Scottish. The adverse opinion quickly caused the SRU to change its policy.

However, the case of Scottish rugby is not isolated. The authors of a recently-proposed Scottish Constitution would grant Scottish citizenship to everyone resident in the country on the day Scotland regains its independence and the constitution comes into force. There might be no need to wait even a year, then. The Irish-born writer, Bernard McLaverty, now resident in Scotland, frequently finds himself in the running for Scottish literary prizes. Lord Byron had a Scottish mother, and so his work might conceivably be included in the canon of Scottish poetry. Sydney Goodsir Smith, on the other hand, was born and raised in New Zealand. Where should the lines be drawn, and by whom?

Some linguists might argue that 'Scottish' is a 'fuzzy semantic category'; that is, at its centre there is a clear set of characteristics, but there are also grey areas at the periphery, as some of these characteristics are compromised. At the core of Scottish Literature, we could have writers who were born and raised and resident in Scotland, writing about Scotland and its people for a largely Scottish audience. The first substantial piece of Scottish literature, John Barbour's *The Brus*, written in the late fourteenth century, would definitely be positioned in the core. So too, presumably, would James Kelman's *How Late It Was, How Late*, which, in 1994, became the first Scottish novel to win the prestigious Booker Prize. Born, raised and resident in Glasgow, Kelman writes about working-class Glaswegians for (so he says) working-class Glaswegians. The wider audience is incidental. Moving towards the edges of our fuzzy category, we might have someone like Muriel Spark or William Boyd, writers with an international reputation, born in Scotland, but not necessarily raised or resident in Scotland, writing for a broad Euro-American audience about a wide variety of themes. All fall into the broader church of Scottish Literature.

Given such diversity, it is difficult to identify particular themes which qualitatively differentiate Scottish Literature from other national varieties. It is perhaps easier if we focus on 'core' texts. There we find the taste for the fantastic which informs the Scottish ballads, and the novels of James Hogg, Robert Louis Stevenson, Margaret Oliphant, David Lindsay, Iain Banks and Alasdair Gray. We find the twin concerns of rural Scotland and urban Scotland: rural issues informing the Kailyard and anti-Kailyard novels of such as James Barrie and George Douglas Brown, as well as the writings of Lewis Grassic Gibbon, Neil Gunn and George Mackay Brown; and urban issues informing the realist novels of such writers as James Kelman, Archie Hind, William McIlvanney, Agnes Owens and Irvine Welsh. What we miss (not always because it's absent but because it's less obviously 'Scottish') is the middle-class novel. We do have William Boyd, Muriel Spark, Ronald Frame, Allan Massie and Candia McWilliam – but these authors are arguably more akin in their technique and their concerns to their southern counterparts. It seems that, like the Scottish accent, Scottish Literature becomes more like its English cousin when you move out of the country and into the urban or metropolitan middle classes.

If we consider Scottish Literature a 'fuzzy category', then its differences from other national literatures can be said to lie in its core concerns and its thematic emphases, but naturally it overlaps in its concerns in other areas. The influence, I would add, is far from one-way. Sir Walter Scott was an overwhelming influence on English Literature and North American literature, as were his near-contemporaries, Thomas Carlyle and John Galt (author of *The Member*, Britain's first political novel, and other fine works).

Adapting Mills on feminist literature, however, reading something *as* a Scottish text may be just as important as classifying its author's nationality or its subject matter (cf. Mills 1995: 31). There may be different justifications for such a reading of a text: the text's language might be Scots, it may have Scottish antecedents, its author might be Scottish by 'affiliation' (presumably birth or adoption), it might be marketed as a Scottish text or, for various sociohistorical reasons, be 'adopted' as a Scottish text (in much the same way as John Galt's works appear in both the Scottish and the Canadian literary canon). But the context of production is only half the story. Something may or may not be read as a Scottish text by certain readers, or it may have such an impact upon Scottish writing that it demands inclusion in the canon. An extreme example of the latter – which few would presumably agree with – is Hugh MacDiarmid's cultural appropriation of 'The Waste Land' on the mischievous grounds that Eliot is 'a Scottish name' (see *A Drunk Man Looks at the Thistle*, ll. 345ff.).

Mills is mainly interested in how texts communicate gender assumptions, discriminating in favour of one group and against another, and how texts might be interpreted in a variety of ways by different genders. But, as she indicates, her richly-contextualised model of reading can also apply to other types of 'affiliation' – national, for example. She writes (1995: 35):

> As feminist readers, therefore, we need two kinds of information to construct the possible readings of a text which might be arrived at. First we need to make a close textual analysis of the text, identifying certain features of form – literary conventions, syntax, lexis, genre and so on: the cues to interpretation. Second, we need to make some generalized predictions about groups of readers' background knowledge – of language, of literary conventions – and of their models of the world. By uniting these two kinds of information, it should be possible to build up a picture of how specified social groups might read a text.

If we substitute the word 'Scottish' for the word 'feminist' in the above quotation, we can reconfigure Mills' project for a different 'affiliation'. Scottish readers bring to the text knowledge and assumptions which may trigger different interpretations and evaluations from those arrived at by members of other communities of readers. This does not mean that all Scottish readers will arrive at identical interpretations of works – just that if community and shared knowledge of the world mean anything at all, then they will influence interpretations up to a point. It is part of the project of this book to consider both types of information – the textual and the background knowledge – in the context of Scottish texts, and how they might be interpreted by Scottish (and other) readers. Most of the chapters deal mainly with textual organisation, but questions of background knowledge will increasingly intrude, and Chapter 10 will deal directly with ways of investigating background knowledge.

FROM MOSCOW TO GLASGOW

In this book, then, I shall assume that insights from literary linguistics are valid and useful – and that obtaining them is often indeed enjoyable. However, I shall try to avoid claims that stylistics is purely a mechanistic and objective means of arriving at a preferred reading of any given text. And while noting that such applications may be broadened to embrace a whole set of non-linguistic signals, I shall largely restrict myself to textual data. Some of the later chapters, however (for example, on stereotypes and tartanry), touch on a wider set of social semiotics.

The first two chapters have been, at times, rather an abstract introduction to the topic: subsequent chapters will focus more on the acquisition of analytical skills, putting into practice the types of theories that Jakobson, Halliday, Widdowson, Mills and others propose. To do this, we shall be considering a variety of different texts from throughout the history of Scots: poetry, prose literature, drama, as well as journalism, diaries and areas such as advertising and even scientific writing and weather reports. Some of the texts will be in varieties of Scots (Lallans, the Glasgow vernacular, etc.); some texts will be in Scottish Standard English. In each case, we shall consider how linguistic theories can be drawn upon to raise to consciousness the normally automatic procedures used to interpret the texts.

3

———— • ————

ANALYSING GRAMMAR

This chapter introduces two strategies for the analysis of the grammar of a text: transitivity analysis, and the analysis of modality. Both strategies link grammatical analysis to the analysis of meaning.

In Chapter 2, language was described as having a variety of general functions, one of which is referential – that is, one of the things that we use language for is to describe events and states in real or imaginary worlds. The first part of the present chapter considers how this referential function influences the selection and organisation of grammatical structures. At this specific level, the level of grammar, the referential function is sometimes labelled the ideational function (e.g. Halliday 1985). The basic idea is the same: the term 'ideational' simply denotes that the internal organisation of sentences is determined partly at least by the speaker's or writer's attempt to describe events and states in a particular way.

Consider the following sentence, taken from a motor insurance claim form:

A pedestrian hit me and went under my car.

This sentence is completely grammatical, and it communicates two consecutive actions perfectly adequately. And yet most people would agree that there is something odd about it: the description of the processes conflicts somehow with our common-sense knowledge of how things are. The techniques described in the first half of this chapter are a step towards a descriptive framework for analysing such sentences and explaining why they seem odd.

CLAUSE CONSTITUENTS

In simple terms, sentences are made up of clauses. Each clause is a set of constituents (subject, object, complement, adverbial) clustered around a verb (or predicator). Simple sentences contain one clause, for example:

S	P	S	P	C
Bruce	fled.	He	was	depressed.

S	P	O	A	S	P	A
He	saw	a spider.	The next day	he	returned	to battle.

Complex clauses can be made in two ways. One way is to put a coordinating conjunction (i.e. 'and', 'or', 'but') between two simple clauses to make one compound clause:

{[S   P   O   ]   &   [A   S   P   A]}

Bruce saw a spider   and   the next day he returned to battle.

The second main way of combining clauses is to insert one clause inside another, so that the embedded clause, or 'subclause', becomes a constituent of the main clause (in other words, the subclause functions as S, O, C, or A in the main clause). Such subclauses are usually introduced by a subordinating conjunction (e.g. 'when', 'if', 'although', 'while', 'since', etc.). Subclauses have their own structure within the main clause:

A				S	P	A
	S	P	O			
Because	he	saw	a spider,	Bruce	returned	to battle.

Here, the subordinating conjunction 'Because' introduces the subclause 'he saw a spider', which has its own clause structure (SPO). This subclause also acts as an Adverbial (A) in the sentence as a whole (which has the structure ASPA). The opening Adverbial gives the reason why Bruce returned to battle. This is the kind of information that Adverbials often provide.

It is necessary to analyse (or, in traditional terms, to 'parse') sentences into clause constituents if we wish to take the first steps towards accounting for the way in which grammar represents a real or fictional world.

FROM GRAMMAR TO MEANING

The phrases and subclauses which we label S, P, O, C and A are grammatical constituents of the clause. When we are looking at the ideational function of language, these grammatical constituents are related to semantic clause components, that is, clause components which try to account for the meaning of the grammatical constituents.

Each clause represents an event or a state. We shall refer to these as processes, which have participants and circumstances. The verbs (P) determine the type of process, which in turn determines the type of participants (usually S, O, C). For example, the verb 'tell' would be a verbal process, which usually suggests that there is a Sayer (possibly realised by the grammatical subject) and perhaps a Receiver (often realised by the object). Circumstances (realised by adverbials) give additional information about the process.

The table below (based on Halliday 1985) shows the main types of process and related participant in English:

Processes	*Participants*
Material processes:	Actor
events and states in the world	Affected
	Beneficiary
	Goal
Verbal processes	Sayer
	Verbiage (i.e. what's said)
	Target (i.e. what's being talked about)
	Receiver
Mental processes	Senser
	Phenomenon
Relational processes:	Carrier
processes of being	Attribute
	Possessor
	Possessed
	Token
	Value
Existential processes:	Existent
clauses with 'there is/are ...'	

Examples of some of these functional categories are given below:

1. | *Actor* | *P: material* | *Goal* |
   | George | was whistling | a tune. |

2. | Actor | *P: material* | *Beneficiary* | *Affected* |
   | George | gave | Alice | a slim volume of poetry. |

In these two sentences, the verbs realise a material process. 'George' is the Actor in both: he is responsible for the actions. In (1), the other

participant in the process, 'a tune' , is the result of the process of whis-
tling, and is labelled Goal . However, in (2), neither 'Alice' nor 'a slim
volume of poetry' results from the process of giving. The participant 'a
slim volume of poetry' is 'Affected' by the process (insofar as its ownership changes), and Alice is the Beneficiary of the process. These types
of participant – Actor, Goal, Beneficiary and Affected – are the most
common types associated with material processes.

3. *Sayer*	*P: verbal*	*Receiver*	*Verbiage*
Alice	told	George	that the poems were awful.

4. *Sayer*	*P: verbal*	*Target*	*Verbiage*
George	called	Alice	a philistine.

In sentences (3) and (4), the verbs express verbal processes. Each process has a participant who is responsible for the act of saying: Alice in (3)
and George in (4). In (3), the act of saying is directed towards a participant (George, the Receiver), and the subclause expresses what is said
(the Verbiage). In sentence (4), the act of saying is about another participant, the Target, and again we are told what is said, the Verbiage.
Sayer, Receiver, Target and Verbiage are the most common participants associated with verbal processes.

5. *Carrier*	*P: relational*	*Attribute*
He	was	furious and upset.

6. *Token*	*P: relational*	*Value*
Alice	was	the love of his life.

Sentences (5) and (6) are examples, together with (9) below, of relational processes, that is, processes of being. Sentence (5) describes a
participant – in other words, a Carrier ('he') is given an Attribute ('furi-
ous and upset'). In sentence (6), the participant, 'Alice', is not described
– her characteristics or attributes are not expressed – but she is given a
Value . In this sentence, Alice is therefore a Token.

7. *Senser*	*P: mental*	*Phenomenon*
Alice	saw	that George was out of control.

8. *Senser*	*P: mental*	*Phenomenon*
She	thought	he had gone mad.

9. *Possessor*	*P: relational*	*Possessed*
Alice	had	a gun.

Sentences (7) and (8) contain mental processes, processes of perception
and thinking. Each has a Senser and something that is perceived or

thought, the Phenomenon. Sentence (9) is another relational process, this time of possession – a special type of being. Participants associated with this type of relational process are Possessor and Possessed.

10.	*P: existential*	*Existent*
There	was	a loud bang.

The final type of process exemplified here is an existential one: only one participant is given, and all that we are told about it is that is exists. The grammatical subject of this sentence is in fact the semantically empty 'there'.

Note that the semantic categories of the clause, as illustrated above, are not nearly so watertight as the grammatical categories (S, P, O, C, A). Halliday (1985) offers criteria for distinguishing between categories, but there is often scope for argument. Many scholars offer different sets of categories for understanding the main types of process, and some have finer distinctions than are given here (see, for example, Traugott and Pratt 1980; Wareing 1990; Fowler 1990). However loose the categories, though, even a rough analysis of them can be revealing of the expression of responsibility for events in a text.

CIRCUMSTANCES

Circumstances (realised by adverbials) give extra information about the process. The most common types of circumstance are:

place	time	extent
manner	means	accompaniment
reason	cause	purpose
role	condition	concession
result	frequency	etc.

Examples of some of the above Circumstances are:

Actor	*Process*	*Circumstance*	*Circumstance meaning*
I	shall go	to the party	PLACE
		by bus	MEANS
		quickly	MANNER
		often	FREQUENCY
		all the way	EXTENT
		if you will	CONDITION
		etc.	

TRANSITIVITY ANALYSIS

Armed, now, with a vocabulary to describe how grammar might represent the world (real or fictional), we can begin to analyse the grammatical organisation of sentences in different texts. For example, what is odd about the description of an accident, mentioned at the opening of this chapter? First, consider the clause constituents:

S   P   O   +   P   A
(A pedestrian) (hit) (me) (and) (went) (under my car.)

This is a compound sentence consisting of two coordinate clauses linked by the conjunction 'and'. The verbs are 'hit' and 'went', and the subject, 'a pedestrian', remains the same in the two clauses (and for that reason is omitted in the second). In the first clause the object is 'me', and in the second clause the adverbial (of place) is 'under my car'.

Having determined the clause constituents, we then assign semantic labels to them:

Actor   P: *material Affected* + P: *material Circumstance: place*
(A pedestrian)(hit)   (me)   (and)(went)   (under my car.)

The semantic labels begin to make the anomaly clear. In contradiction to our real-world knowledge, the pedestrian is represented as the Actor, that is, the pedestrian is presented as in some way responsible for the actions described: hitting the car and going under it. The driver ('me') is represented as Affected by the action of hitting. The presentation of responsibility for the actions and the Actor/Affected relationships contradicts our real-world expectation, that is, that drivers are more often responsible for hitting pedestrians than vice versa, and our knowledge that it is the pedestrian who is likely to be more 'affected' than the driver.

So far, this descriptive framework might seem a cumbersome instrument for explaining a fairly obvious howler. However, this kind of analysis, known as transitivity analysis, can shed light on aspects of language which otherwise might only be grasped intuitively or subconsciously. Consider the following extracts from two Scottish texts, the first a novel and the second a short story. Although they are by different writers, they share the topic of 'sexual encounter' (cf. Burton 1982; Wareing 1990, 1994; Mills 1995). A transitivity analysis of each text helps show how the fictional worlds are represented by different writers.

A systematic transitivity analysis often follows the steps given below:

1. Analyse each sentence into its grammatical constituents, i.e. S, P, O, C, A.

2. Identify the functional components of (a) the main clauses and
   (b) the subclauses, i.e. the processes, participants and circumstances.
3. What kinds of Processes predominate in each text?
4. What kinds of Actors predominate?
5. What types of Affected participants are found?
6. What types of Circumstances are found?

In addition, we can ask whether or not there is a general pattern which
emerges from any given text, or whether each text is distinctive in the
way that it represents the actions and states described.

From James Kelman, *A Chancer* (Picador, 1987)

Vi smiled at him for a moment then she looked at the fire.

He put the toast back down. He stepped towards her and he
took both of her hands in his and leaned to her but she rose from
the settee. They put their arms round each other, clinging together,
then he kissed her neck, and upwards to the lobe of her ear, and
she moved her head a little, till they were kissing each other's lips;
then they broke away and clung with their arms round each other
again and Vi chuckled.

Vi, he said. He sighed and lifted her up off the floor, walked
forwards still holding her.

Put me down, she said and she had to raise her feet to avoid
kicking something.

He laughed, but continued towards the recess and as she toppled
onto the bed he went with her, landing almost on top of her, and
they were kissing again. She arched her back from him when he
attempted to unloosen the strap of her bra but tugged her jumper
back down when he pulled it up.

She pushed him from her and he stood down.

It's okay, she said. Just …we'll go into bed first.

Aw, Christ. He shook his head and turned away.

From Janice Galloway, 'David' in *Blood* (Minerva, 1992)

His palm was clammy. I touched once. Then he laced his fingers
into mine till they were tight.   The wood at the side of the door,
biting my spine. He came closer so slow I wasn't sure if he would or

Our teeth touched, mouths open. I felt him swallow, the skin
on my lip stretch till it split, a sudden give from the tightness and
I was sliding my hands, tugging on the thin shirt: ridges of warm
rib beneath my fingers rubbing my palms on the warm sides of his
jeans, the length of seam. He pulled his head back and looked, the

blue eyes and smooth temples. Flecks of blond on the backs of his hands, his nails trailed over the blouse, the nipple stiffening where he let his hand wait and I said something I don't remember. Then there was my mouth on his neck, salt nipping the torn skin of my lip.

A comparison of the two passages demonstrates how a transitivity analysis can be carried out. First of all, consider the verbs in the Kelman passage. They represent a limited number of types of process: mainly material and verbal:

Material processes		*Verbal processes*
smiled	lifted	said [three times]
looked	walked	
put	holding	
stepped	(had to) raise	
took	toppled	
leaned	went	
clinging	landing	
kissed	arched	
moved	attempted to unloosen	
were kissing	tugged	
broke away	pulled	
clung	pushed	
chuckled	stood	
sighed	shook	
	turned	

It is obvious from the lists above that material processes, particularly those which express behaviour ('smile', 'chuckle', 'kiss', 'laugh') and movement ('step', 'lean', 'move', 'break away', 'lift' etc.) dominate the passage. There are a few verbal processes, and no relational or mental processes. The nearest to a mental process is 'look', but this is not so much a mental process as a material process which precedes perception (it is possible to look without seeing). The passage, then, presents a predominantly external view of the fictional world: we are allowed to observe the characters' actions and listen to what they are saying. We are not offered much in the way of description or evaluation (which would normally be expressed by relational processes); nor are we given direct access to the thoughts or emotions of the characters – a significant absence, given the emotional topic. The only evaluation in the passage is spoken by a character – Vi's 'It's okay'. The narrator chooses to exercise restraint.

Further analysis reveals that the sentences are largely in the active voice and the grammatical subjects therefore correspond with the Actors of the material processes. These Actors turn out consistently to be the participants, realised as whole, indivisible beings: 'Vi/she' and 'he'. As we shall see, this is in marked contrast to the Janice Galloway passage.

The extract from 'David' also describes two characters kissing, but the mode of representation is very different. Most obvious is the choice of narrator, here a first-person narrator as opposed to the invisible third-person observer in the Kelman passage (for a more detailed discussion of narrative voice, see Chapter 9). The choice of first-person narrator allows us access into the mind of one of the characters at least. Several mental processes therefore accompany the material processes (which are still the majority), some relational processes and – notably – an existential process at the end of the extract:

Material processes	*Mental processes*	*Relational processes*
touched	felt	(His palm) was (clammy)
laced	(don't) remember	(they) were (tight)
biting		(I) wasn't (sure)
came		
touched		
stretch	*Verbal process*	*Existential process*
split	said	there was (my mouth ...)
was sliding		
tugging		
rubbing		
pulled		
looked		
trailed		
stiffening		
(let) wait		
nipping		

The fictional world here is portrayed with reference to the sensations and feelings of the narrator ('His palm was clammy ...I felt him swallow'). The material processes have less to do with behaviour and movement, and more to do with tactile, and sometimes violent, actions ('touch', 'bite', 'split', 'slide', 'rub', 'trail', 'nip') . The final existential process is an interesting way of representing an action that might well be otherwise expressed. Compare four possible ways of expressing this event:

He kissed me.
I kissed him.
We kissed.
There was my mouth on his neck.

The different versions shuffle around the responsibility for the action. In the final version, the responsibility for the action is not made explicit, and we are left with an event which seems almost to happen by itself: the narrator notes that her mouth is on the boy's neck, but she does not acknowledge responsibility for putting it there. Compare the passage from *A Chancer*, where the man, Tammas, takes the initiative ('he kissed her neck') and she responds ('they were kissing each other's lips').

That a denial of responsibility is evident elsewhere in the extract from 'David' is clear if we consider the Actors of the material processes. In the Kelman passage, we saw that the Actors were consistently the characters, realised as whole people (he/she/Vi). In 'David', however, whole individuals perform some of the actions (e.g. 'I touched once'), but others are performed by inanimate objects ('The wood ... biting') or, more commonly, parts of the body ('Our teeth touched ... I felt ... the skin on my lip stretch ... my fingers rubbing ... his nails trailed ...'). Whereas Kelman presents his characters as having responsibility for their actions, Galloway, in this passage, presents her narrator as being less directly responsible: the grammar of the passage reduces the sense of personal responsibility and increases the sense of being caught in the midst of uncontrollable events and sensations.

Other observations could be made about the two passages: for example, that the Circumstance Adverbials in the Kelman passage are largely locative, the strong sense of place adding to the feeling of concreteness; and that in the Galloway passage the use of non-finite verbs (i.e. verbs not marked for tense or person: 'rubbing', 'stiffening', 'nipping') further increases the sense of a series of floating, ongoing processes, not tied down to time or an individual participant. But enough has been said to indicate that such analyses can help to reveal differences in the stylistic strategies of different texts, and that they can provide a powerful descriptive framework with which to communicate these differences.

MODALITY

Grammar does not only represent a view of things. Jakobson's six functions of language include an emotive and a conative function; that is, two of the things that language does are to express something about the attitudes and emotions of the addresser (the emotive function), and to direct the addressee, by commands, requests, question or pleas (the conative function). These two functions, emotive and conative, are collapsed in Hallidayan grammar into one function, the interpersonal.

To say that language has an interpersonal function, then, is simply to say that language expresses the addresser's relationship with the addressee and the addresser's attitude towards what he or she is saying. It is here that we begin to see some superficial differences in the way that the grammars of Scots and Southern English realise these functions.

Grammatically, there are different means of expressing emotion and attitude in the grammar of a language. Two of these means fall into the grammatical category of modality. Modality refers to a certain class of adverbs (modal adverbs) and a certain class of verbs (modal auxiliary verbs). Both perform similar functions. A third way of expressing attitude is through the choice of certain main verbs and adjectives. A fourth way of expressing attitude is by way of rhetorical questions, commands, pleas and so on. We shall consider these possibilities in detail, beginning with some examples of Scots and English modal adverbs.

MODAL ADVERBS IN SCOTS AND ENGLISH

Modal adverbs express attitudes towards what is being said. Such attitudes might be expressed roughly as degrees of certainty and uncertainty, desirability and undesirability, importance and unimportance, propriety and impropriety, real and unreal, and so on. Some examples of Scots adverbs which express three of these areas of meaning are given below, followed by their English equivalents:

	Degrees of reality	*Degrees of certainty*	*Degrees of desirability*
Scots:	ackwallie	certie	howpfullie
		shuirlie/fairly	(un)happilie
		aiblins	
		mibbie	
English:	actually	certainly	hopefully
		surely	(un)fortunately
		perhaps	
		maybe	

The function of these modal adverbs, and others like them, is to express the speaker's attitude towards the proposition expressed by the sentence. Compare the following examples, with and without modal adverbs:

Glesca's the capital o Scotland.   Glesca's mibbie the capital o Scotland.

Embro's the capital o Scotland.   Shuirlie Embro's the capital o Scotland.

| | Ackwallie, Embro's the capital o Scotland. |
| Things'll (no) chynge. | Howpfullie, things'll (no) chynge. |

It is important to remember that the unmodalised sentences still implicitly express an attitude on the part of the speaker: bald generalisations express complete certainty. But the modalised sentences express the speaker's attitudes explicitly, by way of the modal adverbs.

MODAL AUXILIARY VERBS

Modal auxiliary verbs, such as 'might', 'could', 'should', 'will' and 'would', function in a similar way to the modal adverbs: they add a layer of attitudinal meaning to any proposition. The system of modal meanings is complicated in southern English, and the situation is further complicated by the fact that in Scots the same words can have a different range of meanings. The main points of both systems are summarised below (cf. Palmer 1979; Lewis 1986; Leech 1987) .

THE ENGLISH MODAL AUXILIARY SYSTEM

Modal auxiliary verbs express a range of attitudes. Most modal auxiliaries fall into pairs, and can be labelled 'near' or 'distant' modals. Near modals express proximity in time, factuality and social familiarity. Distant modals express distant time (usually in the past), hypothesis rather than fact, and social distance (in other words, politeness).

Consider the different meanings of 'can' and 'could' in the following sentences:

1. Can I borrow your dictionary?
2. Could I borrow your dictionary?
3. Liz can win a gold medal in Tokyo next month.
4. Liz could win a gold medal in Tokyo next month.
5. I can swim two lengths of the pool these days.
6. I could swim twenty lengths when I was wee.

Sentences 1 and 2 ask *permission* of the hearer. The difference between the two sentences can be explained in terms of *social distance*: in the first sentence we assume that both speakers are on equal terms, whereas, in the second sentence we assume that the hearer has superior status (or is being accorded superior status as a token of politeness). Sentences 3 and 4 both express *possibility*. The difference between these sentences can be seen in terms of *distance from reality*: sentence 3 expresses a stronger possibility than sentence 4, which is more hypothetical. Notice that in sentence 4, 'could' does not indicate the past: as in sentence 3, the speaker is referring to a potential event in the future. The final two sentences express *ability*, and the difference between these sentences can be considered as *distance in time*: sentence 5 indicates the present, and, in sentence 6, 'could' now indicates the past.

As these examples illustrate, the modal auxiliaries are very sensitive to context; however, their meanings are relatively stable, and they fall into two general categories of near and distant.

The table below shows, in a very simplified manner, the basic meanings of the primary modal verbs in English. It should be borne in mind that the meanings denoted do tend to shade into each other, and that some speakers might use several of the modal auxiliaries in different ways to others. Note that not all auxiliary verbs fall into neat pairs.

Meaning	Near modal(s)	Distant modal(s)
ability	can	could
possibility	can/may	could/might
permission	can/may	could/might
obligation/	must/have (got) to	had (got) to
requirement	need to	needed to
		ought to
		had better
deduction	must/have to	had to
prediction/	will/shall/be to	would/were to
hypothesis		
intention	will/shall/be going to	would/was going to

THE SCOTS MODAL AUXILIARY SYSTEM

Not all language varieties have the same distribution of meaning for the modal auxiliary verbs. Indeed, the Scots system is slightly different from the southern English one (cf. Aitken, in T. McArthur 1992: 904–5). For *permission*, 'can' is normally used instead of 'may', and 'must' expresses *deduction* more often than *obligation*. Although 'sall' (meaning *intention* with the first person, and *prediction* with second and third person) is quite common in written Older Scots, it is now mostly obsolete. A reduction of 'sall' to '-'se', (used with the first person, e.g. 'I'se warrant …') became used as a kind of emphatic present in the late eighteenth and nineteenth centuries. 'Will', used with the second and third persons, can indicate the speaker's *intention* (e.g. 'Aye, ye will so go!'), but it simply expresses *prediction* when used with the first person (e.g. 'I'll see you the morn's mornin'.). Highland English speakers might use 'will' to make a tentative *hypothesis* (e.g. 'You'll have had your tea'; 'Will you be a student, then?').

In the west and south of Scotland, 'can' and 'could' are sometimes treated as main verbs, and therefore they might be combined with other auxiliary verbs (e.g. 'Will ye can fetch us the paper?'; 'I micht could dae that'). Scots might notice some other divergences from the English system in their own usage. The main Scots and southern English usages are summarised below:

Meaning	Near modals		Distant modals	
	English	Scots	English	Scots
ability	can	can	could	could
possibility	can/may	can/will maybe 'll mibbe	could/ might	could/ might micht
permission	can/may	can	could/might	could
obligation/ requirement	must have (got) to need	maun have (got) to need to	had (got) to needed ought to should	had (got) to needed to ought to/ ocht to should/ would had better
deduction	must have to	must have to	must have had to	must have had to
prediction/ hypothesis	will/shall/ be to	will/sall [rare] be to	would/ was to	would/ was to
intention	will/shall/ be going to	will/ be going to	would/was going to	would/was going to

The modal system (in Scots and English) is a complex one, and so it is not always possible to limit the meanings expressed by a particular verb. The result is that when, for example, the sentence 'You can leave now' is taken out of context, the auxiliary verb 'can' might be expressing permission, possibility or ability. Even in context, a definitive meaning might well be elusive – the following sentence might still express any of the three possible meanings: 'Your visa has been processed; you can leave now'. The sentence might also express other meanings depending on the context: for example, if spoken sarcastically by a secret service-man, it might be taken as an implied threat. The effect of context on speaker meaning is considered in detail in Chapter 6.

PROCESSES AND ATTRIBUTES

Sometimes the attitude of the speaker or writer is explicitly expressed in the choice of a main verb describing a mental process, or in the choice of an adjective describing a mental attribute. Compare the following ways of expressing *certainty*:

1. The government *will* take action now.(Predictive modal auxiliary)
2. *Surely* the government will take action now. (modal adverb)
3. I am *sure* the government will take action now. (mental attribute)
4. I *believe* the government will take action now. (mental process)

Such verb and adjective phrases all express subjective mental processes and states. Grammatically similar are modal processes and modal attributes. These are realised by verbs and adjectives which fall into the areas of meaning which are tabulated above, and would include the following:

1. The goverment *requires* to take action now.
2. I am *obliged* to cooperate.
3. What is *needful* is a better understanding of the problems.
4. It is *possible* that we shall have to reconsider.

RHETORICAL QUESTIONS AND COMMANDS

Falling outside the realm of grammar proper, but still worth considering here, are rhetorical questions and commands. These are 'interpersonal' insofar as they do two things:

1. they increase the sense of personal interaction between speaker and listener, or writer and reader;
2. they can be revealing of the assumption of the speaker/writer: for example, the rhetorical question 'Are they crazy?' assumes that 'they' are acting as if they are; and the appeal 'Help save our Scottish Regiments' embodies the speaker's assumption that the regiments should be saved.

MODALITY AND AUTHORITY

It is obviously important to look at the way in which modality is expressed in texts. It is also important to consider modality where explicit modal expressions are relatively few. Let us consider a text where the writer assumes some degree of authority with respect to the reader. The text is an extract from an editorial, from *Lallans*, a magazine which publishes poetry and prose in literary Scots. On these – and similar – texts, the following activities can be carried out:

1. Identify all modal adverbs in the text(s). What kind of meaning do they express? Do any patterns of modal meaning emerge?
2. Identify all modal auxiliary verbs in the text(s). What kind of meanings do they express? Are they near or distant modals? Does any pattern emerge?
3. Identify any modal or mental processes/attributes in the text(s). Does the writer present him/herself as *certain* or *uncertain* about his/her propositions?
4. Comment on the assumptions underlying any rhetorical questions, commands or appeals in the text(s).

The following extract is by David Purves, from the Editorial of *Lallans* 41 (Mairtinmas 1993, p. 4). Like Neil MacCallum's letter reprinted in Chapter 1, this editorial takes issue with the Director of the Scots Language Resource Centre's pronouncement that it it is not necessary to teach children standard Scots; it is, however, necessary to help children understand dialects other than their own.

> The onlie kynd o Scots that coud be taucht is the leiterarie Scots that is no ferr aff a standart that awbodie can unnerstaun. This is the leid that haes been uised for poetrie by skreivars frae Allan Ramsay til Willie Soutar. It is, forby, the leid o the ballads, proverbs an sangs in Scots. Whan we read that, 'Willie's gaen tae Melville Castle, buits an spurs an aw,' an that 'he kissed the lassies aw fareweill afore he gaed awa,' we ir no daelin wi onie dialect. This is no a leid that is aucht onie parteiklar district o Scotland. For aw that, this is no tae say that the lave we hae o spoken Scots in dialects lyke Caithness, or what is spoken in Glesca bi Rab C. Nesbitt, is no important. What is needfu is ti mak guid again the brukken link atwein the speik in the playgrunds an the national heritage o leiterature in Scots.
>
> Ti try ti teach dialects in skuils insteid o a mair standard kynd o Scots based on the leiterature, is shuirlie ti pit the cairt afore the horse an expek it ti pou.

There are remarkably few explicit modal markers in this passage, which is to be expected in texts expressing authority. Such texts are likely to express confident assertions, untinged by doubt and probability. Such confident assertions are:

> This is the leid that haes been uised for poetrie …
> It is, forby, the leid o the ballads …
> …we ir no daelin wi onie dialect.
> This is no a leid …
> For aw that, this is no tae say …

It is the absence of explicit modal markers here that implicitly communicates the authority of the editorial: the assertions are presented as facts. Some explicit modal markers (e.g. the adverb 'shuirlie' and the adjective 'needfu') support this sense of authority: 'shuirlie' expresses *certainty*, while 'needfu' indicates a *requirement*. It is part of the construction of an authoritative persona to state what is certain and what is needed.

Nevertheless, even in editorials, a measure of modal expressions of desirability, speculation and prediction will be evident from time to time. Here, the initial sentence contains the only two modal auxiliaries, 'coud' and 'can', expressing distant possibility and present ability respectively. These are key points in the argument. The basis for the assertion that 'leiterarie Scots' is not a dialect is made on the grounds of *ability*, in this case its intelligibility: 'awbodie can unnerstaun [it]'. And for this reason, the opening point is made about the *possibility* of teaching Scots: 'the onlie kynd o Scots that coud be taucht is … leiterarie Scots'. It is perhaps ironic that this possibility is expressed by the more distant, speculative 'coud'. The choice of the modal 'can' would have brought the concept of teaching Scots in schools much closer to the here-and-now.

What we have here, then, is a text which is a linguistic construction of authority as communicated by a writer of editorials: the writer might begin by expressing possibilities, but he concludes with a series of assertions, marked by a signal of strong certainty. He has the knowledge necessary to state facts and possibilities, and he has the insight to state what is required in the situation discussed. He expects to be agreed with.

Authority can be constructed in different ways. Compare the relatively unmodalised editorial with this extract from a seventeenth-century sermon by Alexander Pleden, a non-conformist field preacher. Pleden lived a nomadic life because of his religious views, and at different times was a refugee in Ireland, a prisoner on the Bass Rock, and a fugitive living in a cave by the River Ayr (see Reid 1982: 171ff.).

Now people of God in Scotland, there is another thing that I have to tell you, and that is this, I would have you get preservatives, for ye walk in a pestellentious air and are nearer unto hazard nor ye are aware of. If any of you were going throw a citie where the plague were hot, ye would seek something to be a preservative to put in your mouths and noses to keep you from being infected with the smell. There will be need of this in Scotland err long, Sirs. I know ye think me a fool for saying these things, but I man tell you this in the name of the Lord, who sent me this day to tell you these things, that err it be long the living shall not be able to bury the dead in thee, O Scotland, and manie a myle shall ye go and ride and shall not see a fire house, but ruinous wastes for the quarrel of a broken Covenant and wrongs done to the Son of God in Scotland. And then the testimonie of a good conscience will be a good feast in that day …

Here, there is much more evidence of modalised expressions:

I have to tell you
I would have you
If any of you were … you would …
There will be need of this …
I man tell you this
the living shall not be able to bury the dead
manie a myle shall ye go and ride
and shall not see
the testimonie of a good conscience will be a good feast in that day.

The modality of the extract shows the preacher constructing himself as a man with a spiritual *compulsion* to spread the word of God ('I have to/ man tell you …') . This preaching lays a set of *obligations* and *requirements* upon the congregation ('I would have you …There will be need of this …'). The requirement, to 'seek preservatives', is supported by the *hypothetical conditional* ('If any of you were … you would …'), and by the horrifying *predictions* which conclude the extract. The key to the authority of this sermon is the expression of obligations – the preacher is obliged to disseminate God's will, and the congregation, on hearing the Word of God, is obliged to act. This contract is predicated on the assumption that the preacher has access to God's will – an assumption supported by the use of verbs expressing mental processes: 'I know ye think me a fool …'. In this sentence, it is the congregation that 'thinks', but the preacher who 'knows'. The emotional appeal of the sermon is heightened, too, by the rhetorical address to 'thee, O Scotland'. The extract is a good example of authority being constructed in a highly modalised and rhetorical fashion.

Modality, then, as we have seen, involves the linguistic construction of a relationship between the addresser, the addressee and the text. So far, we have concentrated on texts which construct the addresser as having authority over the addressee, and a strong degree of certainty about what is being asserted in the text. Editorials are a useful place to begin an exploration of this kind of modality, because they are a genre whose function is to pass judgement on an item of current interest. Other genres, such as sermons, political speeches and election broadcasts, are equally fertile grounds for such an analysis. In these texts, authority can be constructed in a variety of ways: by appeals to reason, to emotion or even to supernatural knowledge. We shall return to the issue of modality in literary texts in Chapter 9, where it will be placed in the wider context of narrative technique.

4

———— • ————

QUESTIONS OF VOCABULARY

USING WORKS OF REFERENCE

A brief word is due, at the start of this chapter, on the use of works of Scots dictionaries in stylistic analysis. We are fortunate in having a range of exceptionally good and increasingly accessible dictionaries of Scots to hand. I refer in most of the following analyses to the concise versions of the Scots and Oxford English dictionaries, since these are the ones that readers of this book are most likely to be familiar with. For those readers with access to good libraries, the standard reference works on Scots are the *Scottish National Dictionary* (*SND*), which aims to cover the language from 1745 on, and the *Dictionary of the Older Scottish Tongue* (*DOST*), which, when completed, will cover the language from the fourteenth to the eighteenth centuries. The *Concise Scots Dictionary* (*CSD*) and its pocket version both draw on the larger, multi-volume works, and they share some of their strengths and weaknesses.

It is worth looking at a single entry from the *CSD* and considering the kind of information that it gives. The entry for 'misfare' is as follows:

> **misfare &c** [mɪsˈfer; *pt* -før; *ptp* -ˈfor(ə)n, *-ˈfer(ə)n] *vti* **1** misfare, come to grief *la14-, now Sh.* **2** *of an enterprise* go amiss, miscarry, fail *la 14-e16, only Sc.* **3** *vt* impair, bring to ruin; mismanage *la15-16, only Sc.*
> *n* misfortune *15-19.* [ME; OE *misfaran*, ON *misfara*]

The beginning of the entry gives information, in the International Phonetic Alphabet, about the pronunciation of the item, its past tense form, and two possible past participles. The pronunciation marked with the asterisk is believed to be no longer current. Then grammatical information is given: the word can be an intransitive verb, that is, a verb which is not followed by an object. The meaning of this form, 'to come to grief', and the substantive form (that is, the noun meaning 'misfortune'), are shared with English. The *Shorter Oxford Dictionary* defines the word so:

Misfa·re, v. [OE *misfaran* = OFris. *misfara*, MHG *missevarn*, ON *misfara*. See MIS-', FARE, *v*,'] 1. *intr*. To fare ill, come to grief – 1633. 2. To go wrong; to transgress – 1487. So †Misfa·re *sb.* going wrong; misfortune –1596

The *CSD* shows us where the two language varieties, Scots and English, overlap: the etymology of the word is shared, and up to a point its meanings are also common to each variety. However, as the *CSD* shows, the 'common core' meaning of the item is now found only in Shetland, and from the fourteenth and sixteenth centuries, further meanings and possibilities were developed: the word was used particularly to refer to the failing of an enterprise – in other words, it was associated with the domain of business – and it could be used transitively, that is, with an object, to mean 'to bring [something] to ruin'. These latter meanings are specific to Scots.

The *CSD*, then, contains a wealth of extremely useful information. Its parent dictionary, the *SND*, is an even greater achievement; however, each dictionary covers only those areas of Scots which are not dealt with by standard English dictionaries, and the *SND* omits many Scots slang items. This serious omission is shared to a lesser extent by offspring such as the *CSD*. For modern urban slang, therefore, a dictionary from another stable, such as the diminutive but useful *Collins Gem Scots Dictionary*, or a semi-serious word-list such as *The Patter*, might in some cases be more helpful than a more rigorously academic work.

The *DOST* is encyclopedic in its reference, particularly in later volumes, since it aims to include the full range of Older Scots vocabulary, including slang and common core items. For those letters still not covered by the *DOST*, and indeed for a wealth of information on Scots items in general, it is still worth consulting the complete multi-volume second edition of the *Oxford English Dictionary* (*OED*). The *OED* also has the advantage of suggesting different patterns of development for Scots and English 'common core' vocabulary items. The latest edition of the *OED* is available in electronic form, which allows it to be searched in various new and interesting ways: for example, all the citations in the dictionary by a particular Scottish writer can now quickly be put on screen. There are plans afoot to make the *SND* similarly available.

The *Scots Thesaurus* (*ST*) is again a selective work of reference, being based on the material of the *Scottish National Dictionary* and the *Concise Scots Dictionary*. It is nevertheless useful, as we shall shortly see, in providing a rudimentary 'map' of Scottish culture by outlining the areas of meaning which are important in Scots. We also see more clearly the range of possible vocabulary items from which a particular Scots item has been selected.

Lexicography is undergoing a revolution as new technologies allow more text to be processed more quickly and efficiently. Dictionary-making on the scale of the *DOST*, the *SND* and the *OED* is a project that nevertheless spans generations, and the procedures and quality of different volumes of multi-volume dictionaries will be variable. When looking up words, it is therefore useful to consult more than one work of reference in order to obtain a fuller appreciation of the denotative and connotative value of any lexical item. It is worth bearing in mind that even the best dictionaries are fallible, but a judicious survey of information about key words can greatly assist the interpretation of a difficult text.

SCOTS: A DIMINISHING RESOURCE?

It can be argued that the vocabulary of modern Scots is limited, insofar as it is restricted to certain everyday topics and traditional occupations. A glance at the categories covered by the *Scots Thesaurus* will reveal rich lexical categories dealing with parts of the body, physical states, farm-ing, fishing, social behaviour, traditions and festivals. However, catego-ries do not exist for science, technology, computing, psychoanalysis, literary theory, and so on. It is sometimes considered to be part of the project of promoting a standard Scots to extend the scope of the language by encouraging writing in domains such as the scientific. How feasible is this? Imagine, for example, writing a user's manual for an Apple Macintosh computer in Scots. The first lines of my own manual read:

> The equipment described in this manual generates, uses, and can radiate radio-frequency energy. If it is not installed and used properly – that is, in strict accordance with Apple's instructions – it may cause interference with radio and television reception.

Now, with some help from the *Concise English–Scots Dictionary* (*CESD*), I can hazard a rough translation of this:

> The gear descreivit in this leerin buikie generates, yaises, and micht gie aff a lowe o radio-frequency energy. If it is no settlit in and yaisit wicelike – that is, stricklie conform tae Aipple's instruc-tions – it micht pit yer radio and television reception in a spin.

I make no claims for this rough translation: it is crudely done by trying to substitute one word for another, always a dubious practice. The point is simply to summarise one of the main issues in the analysis of

Scots vocabulary. In the *CESD*, I found no equivalents of 'radio-frequency energy', 'television', and so on. There is a word for 'reception', but it has the sense of 'welcome'. Eyebrows might be raised at my use of 'settle' for 'instal' – the Scots word really should be used for the 'installation' of a minister. I am rather fond of 'gies aff a lowe' (literally, 'gives off radiance') for 'radiates', but I remain unsure if it would be accepted as technical vocabulary. Possibly, as Tom Leonard might say, in 'Unrelated Incidents (2)':

> a doant kerr
> fyi caw it
> an apple
> ur
> an aippl –
> jist leeit
> alane!

Nevertheless, there are some good reasons for attempting such a task as this. First, it is important to recognise that within a single language variety (whether Scots or English) there are various constraints determining choice of vocabulary. We shall consider these shortly under the heading of register analysis. Second, when two varieties, such as English and Scots, exist simultaneously, sharing a 'common core' of vocabulary and grammatical items, it is important to realise that there is not a one-to-one correspondence between the Scots items and the English ones. The brief activity above is an attempt to illustrate this: for example, the Apple user's guide contains the word 'use' in its instructions. The direct Scots equivalent is 'yaise' (or one of its variants). However, it is possible to argue that 'yaise' is inappropriate to the context of formal, technological written discourse – that (for historical reasons) the English form is what a Scot would use in such contexts, reserving the Scots word for speech, or for informal contexts – although perhaps it might be used in formal, even written, contexts when the activity or subject matter is viewed as typically Scottish (e.g. crofting rather than computing).

This point is further complicated by the fact that a Scot might write 'use' but pronounce it 'yaise', if moved to read the word aloud. Which form is then being used? Either case can be argued. Moreover, some Scots language activists might argue that restricting Scots to certain subject areas is an unhealthy way of putting the variety in a linguistic 'ghetto', and that, the cringe factor notwithstanding, Scots should be employed in writing technological documents and the like in the mither tongue. Two examples of the latter approach are the SNP's occasional policy of having a Scots version of some of its documents, as well as English and Gaelic ones (see the letter reprinted in Chapter 1), and Billy Kay's BBC Scotland radio series, *Amang Guid Company*, featuring conversations in Scots with such as investment bankers about investment banking (admittedly this was still spoken mode, but the topics were unusual in that they fell outwith the 'traditional' domains of farming, fishing and crafts, and the speech genre was a radio interview rather than a casual conversation). The lexical situation in modern Scotland is undoubtedly complicated. How can we begin to make sense of it? There are various avenues of approach.

DENOTATION AND CONNOTATIONS

When analysing the meaning of words, linguists distinguish between the generally accepted literal meaning of a word, its 'core' or 'dictionary' meaning (i.e. its denotation), and the additional associations that the word might accumulate, perhaps for individuals or groups of people, over time (i.e. its connotations). If the connotations of a word become sufficiently well established and widespread, they could become part of its denotation, or they could become a new denotation – that is, its 'dictionary' definition would either change or be added to. It is to be expected that even in cases where Scots and English vocabulary items have common roots and, initially, common denotations, the development and distribution of meanings north and south of the border might well diverge. To take the example of 'pudding', present-day Scots and southern English both have the sense of (a) a kind of sausage and (b) a dessert. However, the former meaning is more prevalent in the north. Similarly, the transferred meaning, probably connotational in origin, of a 'pudding (head)' being a stupid person, survives in the common Scots insult 'ya puddin', while equivalent insults are evidently less frequent in the south.

ASPECTS OF REGISTER

'Register analysis' is the name given to the study of language variation according to situation. Although it can be applied to both grammar and vocabulary, we shall concentrate on the latter here. There are three main aspects of register:

> *Domain* (sometimes called 'field'): some terms might be restricted to certain topics, subjects or activities. For example, the word 'forisfamiliate' ('of a minor, living independently of his or her

parents because of being married') is a term only found in legal contexts. We can say, then, that this term is in the domain of law.

Tenor: the interpersonal characteristics of words (e.g. are they formal, informal, intimate, abusive?). Terms of address and endearment are obvious examples of tenor. For example, 'croodlin doo' (literally 'wood pigeon') is recorded as a term of endearment in Scots, obviously expressing intimacy.

Mode: refers to the question of whether words are found in written or spoken discourse, or both. A good dictionary will often give words labels such as 'literary' – which would suggest that the term is now probably found only in written texts (or, at most, texts written to be recited or read aloud). An example of this would be a modern occurrence of 'puirtith' meaning 'poverty' – now only found in literary Scots.

A careful consideration of the patterns of domain, tenor and mode of vocabulary items can tell us a great deal about the intended impact of a text: what context we are supposed to put it in, the relationship between speaker and hearer or writer and reader, and whether the text is intended to be understood as spoken, written, conversational, literary, journalistic etc.

COLLOCATION

Consideration of the collocations of words (that is, the words that they are found with, or sometimes combine with) can tell us more about the associations of the word under scrutiny. For example, the *CSD* tells us that 'kirn' in the sense of 'a celebration marking the end of the harvest' can combine with 'dollie' or 'baby', the combination meaning 'a decorated female effigy' made from the 'kirn cut', or last sheaf or handful of corn to be cut. Other possible collocations include 'kirn supper' and 'win the kirn' (that is, to gain the honour of cutting the last sheaf). These collocations suggest something of the ritualistic, communal and competitive characteristics of harvesting – characteristics which might now be less in evidence given the widespread mechanisation of agriculture.

EXPANDING SCOTS VOCABULARY: OUT OF THE GHETTO?

Writers who employ literary Scots, or Lallans, tend to be those who are most concerned with the elaboration of the language – that is, the use of Scots beyond the traditional domains in which it is now largely used. We can identify various strategies for increasing the range of Scots vocabulary (cf. Macafee c. 1989: 12ff.). First of all, the status of Scots as a medium of communication can be raised by the translation of prestige literature into Lallans. This general activity can lead to more specific strategies: the revival of archaisms, possibly by 'dictionary-dredging'; borrowing of words from other languages; and the creation of new words, or 'neologisms'. Let us consider these strategies in turn.

TRANSLATION OF PRESTIGE LITERATURE INTO SCOTS

Literary translation into Scots is a long-established practice. Gavin Douglas observed in the sixteenth century that the Scots word-stock is stretched by such projects. The desired effect of such translations is not simply that new words are created and old words revived – current words are also given new associations. For instance, a writer may take a word which is associated with a particular register of Scots, possibly a low register, and include it in a high-style passage in a translated text – and in so doing begin to change the expectations that people have of the suitability of those lexical items for particular situations. A good example of a recent translation into Urban Scots is Edwin Morgan's version of Rostand's *Cyrano de Bergerac*, an adaptation that demonstrates that the much-derided medium of Glaswegian Scots is equal to the task of providing an idiom for the legendary, long-nosed soldier, poet and lover. The translation revives, or possibly reinvigorates, such Scots items as 'gloamin' (twilight), 'dauner' (wander) and 'stravaigin' (travelling aimlessly). The value of the Scots items is increased by collocating them with such high-style Latinate items as 'forbearance' and 'protuberance', and, of course, by their very appearance in a translation of a highly-regarded play:

CYRANO: Look at me, ma freen, whaur's the forbearance
Wid circumvent this auld protuberance?
Oh, a kin huv nae illusions. Christ though,
The gloamin winkles oot some weel-faur'd show
Of feelin, when Ah dauner by the trees
And wi this Beelzebub o a nose release
The *Quelques Fleurs* o April, and watch a perr
Stravaigin in the muinlicht. Who'd no prefer
Tae walk wi his ain love, spring or fall,
Unner the muin? Ah dream o that scenario,
Forget Ah'm no cut oot fur a Lothario –
Then see ma shedda-profile oan the wall!
(Rostand/Morgan 1992: 33)

RESURRECTING ARCHAISMS

Words like 'dauner', 'gloamin' and 'stravaigin' are still heard in non-literary use in parts of Scotland. However, other words which have generally lost their currency (or possibly which never had much currency outside literary contexts) might be resurrected in modern contexts, particularly by Lallans writers. When archaic or obsolete vocabulary is lifted straight from an earlier piece of work, there may well be an allusion to the earlier text. Macafee (c. 1988) points out the similarities between William Dunbar's 'Ane ballat of Our Lady' and Sydney Goodsir Smith's 'The grace of God and the meths drinker':

> Hale sterne *superne*! Hale, in *eterne*,
>   In Goddis sicht to schyne!
>
> > (Dunbar)
>
> > There
> – But for the undeemous glorie and grace
> O' a merciful omnipotent majestic God
> *Superne eterne* and sceptred in the firmament –
>
> > (Goodsir Smith)

Alternatively, words can be lifted from dictionaries, as MacDiarmid famously did with dictionaries and glossaries by Jamieson and Wilson. Today there are more and better opportunities for 'dictionary-dredging' than even the modern makars enjoyed. However, as the quotation below suggests, this strategy can cause irritation.

> Those who feel that a pure English does not wholly encompass the Scottish experience as mediated through language may by all means introduce a peculiarly Scottish word, if the situation calls for it in their judgement. Those who feel impelled to write in dialect are equally entitled to do so. But let us cast aside this falsification – for such it is – that a reconstructed Scots is feasible or, indeed desirable. ...
>
> A final word: as I said, nobody hears anyone speak of 'aiblins' nowadays. How would it be if a poet writing in English introduced terms such as 'doth' or 'mayhap' or 'verily' into his verse? He would probably be laughed out of court and his poems would find it hard to gain a place in any literary magazine. Why, then, must we have 'aiblins' and 'maun' and such-like inflicted upon us? Let the dead bury the dead. (Youngson 1992: 92)

The attitude expressed here might well be questioned – poets writing in English could conceivably use terms like 'verily' or even 'mayhap' if they wished to give their verse an archaic quality. The language would certainly be mannered, but mannered language has always been a feasible option for poets. The taste for 'unmannered' poetic language is, after all, a relatively modern phenomenon, and literary fashions do change.

BORROWING FROM OTHER LANGUAGES

In his Prologue to the First Book of *Eneados*, Gavin Douglas defends his strategy of borrowing words from other languages to expand Scots:

> Lyk as in Latyn beyn Grew termys sum,
> So me behufyt quhilum or than be dum
> Sum bastard Latyn, French or Inglys oys
> Quhar scant was Scottis – I had nane other choys.
> (Book 1, ll. 115–18)

The argument here is that rather than 'be dumb' in situations where Scots was lacking, Douglas would take from the word-stock of other languages. It is a strategy echoed 400 years later by the poet and translator Douglas Young – with a significant qualification (Young 1946: 23):

> If Lallans fails, coin something from Latin or Greek if you like, as King's English does; if all else fails admit a Hottentotism rather than another Anglicism. This should be our intransigent policy for the next five hundred years or so.

The source language of borrowings is, of course, an important consideration: the cultural history of Western Europe dictates that Greek and Latin borrowings are considered prestigious; the stylistic effect of the distribution of Latinate and native northern items in Older Scots poetry is discussed in Chapter 11. The relatively more recent political history of Scotland and England, and in particular the resurgence of a nationalist sense of a separate cultural identity for Scotland, prompt Young's ban on 'Anglicisms' to the extent that he – grudgingly – would admit 'Hottentotisms' in their place. An example of Young's use of an obvious Gaelic loanword can be seen in *The Puddocks* (1958), his translation of Aristophanes' *The Frogs*. At one point, Dionysus calls Euripides 'puir aiblach' (l. 852; 'poor dwarf'). The *SND* traces the history of this word, from an instance in 1725 when it meant 'mangled carcase', to twentieth-century cases where it means 'worthless or diminutive person'. The Gaelic origins of the expression are still evident one of the twentieth-century citations, and the *SND* observes that the expression is particularly common in the north-east of Scotland. Young's use of a Gaelic loanword here serves to reinforce the nationalistic tone of the translation. Even so, it is difficult for any Scots writer to avoid borrowing from English, as we can see from other lines in the same play. Aeschylus later describes the audience for his plays as 'nae corner-boys and spivs, like nou, far ben in racketeering' (l. 1,015). Young's attempts to avoid the use of Anglicisms were obviously overcome here by the attraction of borrowing English items, such as 'spivs', which express concepts that had been topical in a Britain which still vividly remembered rationing.

NEOLOGISMS

A final strategy for expanding Scots is the use of neologisms, or newly-coined words. As we saw in Chapter 1, the Scottish Nationalist Party drew criticism at its 1993 Conference for using the word 'unthirldom' in a letter in Lallans from the Party Convener. The word obviously carried the sense of 'independence', and was used to Scotticise the slogan 'Independence in Europe' (or 'Unthirldom ben Europe'). Criticism centred on the argument that an alternative word, 'freedom', has existed in both Scots and English since medieval times, and its use in Scots is sanctioned by a famous passage in John Barbour's *Brus*: 'Freedom is a noble thing ...'. In fact, although the sense has been extended, and a nominal form coined, the roots of 'unthirldom' are found in traditional Scots. The transitive verb 'unthirl' has existed in the language since the late sixteenth century, at least in the form 'unthirled' meaning 'unsubjugated', or, alternatively, not bound by 'thirlage' (that is, 'thrall or bondage to a particular mill'; early eighteenth century). Its new use then builds on a sense of 'breaking free from subjugation', a sense not necessarily expressed by the more general 'freedom'.

New Scots words tend to be of four types (cf. McClure 1981c): compounds such as 'ayebydand' ('always-remaining') or 'fause-bounder' (literally 'false-boundary', meaning 'gerrymander); figurative or meta-phorical extensions of existing words, such as 'ice-flume' ('ice-river' or 'glacier'), 'pow count' ('head count', or 'opinion poll'), or indeed 'unthirldom'; words based on sound-symbolism such as 'flichterie-fleeterie' (which sounds like other words meaning light, quick activity, e.g. 'flicht', 'flit', 'fleet'); and calques, that is, words modelled on compounds or idioms in another language, preferably not modern English, but often Germanic: for example, 'yearhunder' ('century'; cf. German 'Jahrhundert'). The use of a Germanic language, the ancestor of present-day English and Scots, bestows some degree of historical 'authenticity' on a coinage. Some usages combine a number of these types: for example, the SNP letter uses the word 'walin' to mean political election, an extension of the Scots meaning, 'choice', in the direction of the German 'wählen', meaning 'to elect'.

QUESTIONS OF VOCABULARY

To summarise thus far, when investigating the vocabulary of Scots, the following questions and procedures might be useful:

1. Does the word in the text have direct Scots/English equivalents, for example, 'use'/'yaise', which are variants of a common root, and 'ear'/'lug', which are etymologically distinct? If so, look up both terms in good Scots and English dictionaries.
2. Is the denotation of the terms the same? That is, do they have the same basic literal meaning(s)?
3. Do the dictionaries tell you anything about the connotations of the terms, that is, what they are sometimes associated with? How do the connotations compare?
4. Do the dictionaries tell you anything about the register of the terms? That is, are they restricted to certain domains, i.e. areas of activity, topics, etc.? Is information given about their tenor, e.g. if they are formal, informal, slang? (As mentioned above, the *SND* unfortunately excludes much slang.) Is there anything indicated about the mode (are the terms usually spoken, written or both)?
5. Do the dictionaries tell you anything about the collocation of the term, i.e. words or phrases that it might be found with?
6. Is there other useful information not covered by the above, e.g. about the currency of the terms (are they obsolete or rare); are they specific to a particular region; what is their etymology, etc.?
7. If a compound word is not found in the dictionary, are its component parts there? Are synonyms for the compound available in Scots? If so, why haven't they been used?
8. If a word which is not a compound is not in the dictionary, is it slang; or is it a neologism based on metaphor, or sound-symbolism; or is it an expression based on a word or phrase in another language?

The answers to these questions help in a stylistic analysis of a text, once we also ask the question 'Why?' Given the possibility of selecting from a range of vocabulary items, why is a particular choice made?

'ADDRESS TO THE HAGGIS': A LEXICAL ANALYSIS

As a demonstration of a simple lexical analysis of a well-known Scots poem, consider the italicised words in the opening two verses of Burns's 'Address to the Haggis':

> Fair fa' your honest *sonsie* face,
> Great *Chieftain* o' the *puddin*-race
> Aboon them a' ye tak your place
>   *Painch*, *tripe* or *thairm*;
> Weel are ye wordy of a grace   5
>   As lang's ma airm.
>
> The groaning *trencher* there ye fill,
> Your *hurdies* like a distant hill,
> Your pin wad help to mend a mill
>   In time o' need,   10
> While thro' your pores the *dews distil*
>   Like amber *bead*.

'Sonsie' is of course a Scots item, deriving from Gaelic, and cognate to the noun 'sonse' (good luck) which is found in blessings such as 'sonse fa' ye', which in turn is echoed in the opening line. The haggis is being marked as a particularly Scottish dish; it is being wished luck, but it is also a bringer of luck.

'Chieftain' is a word shared by both Scots and English. The denotation is, of course, 'leader'. However, whereas the *CSD* refers to the possible connotation of 'clan leader', my edition of the *Concise Oxford Dictionary* suggests the possible meaning 'leader of brigands or bandits'. The different possibilities here suggest – however tenuously – a divergent north/south sensibility about clan or tribal chieftains: in the context of Jacobite sentimentality, they are 'great leaders'; in the context of English demonology, they are 'brigands'. The point here is that although 'chieftain' is a common core item, shared by Scots and English, its connotative value might be different in each case.

'Puddin' is another common-core item, although, as noted earlier, its semantic development is different in English and Scots, Scots still allowing the earlier meaning of 'offal-filled sausage'. Falling into the domain of food, it collocates with similar fare: 'painch' and 'tripe' (which are synonyms for animal entrails used as food) and 'thairm' (animal gut used as the skin of a sausage). Denotatively, these items share similarities in ingredients; connotatively, they are associated with poor or homely food. Such fare would probably not have merited much culinary praise – tripe, particularly, now has the transferred meaning of 'rubbish'. That Burns is celebrating haggis, in the company of related foodstuffs commonly considered of little worth, is the key to the tone of the poem. Either the poet is being ironic, or he is encouraging a revision of attitudes to this type of food – or possibly he is leaving open a dual interpretation. An ironic reading is supported by the fact that the genre of the poem, an address, raises expectations of a noble addressee – expectations deflated by the subject of the poem. On the other hand, the use of the word 'honest' in the first line suggests that in this poem (as elsewhere in Burns) it is the unpretentiousness of the Scottish fare which is being celebrated.

'Trencher' also falls within the domain of food – it is a word now apparently obsolete in both Scots and English. Literally meaning 'a wooden serving-plate', it does survive in the compound 'trencherman', meaning 'someone with a good appetite' or 'someone with good taste in food'.

'Hurdies' ('buttocks') is interesting because of its tenor. The fact that it sounds like a familiar diminutive, and the fact that it refers to a vulgar part of the body, suggest that the speaker has a familiar or even intimate relationship to the personified haggis. This is not a formal celebration. The informality complements the slightly mocking knowledge that the object of celebration is commonly considered to be of low culinary status.

Lines 11 and 12 contain several individual vocabulary items, which, taken together, suggest a metaphorical reading. 'Dews' denotatively refers to droplets of moisture, but can also refer to 'mountain dew' or illicitly-produced Scotch whisky. This possible reading is reinforced by the adjacent word 'distil', which is technically appropriate to both readings, but is perhaps associated more with the latter. It is often as instructive to consider which word a writer has not chosen to use, as to consider which word the writer has chosen. Burns might have used the word 'draps' instead of 'dews' in the eleventh line of 'Address to the Haggis' – the word would have sounded more Scottish, and it would have maintained metrical and alliterative patterns. But 'dews' was preferred, partly for its associations with a high-style register, and partly for its specifically alcoholic connotations. The 'bead' in line twelve can again refer to moisture, but it also has the possible meaning of alcoholic beverage, a reading again reinforced by the epithet 'amber'. There is a fairly strong case, then, for arguing that in these two lines the haggis is being compared to whisky – a drink which is both intoxicating and, again, markedly Scottish. There is a slight shift in register here too – towards a more euphemistic, 'poetic' language, which is once more at odds with the homeliness of the subject.

We have confined ourselves to a sample of the vocabulary items from two stanzas of Burns's poem. However, we have, I hope, seen enough to illustrate some relevant points. First, the selection of vocabulary in the poem celebrates the haggis as a markedly Scottish dish. The specifically dialect vocabulary, obviously, contributes to this, but so do the Scottish connotations, distribution and relative currency of some of the 'common core' items such as 'chieftain' and 'puddin'.

Second, the register of the items helps us to account, in part, for the comic tone. The domain, represented by a low-status foodstuff – 'haggis', 'painch', 'tripe', 'thairm' – is in contrast to the celebratory function of the ode. The familiar tenor of items like 'hurdies' suggests the intimacy of the speaker with the object of his adoration. The mismatch between poetic genre and the unexpected tenor and domain mean that we have to reassess received opinion about this type of food, elevating its status, or we have to read the poem as ironic. Either reading is possible, and each can be supported by the linguistic evidence.

ORGANISING LEXIS

So far in this chapter, we have looked at some general questions of vocabulary: the difference between connotation and denotation; the register of certain items; and ways of expanding Scots vocabulary. Most of these questions have considered lexical items in isolation. We shall now move on to consider lexis in context.

Lexical items in isolation will not give much information about their meaning. Think, for a moment, about the meaning of the word 'big'. How might the term be defined: by sense relation (for example, by reference to a word with a similar or contrasting meaning), or ostensively (e.g. by referring to something that typifies the word), or in some other way? Now consider the dictionary definition found in the *CSD*: It begins:

> **big**[1] **&c; bigg** *la16-e20* … *vti* … **1** build, construct, erect *la14-*. **2** *of birds* build nests *15-*. **3** *vt, also* ~ **on** *la16-17* build, make (a fire) *16-*. **4** occupy (land), *esp* by building on it; build on (land or ground) *15-16*. **5** stack (hay, corn *etc*) *la19-*.

If you did not choose any of these five meanings, it is hardly surprising – deprived of a context, most people would choose the most familiar meaning of any word, here probably something like 'not small'. Context constrains the range of meanings that can be chosen. You might have come up with a different definition if asked to define 'big' in the context of the following anonymous translation of the Song of Solomon 4:4 (1860; reprinted in Tulloch 1989: 128):

Thy neck is like the toor o' David, bigget for an armourie, whauron hing ae thoosan' bucklers, a' shields o' dochtie men.

Here, the form of the item ('bigget'; the past participle of the verb) and its collocates (buildings such as 'toor' and 'armourie') narrow down the choice of meaning to something like 'build', 'construct' or 'erect'.

The meanings of lexical items in literary texts, particularly poetry, may not always be so easy to specify unambiguously: the 'richness' of some poems lies partly in their play on multiple senses and subtle connotations, and the contexts are often unusual, for example:

This is the laund that bigs the winds; winds big the cloods.

Here, the core meaning is again 'build', but the process is metaphorical. Possibly the second clause ('winds big the cloods') suggests the meaning 'stacks', and we might visualise the wind stacking the clouds in pre-mechanisation hayrick-shapes. Dictionaries do not always suggest subtler possibilities; and poetry does not always allow us to narrow meanings down, even if we should want to.

COLLOCATION

So far, we have considered collocation only briefly. The 'collocates' of a lexical item are those words with which it occurs: 'big' in the sense of 'build' often occurs with items referring to types of building. It is less likely that it will occur with items like 'winds' and 'cloods'. The frequently-occurring collocates give us a sense of the denotation of the item; the rarely-occurring items give us a sense of the connotations.

In this chapter, I have relied mainly on intuition when deciding whether or not a lexical item's collocates are likely or unlikely, normal or deviant. However, it is worth bearing in mind that computerisation now allows us, at least in principle, to accumulate vast bodies of text (called corpora) which can then be manipulated quickly and easily. The immediate collocations of an item (i.e. the words immediately adjacent to it) can quickly be displayed in this fashion (cf. Kirk 1992/3; and Chapter 11 below).

LEXICAL SETS

Some lexical items co-collocate; that is, they appear with a similar range of items. 'Wind' and 'cloods', for example, will share many collocates, meteorological items such as 'blouster' (squall), 'flocht' (sudden gust), 'rain', 'blash' (a drenching shower), 'onding' (downpour), etc. These lexical sets are the basis for reference works such as the *Scots Thesaurus*.

As noted earlier, lexical sets provide a kind of 'map' of the culture which communicates by using a particular language or language variety. Cultures will generally produce many lexical items to express meanings which are important to them. A revealing exercise is to look at tabloid newspapers and count the number of lexical items which refer to parts of the female body and compare with the number of lexical items referring to parts of the male body. Then you can categorise the parts that are most frequent, and, by implication, most important. Most exercises of this kind will quickly demonstrate that 'tabloid culture' focuses on the female body much more than the male body, which speaks volumes about the readership and its abiding concerns.

The *Scots Thesaurus* can also be used in a similar way: there are categories for 'wind, storm' (5.2.2) and for 'rain, mist, snow, frost' (5.2.3), and a smaller one for 'thunder and lightning' (5.2.4). 'Hot weather' does not merit a separate section and appears only under 'general weather states' (5.2.1). Again, this linguistic fact is revealing of general cultural concerns.

LEXICAL COHESION

The presence of lexical items which co-collocate in a text is one way of giving it cohesion; that is, the presence of items which share a range of collocations supplies 'chains of meaning' which tie a text together (cf. Halliday and Hasan 1976). In practice, if we come across a particular lexical item in a text, then we would expect to find other items which pick up on it in some way: the item 'blash' might be picked up by other weather words, and the item 'hungrysome' might be picked up by other items referring to appetite or thirst (e.g. 'drowthy', 'stappit') or by items in the related lexical set of food. By identifying lexical sets and considering how they develop in cohesive 'chains', we can isolate themes in texts and observe how they are developed.

There is a noticeable weather theme running through this chapter, largely because it is a fairly well-defined area of meaning which often features in Scottish literature and, indeed, everyday life. To demonstrate a simple activity involving collocation and cohesion, we shall look at two texts – a weather forecast and a poem – and consider which lexical items are used, and how they are used.

The first text is a transcript of a weather forecast broadcast on 18 April 1994. It was broadcast on ITV's *Scotland Today*:

Scotland Today

Good evening. Well, those of you with barometers will notice a slow but sure drift to the left tonight and tomorrow, but for a change strong winds and driving rain are not on the agenda. So onto tonight and though a good deal of cloud across the region bringing a few showers mostly across Strathclyde and Central, the odd one possibly heavy later on, but despite the showers the cloud should break at times especially as we progress eastwards. The temperatures not falling too low tonight thanks to the cloud and a gentle westerly breeze, the lowest values around 3 to 4 degrees Celsius so perhaps maybe the odd isolated patch of ground frost around. Tomorrow, then, quite a bright day in store and most if not all of us should see something of the sun. A few showers'll be floating around for much of the day. The odd one could be heavy, and prolonged, but having said that they're going to be well scattered, and the east of the country should on the whole see fewest showers. Now given some sunshine we could see temperatures up to twelve or even thirteen degrees Celsius, and with only gentle breezes it should feel pleasant enough. Any showers however will pull the mercury down a few degrees. Well that's all for now; I'll be back later with an update, but in the meanwhile here's the summary.

A BRIGHT DAY
SOME SUNSHINE

SCATTERED SHOWERS
LOCALLY HEAVY

LIGHT WINDS

Adapting some of the categories from the *Scots Thesaurus*, we can group the weather-related vocabulary as follows:

Scientific instruments	*Climatic change*
barometer	slow but sure drift
mercury	for a change
satellite	changing
	falling
	pull (the mercury) down

Rain, wind, cloud	*Sunshine/clear weather*
wind	a bright day
rain	the sun
cloud	sunshine

shower
patch of ground frost
breeze

Temperatures	*Types of shower/rain*	
temperature	(frequency:)	a few/fewest
value		the odd
Celsius		well scattered
degree	(force:)	heavy
		light
		driving
	(duration:)	prolonged

A full lexical analysis of this text would go beyond weather words to classify, for example, words referring to places ('the region', 'Strathclyde') or direction ('westerly'). But the focus on weather words alone, here, is probably sufficient to confirm our expectations about the communicative purpose of the text: it is designed to convey information about what kind of weather to expect, what temperatures to expect, the duration of particular types of weather (here, mainly showers), and how the weather and the temperatures might change. Perhaps to lend some authority to the forecast, there is also a reference to a scientific instrument ('barometer'). This analysis might seem like a lot of effort to state the obvious, and, given the simple and highly-constrained nature of most weather forecasts, such a complaint carries some weight. However, weather forecasts are a good example of 'everyday language' against which to profile examples of 'literary language' which also use weather vocabulary. An example of this is Kate Armstrong's 'This is the Laund':

> This is the laund that bigs the winds; winds big the cloods;
> the cloods, the weit, the weit, the grun; an antrin steer
> o syle an rain. Thon frimple-frample watter rowin
> frae Kenmore tae Dundee is cried the River Tay.
> It's no the Tay ava. The get o aa the oceans   5
> fae Mexico tae Greenlaun, gift o a cloodit warld
> an we wid awn it, screive it. Siccar the wather-man
> ettlin tae shaw the springheid, warstles wi his isobars
> an seeks tae trammel fer ae day the fricht o kennin
> the yird's sclenter. Tae whitna maitter scarts atween
>   these banks   10
> on loan a whilie, we sall gie particlar name. But gif
> the medium be the message, raither mind hoo thocht
> or scoukin haar kenna the immigration laws.

Frae muckle warld tae muckle warld, bairnie tae mither,
spicket tae seiver, onding tae quernstane,   15
sae Scotland's fowk, skailt frae ae clood or ither
intil a sheuch descrives them as her ain;
sae ilka braith an ilka tear ye share, an antrin steer
o rain an syle, a thocht baith gied an taen.

This poem might seem opaque to many readers at first sight – indeed, its Scots is so dense that it may be incomprehensible without
recourse to a glossary. Rather than simply looking words up, however,
we can again sort them into groups of items with related meanings.
One thing which strikes us on a close examination of the vocabulary of
this poem is that there is a greater variety of lexical sets than are found
in the weather forecasts: we do not only find words for rain, wind and
cloud, but also for offspring, possession and violent activity, as we can
see below (line numbers are given after each item):

Rain, wind, cloud
laund (1)
winds (1, 1)
cloods (1, 2, 16), cloodit (6)
rain (3, 19)
haar (13)
onding (15)

Geography and topography
grun (2)   Greenlaun (6)
syle (3, 19)   warld (6, 14, 14)
watter (3)   yird [?] (10)
River Tay (4)   sclenter [?] (10)
the Tay (5)   maitter (10)
oceans (5)   banks (10)
Mexico (6)   sheuch (17)

Confused/violent activity
steer (2, 17)
rowin [?] (2)
frimple-frample (3)
warstles (8)
trammel (9)
sclenter [?] (10)
scarts (10)
skailt (16)

Offspring
get (5)
bairnie (14)
mither (14)

Possession
gift (6)
awn (7)
on loan (11)
her ain (17)
share (18)
gied (19)
taen (19)

Communication
screive (7)
shaw (8)
gie … name (11)
medium (12)
message (12)
descrives (17)

People (see also *offspring*)	*Seasons*
wather-man (7)	springheid (8)
Scotland's fowk (16)	

Meteorology	*Mental state*
isobars (8)	fricht (9)
	kennin (9)
	mind (12)
	thocht (12, 19)
	kenna (13)

Physical activity	
braith (18)	
tear (18)	

Legislation	*Man-made water chanels*
immigration laws (13)	spicket (15)
	seiver (15)

The classification of the lexical items into sets here is more thorough than that attempted for the weather forecast, partly because the communicative purpose of a poem is harder to specify – obviously the poem is not only about the weather. Parts of a weather forecast can be neglected if they are irrelevant to the needs of the viewer (who might only be interested in a particular geographical area, and who might or might not be interested in gardening, for example). But if poetry, as Jakobson suggested, is written and communicated for its own sake (see Chapter 2), then none of the lexical sets noted above, large or small, can be considered inessential.

The poem shares with the weather forecasts some areas of vocabulary: rain, wind, cloud and geography, for example. However, other areas of meaning are prominent in the poem, notably words for confused activity, and – perhaps less obvious when we actually read the poem – words in the lexical sets of possession and communication. Collecting the lexical items into sets such as these can help to display prominent themes in a text, and the sets can support arguments about the interpretation of the poem. On the basis of the lexical sets, we might argue, for example, that the poem is about the great natural cycle: the global transformations of earth to air to water to earth (a cycle paralleled by that of mother to child). People (here 'Scotland's fowk', typified by the 'wather-man') try to possess this terrifying, confused and violent process by naming it: 'awn' (own) is linked to 'screive' (write) as if one is a paraphrase of the other. However, the poem's speaker asks us to remember that natural cycles, like thought itself, cannot be pinned down or channelled by the laws, labels and limits of humankind, and that, despite our claims of ownership, we are equally part of the great cycle, our breath like the wind, our tears like the water.

This kind of analysis can be revealing, but we should not be misled into thinking that it is purely objective. The setting-up of categories implies that I already have an idea of what might be interesting, and during the process I was aware that others were possible (I could have had a category of water-channels which took some items from topography and absorbed all of the man-made ones; I do not think it would have changed my overall interpretation, but it might have emphasised different nuances in the poem).

The activity of sorting a text's lexis – particularly a poem's lexis – into semantic categories also points up the ambiguity of some items. A weather forecast is or should be unambiguous: people want to know what the weather will be tomorrow. As noted earlier, a poem's richness is partly derived from deliberate (or perhaps, sometimes, fortuitous) ambiguity: multiple meanings are equally valid. Two tricky terms to classify in 'This is the Laund' were 'rowin' (3) which could, according to the *CSD*, mean simply 'rolling', or possibly 'lurching', or 'tossing and turning relentlessly', or perhaps even 'rowing (a boat)'. More atmospherically, 'the yird's sclenter' could mean the movement of the earth, or possibly a hillside grave, depending on how you interpret 'yird' (earth; grave) and 'sclenter' (the *CSD* defines this as meaning 'loose stones', or 'a stony hillside'; the poem's glossary suggests 'movement', since the word seems to be related to 'slidder' or 'slither'). A lexical analysis of poetry need not necessarily restrict the number of possible meanings; rather it should, within reason, multiply them.

As we have seen, simply grouping lexical items into sets can be revealing in a number of ways. If the *Scots Thesaurus* gives us a map of Scottish culture, then, on a smaller scale, the lexical analysis of individual texts can give a profile of their primary concerns – their themes – and can highlight the nuances and ambiguities that are specifically part of a literary interpretation.

5

METAPHOR

A fuller consideration of metaphor follows naturally on from a discussion of words and their literal meanings. Metaphor is a figure of speech, that is, a non-literal use of language which involves a transfer of meaning. Since Aristotle's *Poetics*, metaphorical uses of language have been seen as inspired deviations from ordinary language: striking metaphors have been applauded as part of the poetic function of language, while often-used 'dead metaphors' and 'mixed metaphors' have been attacked as clichés and as evidence of muddled thinking. As we shall shortly see, the long-standing view of metaphor as literary ornamentation has radically changed in the past few decades.

The traditional view of metaphor is set forth by Adam Smith, now widely remembered for founding the discipline of economics, but who also lectured on Rhetoric and Belles Lettres in the Philosophy Department of Glasgow University, at various times between 1748 and 1763. In his sixth lecture, he defines metaphor thus:

> In every metaphor it is evident there must be an allusion betwixt one object and an other. Now as our objects are of two classes, intellectuall and corporeal, the one of which we perceive by our mind only and the other by our bodily senses; it follows that metaphors may be I of four different kinds. Ist when the Idea we borrow'd is taken from one corporeal object and applyed to another intellectuall object; or 2dly from one intellectuall object to an other corporeal; or 3^d betwixt two corporeal, or 4th betwixt two intellectual objects. When we say the bloom of youth, this is a meta<phor> of the 3^d kind. When we say one covets applause, this is a<n> instance of the 4th sort of metaphor. The lust of Fame is an instance of the Ist kind, betwixt a corporeal <and> an intelle<c>tual object. {The lust of fame is a transposition of a word from denoting a Corporeal Passion to another Mentall equally gross

and indelicate.} And when we say in the script<ure> language, The fields rejoiced and were glad, The floods clapt their hands for joy, [an] are an example of the 2ᵈ kind. ...

One thing farther that we should observe is that two Metaphors should never be run and mixed together as in that case they can never be both just. Shakespeare is often guilty of this fault, as in the line immediately following that before cited, where he goes on, or bravely arm ourselves and stem a sea of troubles. Here there is a plain absurdity as there is no meaning in ones putting on armour to stem the seas. (Smith 1983: 29–30)

Smith goes on to criticise a few lines of Thomson's *The Seasons* for similar 'absurdities', which, he argues, are admired 'because few take the pains to consider the authors reall meaning or the significance of the severall expressions, but are astonished at these pompous sounding expressions' (ibid., p. 31). In Smith's irritation here, we can see the application of logic to language which characterised the eighteenth century: mixed metaphors are outlawed along with such solecisms as double negatives. Adam Smith believed in a clear, 'transparent' style of language; his second lecture begins: 'Perpicuity of stile requires not only that the expressions we use should be free from all ambiguity proceeding from synonimous words but that the words should be natives if I may <say> so of the language we speak in' (ibid., p. 3). The call for clarity and a good, honest native diction survives right through to this day, and is forcefully expressed in, for example, George Orwell's well-known essay, 'Politics and the English Language' (1946). Both Orwell and Smith deride mixed metaphors, and both hold the view in common that metaphorical language is outside the conventional use of language: it is characteristic of the literary or poetic.

The English literary critic I. A. Richards introduced the terms 'tenor' and 'vehicle' to distinguish between the two terms which are being linked by metaphor, and 'grounds' for the reasons for linking them (Richards 1936). Thus:

A   is described as if it were B on account of certain similarities.
(Tenor)   (Vehicle)   (Grounds)

An example of a poetic metaphor would be the first line of Edwin Muir's 'Scotland's Winter':

Now the ice lays its smooth claws on the sill.

Here, 'ice' (tenor) is described as if it were a bird of prey, or possibly another clawed creature (vehicle), on the grounds that its shape on a window-sill resembles claws. It is the originality of poetic metaphor that is the source of pleasure: we are surprised into looking at the world anew.

However, not all metaphors give us this pleasure. To call the supporting part of a table its 'leg' also involves metaphor: the table is described as if it were an animal on the grounds that its supports perform a similar function to an animal's legs. But the phrase is so conventional that it has lost its power to provoke. This is not to say that the metaphor cannot be revived: if I were doing some elementary carpentry I might say that I was 'amputating' the table-leg; or if I were describing a hallucinatory experience I might describe the table crawling towards me on its squat little legs. But on the whole, phrases like 'dead' and 'moribund' describe metaphors that have become routine. Surprising metaphors are usually considered the province of poetic or literary usage.

A distinction is traditionally made between metaphor and simile: in the latter case, the comparison between tenor and vehicle is made explicit by the use of the signals 'as' and 'like', as in Burns's 'My luve is like a red, red rose'. Other, related, figures of speech include synecdoche, whereby the part is taken to signify the whole (for example, a worker might be referred to as a hand); and metonymy, whereby something is referred to by something else which is associated with it (for example, a diner in a restaurant might be referred to by the meal which he or she has ordered: 'The vegetarian haggis has asked for the bill'). It should be evident from the examples given that simile, synecdoche and metonymy are, like metaphor, not restricted to high-flown literary discourse.

LINGUISTIC AND CONCEPTUAL METAPHORS

More recent work (G. Lakoff and Johnson 1980; G. Lakoff 1987; G. Lakoff and Turner 1989; Steen 1994) has sparked a renewed interest in metaphor, both as an integral part of everyday thought and language, and as a literary trope. Lakoff, Johnson and Turner argue that literary metaphor is an extension of a thought process that also finds its realisation in everyday language. This argument shifts the basis of metaphor from the linguistic to the conceptual domain. Richards' definition of a metaphor as having a tenor, vehicle and grounds belongs in the realm of textual linguistics. Lakoff, Johnson and Turner claim that such linguistic phenomena are the product of a mental or cognitive operation, whereby one structure of thought is 'mapped onto' another structure of thought, creating, effectively, a new kind of understanding. This cognitive operation is a conceptual metaphor. So, in the example given earlier from Edwin Muir, the linguistic metaphor in the poem is the result of a conceptual metaphor: the poet has combined the two separate mental structures, and his understanding of the relationship between birds-of-prey and ice result in a novel perspective of the world. The presence of the linguistic metaphor prompts the reader to combine the separate mental structures in a similar way, and so we attempt to reconstruct the poet's new understanding: possibly that ice on a window-ledge is in some way beautiful but threatening, as a bird of prey is lovely but dangerous. (For a further discussion of mental structures and the process of reading, see Chapter 10; for a sympathetic critique of Lakoff, Johnson and Turner, see Steen 1994.)

IS EVERYTHING METAPHORICAL?

By suggesting that metaphor is integral to our everyday understanding, we run the risk of implying that all our concepts are in some way metaphorical. At its most extreme, this claim is unlikely. G. Lakoff and Turner (1987: 134) distinguish between a strong position and a weak position:

The strong position is:

Every aspect of every concept is completely understood via metaphor.

From this it follows that:

Every linguistic expression is completely understood via metaphor.

The weak position is:

Every linguistic expression expresses a concept that is, at least in some aspect, understood via metaphor.

The weak position is the less interesting of the two and it may be correct. For example, we saw above that in understanding dogs as loyal and lions as courageous, we are metaphorically attributing to them human characteristics and thus comprehending them, *in some small part*, in metaphorical terms. The bulk of our understanding of these concepts is, of course, not metaphorical at all. (original emphasis)

In other words, there are certain concepts which we apprehend and understand more or less directly: people, plants, animals, physical and emotional states, and certain experiences (compare Adam Smith's corporeal and intellectual 'objects'). However, when we encode these concepts in language, complex sets of associations, some partly metaphorical, might be added to the core concept. And when we move beyond the immediately perceived and understood, we use the basic source domains to help us understand the target domains. For example, I know what sleep is; I experience it most nights; and so when the screen of my laptop computer goes blank, I suppose that it is sleeping too. I have mapped the domain of *organism* onto the domain of *computers*, resulting in the conceptual metaphor *the computer is an organism*. This conceptual metaphor is at the root of linguistic metaphors like 'My computer's gone to sleep' or even 'My program has a virus'.

METAPHOR AND LEXIS

We shall consider metaphor at the level of lexis before going on to consider its use at discourse level. Some very basic words in the lexicon have a number of different meanings. Take, for example, 'gane' ('gone') in the following contexts (cf. the *CSD*):

1. She's gane awa tae Embro.
2. It was Sunday gane a week. (= It was Sunday past.)
3. He's gane forty-twa. (= He's more than forty-two.)
4. The puir auld fule's gane. (= The poor old fool's crazy.)

Here the dictionary might present the items as an example of polysemy; that is, of multiple meanings which are separately listed. The four examples use 'gane' to mean something like 'departed', 'past', 'over' and 'crazy'. However, the fact that one word, 'gane', is used to express these concepts suggests that our culture categorises them in a similar way. This categorisation is determined by the culture rather than the language itself.

What, then, might be the basis for the categorisation? The 'core' meaning here might be something like 'departed on a journey', which would fit (1) in a literal fashion. The metaphor *time is a journey* might then explain sentence (2): Sunday has taken a week or so's journey into the past. A similar metaphor, *life is a journey*, accounts for sentence (3): he has departed from that point on his journey which corresponds to the age of 42. The metaphor *insanity is elsewhere* accounts for the final example, the 'auld fule' being well on his way to his metaphorical destination. A quick look at the *ST* under the heading 'Madness' (15.6.8) reveals that other expressions making use of this metaphor are 'ajee' (literally 'off the straight'), 'awa i the heid', 'by one's mind', 'cairried', 'in a creel', 'be forby oneself', 'gang by oneself', 'rove', and 'wandert'.

The metaphors bind together the various meanings of 'gane' into a semantic category (i.e. 'departed on a journey'), and also link the meanings with others in similar semantic fields (e.g. 'absence', 'insanity' etc.). Other metaphorical processes are common at the lexical level. If 'Summer's lang gane' makes use of the metaphor *time is a journey*, then 'summer' here is a departed traveller. The season is 'reified' (that is, made into a 'thing'), after which it can be represented as having taken part in an action (namely, 'departure'). A common type of reification is, of course, personification, whereby the 'thing' has the attributes of a person: summer might linger regretfully, and then depart in sorrow.

Reification (the metaphorical process which says *actions are things*) is often accomplished by nominalisation: a verb becomes a noun (e.g. 'to depart' becomes 'departure', 'to look' becomes 'a look', and so on). This way of looking at actions and events is important to our language and thought: it allows us to describe actions in a varied way (e.g. 'a swift and happy departure') and to represent actions as participants in further actions ('The departure was delayed by five hours').

In such examples, much everyday language can be analysed as fundamentally metaphorical. However, it is a moot point whether everyday examples are in fact understood as metaphor. Steen (1994) argues that they are not. His research suggests that 'dead metaphors' are no longer understood by mapping one conceptual domain onto another. If Steen is correct, then the examples of 'gane' given above are simply understood as polysemy, that is, as different meanings of the same word-form. In the literary sphere, too, one person's new conceptual metaphor might well be another person's cliché: much will depend on the individual's familiarity with the literary conventions used in a text. A distinction can be made between the way that an expression such as 'The puir auld fule's gane' can be analysed linguistically, and how it is in fact understood by discourse processors. Linguists may well analyse 'gane' as a transfer of meaning from 'location' to 'insanity'; however, the discourse processor need not actually make this transference every time he or she encounters the expression. To the processor, the expression 'gane' might come to be associated with the domain of insanity, and so no transference of meaning would occur.

Even so, the fact that much everyday language is open to analysis as metaphor can be very revealing of cultural assumptions: the underlying metaphor *insanity is elsewhere* tells us much about our cultural attitudes to madness, even if we do not recognise the metaphor as such, or even if we do not have recourse to a conceptual mapping of different domains each time we use a phrase such as 'Aye, she's gey wandert'. For this reason alone, the new approaches to metaphor are extremely useful in the analysis of texts.

ANALYSING METAPHOR IN DISCOURSE

As we have seen, recent approaches to metaphor argue that metaphor is conceptual as well as linguistic: as human beings, we organise our knowledge in structures or schemata (see also Chapter 10). This means that when we strive to understand something new to us, perhaps something that is beyond our immediate experience, or if we try to understand a familiar concept in a new way, we map elements of one set of schemata onto the new domain. In this process of metaphoric transfer, the language deviates from the norm – although, in time, such deviations might well become conventionalised themselves. It is the analysis of language which has mainly provided the clues to defamiliarise the more conventional metaphors (although see Steen (1994) for alternative research methodologies, borrowing from cognitive psychology).

A particular lexical item will call forth a particular set of schemata: 'clock' will, for example, call forth for most of us a certain type of machinery with certain functions and associations: time-keeping, time-saving, punctuality and clock-watching, etc. If we then wish to present a theory about how the human body reacts to travel across different time zones, we can map onto the domain of the body the domain of clocks: we can talk about 'body clocks' and we know that in some way the body keeps time; it has to be adjusted if the time changes, or it might 'lag' behind the time at the destination. This metaphor is part of a more general one which says that *people are machines* (cf. G. Lakoff and Turner 1987: 132), and can be related to, for example, *the mind is a computer*: 'Sorry, I can't remember her name. My circuits are blown. The file's been wiped.'

Looking carefully at lexical sets is obviously one way of analysing metaphorical transfer: a set of items relating to one domain (e.g. computing) might appear systematically in another domain (e.g. the mind). Looking carefully at the grammar of the text is another way of analysing metaphorical transfer. If *time is a journey*, then journeys have travellers. By another metaphorical transfer, one possible traveller might be a season, and so we can find 'winter' in the Actor slot in a phrase like 'Winter has arrived'.

Let us now turn to some more extended texts, literary and non-literary, and consider how metaphor is used.

From Adam Smith, *The Wealth of Nations* 1937: 383; emphases added)

The manufacturers first supply the neighbourhood, and afterwards as their work *improves* and *refines*, more distant *markets*. For though neither the *rude* produce, nor even the *coarse* manufacture, could, without the greatest difficulty, *support* the expence of a considerable land carriage, the *refined* and *improved* manufacture easily may. In a small bulk it frequently *contains* the price of a great quantity of *rude* produce. A piece of fine cloth, for example, which weighs only eighty pounds, *contains* in it, the price, not only of eighty pounds weight of wool, but sometimes of several thousand weight of corn, the *maintenance* of the different working people, and of their immediate employers. The corn, which could with difficulty have been carried abroad in its own shape, is in this manner *virtually exported* in that of the complete manufacture, and may easily be sent to the remotest corner of the world. In this manner, have *grown up naturally*, and as it were *of their own accord*, the *manufactures* of Leeds, Halifax, Sheffield, Birmingham, and Wolverhampton. Such *manufactures* are the *offspring* of agriculture.

A number of metaphors are evident here, although it is perhaps unlikely that Smith would have granted them that status. The italicised words draw attention to several metaphors: the idea that *processing is refinement* lies behind the cluster of words which see unprocessed goods as 'coarse', 'rude' and processed goods as 'improved', 'refined'. The pervasive metaphor that *commerce is a market* extends what for an agricultural society must have been a common experience, namely market day, into the more abstract, transnational set of economic forces. Expense is something that must be 'supported'; we might characterise this metaphor as *poverty is a burden*.

We must be wary of transferring modern concepts into older texts: in the mechanical age, we might leap upon 'maintenance' used of workers as an example of the *people are machines* metaphor. However, if we look at the entries for 'maintenance' in the *OED*, we do not find entries relating to machines until fairly late: 1884 is the first technological entry (about a telephone company), and from the 1950s onwards there are a few quotations from engineering. Before that, 'maintenance' had to do with 'providing people with the requisites of life' (1389 on), although by 1460 there is the additional sense of 'the action of keeping in effective condition, working order, repair … by the supply of funds or needful provision'. This sense relates chiefly to lands and estates, although there are also references to maintaining lamps in oil, and maintaining troops. Bearing this sense in mind, we may think of Smith's workers as being equivalent to estates, lands, lights or troops, and the possible metaphors *people are property* or *people are assets* suggest themselves more strongly than *people are machines*.

The passage as a whole works out an interesting metaphor by which corn can be thought of as 'virtually exported' if it is eaten by working people (and their immediate employers) who make fine cloth to sell overseas. The specific metaphor might be expressed as *foodstuff consumed in the process of making exported goods is exported foodstuff*. This is a good example of a writer using metaphor explicitly in an attempt to make us rethink a familiar concept.

The reification of 'manufacture', 'agriculture' and 'commerce' as 'things' rather than 'processes' is an example of a common characteristic of scientific writing (*actions are things*), but perhaps the most striking metaphor in the passage is the further elaboration of these reified processes. Once 'manufacture' has been reified, it can 'naturally grow up' ; in a similar way, reified agriculture and commerce can have 'offspring'. This is a further development of the *processes are things* metaphor, and might be expressed as *processes are organisms*. There is an underlying ideology at work here, whether Smith was consciously aware of it or not: by presenting manufacture, agriculture and commerce as organisms, subject to natural laws (growth, procreation), he presents a view of economic history as deterministic, fixed, beyond the control of individual people. This view is a direct result of mapping the target domain of 'processes' onto the source domain of 'living organisms'.

It is interesting to compare Adam Smith's style in his discussion of economics with a newspaper article from the present day:

'View from the Bridge', *The Scotsman*, 14 May 1993

Tide of events rocks boat for EMS

Just as it had begun to look as if the French government had succeeded in restoring confidence in the fragile franc and the European monetary system was safe from imminent disintegration, two more countries have nearly fallen off the raft.

Portugal, which devalued once last year in a desperate attempt to stay on board, did the same yesterday to remain competitive with its bigger neighbour, despite feeling there was no fundamental need to devalue.

Spain is also staying on board, but has devalued the peseta by another 8 per cent to make room for some much needed reflation.

It does leave the ERM in disarray. Greece has never been in the ERM, but the UK and Italy fell out last autumn, and hardly anyone expects the UK to rejoin and give up its newly found freedom to cut interest rates and compete more aggressively at home and abroad.

The Dutch guilder is the one currency which is firmly ensconced in the system.

Eurosceptics will welcome the latest news as further evidence that Brussels bureaucracy is in retreat and argue that the Maastricht Treaty should also be rejected to preserve national independence for all time.

But it is worth pointing out the real risks of throwing the baby out with the bathwater. The ERM turned into a monster partly because it was based on the mark and driven by the special policy requirements of a reunified Germany which were unsuitable for countries suffering from a severe recession and partly because, unlike its predecessor, the European currency 'snake', the flexibility had been removed.

Countries were forced to adopt increasingly painful and inappropriate policies to maintain currencies which became increasingly over or undervalued, until finally and expensively they were overwhelmed by the tide of speculation.

The plain fact is that the Community is not ready to commit itself to a long slow move to a single currency.

But that does not mean that all currencies should go back to floating freely as they did between 1973 and the birth of the snake in 1979.

Free floating encourages massive swings between currencies and discourages the free flow of international trade between natural trading partners.

If EC countries all start competing again on exchange rate policies (as well as actively undercutting each other's wages) it is not difficult to imagine a situation where anti-dumping duties and the paraphernalia of protectionism come creeping back as well.

This is a very different economics text from the previous one. It was written two centuries later for a mass audience publication, and it is concerned with a very specific economic event: the difficulties that different countries were having in 1993 in conforming to the agreed guidelines of the Exchange Rate Mechanism (ERM), a European agreement which, it was hoped, would lead to eventual monetary union (the European Monetary System or EMS).

Here, a relatively arcane subject is being made palatable for a interested but non-specialist reader largely by virtue of an extended nautical metaphor: *economic events are sailing vessels*. Thus events 'rock the boat', countries 'fall off the raft', while others 'stay on board', speculation is a 'tide', and hitherto dead metaphors such as 'reflation' and currencies 'floating freely' are reinvigorated. The nautical metaphors are freely mixed with others such as *the national economy is a patient* (countries 'suffer' recession; policies are 'painful'), and *economic policies are creatures* (the ERM turns into 'a monster', and anti-dumping duties and protectionism come 'creeping back'). Other incidental metaphors in the passage include *currencies are objects* (the 'fragile franc') and *negotiation is war* (Brussels bureaucracy is 'in retreat').

The report is densely metaphorical, despite the fact that it is a piece of broadsheet journalism. The answer to the question of why there are so many metaphors here may well lie in the fact that the topic is specialised, although the intended readers are not necessarily specialists. Extended metaphors have some entertainment value (in Jakobson's terms, the poetic function might be a strong second to the dominant referential function here), but they also help to present a specialist field (the economic processes) to a non-specialist readership in terms with which it might be more familiar, or which it might find more dramatic (sailing, illness, monsters, war, etc.). The idea that metaphors are useful in communicating specialist information to a non-specialist audience does not help us very much with the next text, however:

From Jim Murray, 'Staying Ahead by a Nose', *Scotsman Weekend*, 30 April 1994, p. 6

Oddly, until now, I had never written anything much on Aberlour. When I first knew it, perhaps ten, maybe 15 years ago, it was a 12-year-old in a square bottle with a boring label. It was not a great malt; it lacked balance and polish and a certain bitterness crept into the finish so the last impressions were not favourable ones. But I rediscovered it in the late Eighties as a completely different dram; rich and heavy with strange minty notes making an unlikely but perfect partner for the sherry theme. Furthermore, the ending has you on the edge of your seat in appreciation. There was no comparison with its thin forbear: this was a malt of substance. ...

Aberlour Antique is different to anything that I have tasted, with a spiciness one is more likely to associate with a whisky from north of Inverness rather than the heart of Speyside. It is heavy-duty malt, impressively rich, with a sherry influence which is extremely subtle, allowing the distillery's minty signature to come through. And from an underlying oakiness, it's evident some pretty ancient whiskies, some as old as 24 years, have been tipped into this vatting. Not bad for £24.95. ...

But the real star is the Aberlour 100 proof ... This is a cracking Speysider of immense character. The sweet, honey start gives way to an avalanche of Talisker-like molten whisky which cools to a simmering richness more normally found in ripe Christmas puddings; plummy, slightly burnt and intense. You are not just drinking this whisky, you are riding it. It finishes, eventually, with treacle toffee and leaves you gasping for more. I really didn't know Aberlour had it in it. The £19.95 price tag for a malt with an average age of about nine years makes it worth travelling abroad just to get hold of one.

Here whisky, and the act of tasting it, are conceived in metaphorical terms, and again metaphors are mixed in a cavalier fashion which might be seen as amusing or pretentious, depending on one's inclination. If we disentangle some of the metaphors, we find *whisky is music* (it has 'notes', a 'theme' and a 'signature'), *whisky is a man* (you can 'know' a whisky, it can be a 'partner', it can be 'thin' or have 'character' etc.), *whisky is antique furniture* (it can have 'polish', 'substance', 'oakiness' etc.) and *whisky is food* (there are references to 'honey', 'Christmas pudding' and 'treacle toffee'). Related closely to these metaphors, we find *whisky-tasting is watching a thriller* (when you are 'on the edge of your seat') and – explicitly – *whisky-tasting is riding* (presuming that the whisky is a stallion, or possibly a powerful motorcycle).

What are we to make of these metaphors – again in a factual piece of journalism? Here the topic is not specialised – but it is subjective. The writer needs to communicate what is ultimately a personal experience: how a certain drink tastes. And so, he maps the personal domain onto more public domains. In doing this, he follows a route that other whisky and wine critics have taken, and he therefore satisfies the expectations of a particular (and often parodied) genre. It is interesting to note in passing that some of these metaphors are picked up by whisky advertisers: pictures of whisky bottles and glasses are often set against antique furniture, evoking the 'oakiness' of the taste and the considerable (but hardly 'ancient') vintage of the liquor.

Let us conclude this chapter by comparing such non-literary uses of metaphor with some literary uses: consider two accounts of a rugby match, the first from a novel and the second from a newspaper report.

From Eric Linklater, *Magnus Merriman* (Jonathan Cape, 1934; Penguin, 1959, pp. 137–8)

Rugby can be a game for gods to see and poets to describe, and such a match was this. *L'audace, encore l'audace et toujours l'audace* was both sides' motto, and which was more gallant – England, taller and bulkier-seeming because clad in white: Scotland, running like stags and tackling like thunderbolts in blue – no-one can truthfully say and none would care to know. If Tallent for England was magnificent, Simmers for Scotland was superb. Did

Tallent run the whole length of the field and score? Then Simmers, leaping like a leopard, snatched from the air a high cross-kick of MacPherson's and scored from that. Did Black for England kick like a giant, long, true, and hard? Then see what Logan at the scrum, Smith on the wing, did like giants for Scotland. And each side in turn, tireless and full of devil, came to the attack and ranged the field to score. Pace never slackened from start to finish, and every minute thrilled with excitement till, at the end, wisps of fog came down – perhaps the gods indeed, hiding their brightness in the mist – and in that haze the players still battled with unwearied zeal.

Judge, then, the fervour of the crowd, poised as it were on the broad rim of a saucer, and as thick together as if the saucer had been smeared with treacle and black sand thrown on it. But they were more mobile than sand, and ever and again a movement would pass through them as when a wave of the wind goes through a cornfield. Ever and again, as when walls in an earthquake fall asunder, some twelve or fourteen thousand would shiver and drift away from their neighbouring twelve thousand and then, stability reasserted, fall slowly into place again. And now, like a monstrous and unheralded flowering of dark tulip-beds, the crowd would open to its heart and fling aloft, as countless petals, hats, sticks, and arms, and pretty handkerchiefs, and threaten to burst the sky with cheers. Now they were wild as their poorer neighbours who, some mile or two away, were cheering their paid teams with coarser tongues. Now all Scotland was at one, united in its heat, and only the most sour of moralists would decry that heat because it had been lighted by a trivial game.

The comparisons here are accomplished more by simile than metaphor: the likenesses are thus weakened and are more decorative in nature. The players are described in exaggerated, mock-heroic terms: as powerful and fast animals (stags and leopards), as powerful natural forces (thunderbolts) and as mythological creatures of enormous size and strength (namely, giants). More energy is given to describing the spectators, with emphasis given to their number (numerous as grains of sand), their power (like an earthquake) and their rare beauty (like dark tulips shedding petals). It is worth noting that the comparison of the rugby crowd with the soccer crowd ('their poorer neighbours') is not metaphorical: both domains are inherently similar. Metaphor demands that the domains being likened are inherently dissimilar.

One common metaphor, *sport is war*, is only hinted at in the presence of the words 'attack' and 'battle' in the literary passage. Otherwise the passage is self-consciously 'literary': the poetic function of the report is made clear at the outset, the comparisons are explicitly signalled, and the exaggerated similes and classical references to spectating gods make clear that this is a rhetorical set-piece. The Linklater passage can be instructively compared with a 'real' rugby report.

From *The Sunday Post*, 17 February 1991

Scotland booted out
England 21, Scotland 12
by Fly-Half

Hodgkinson the Hoof booted Scotland out of the Calcutta Cup with five penalty goals and a conversion.

From a Scottish point of view he was not only a goal kicker of unnerving skill, he was also a heartbreaker because Scotland gave away fewer penalty chances than England.

Hodgkinson could hardly miss. Only one went adrift – a testing shot from 50 yards which wavered just outside the posts.

Scotland had a goalkicker, too, in Chalmers, who potted four out of five and wasn't far away with a drop.

Scotland were simply bombed out. Not just by Hodgkinson's boot, but by the accurate line-kicking of their stand-off Rob Andrew.

Scotland couldn't escape from defence often enough to mount any kind of sustained attack.

England's juggernaut forwards saw to that. They gave nothing away in the scrum, exerting the sort of shove which made life a joy ride for their scrum-half Hill.

Sole, Gray, Turnbull, White and Jeffrey all had England at panic stations at odd times, but the defence quickly regrouped and in the end yielded nothing.

The suspicion that the Scots were a bit bare in ideas behind the scrum was borne out. There were individual touches, yes, but few combined movements.

Armstrong robbed Hill at the very first scrum but found the stocky Englishman a difficult customer to pin down. Even so, the Jed man looked as likely as any to punch a hole in the defence.

Chalmers usually chose the right option and handled well, but Andrew read the game so intelligently there was little he could do to alter its flow.

Lineen floated through a few gaps in his old style, but the three-quarter line as a whole could not develop any rhythm against opponents who came at them swiftly and knew how to knock them down.

Gavin Hastings was sorely troubled by Andrew's cunning line kicks, but at least he showed some of the belligerence which the Scots backs lacked.

Had he not been regularly imprisoned in his own half something might have come of his surging runs.

England are still on short rations where tries are concerned with only two in two games, but so long as Hodgkinson keeps thumping them over from all angles and all distances, the Grand Slam must surely be in reach.

Sport and war are two domains which are often linked by metaphor, and this cross-association is evident in a variety of phrases in this report:

Scotland were simply bombed out.

Scotland couldn't escape from defence often enough to mount any kind of sustained attack.

Sole, Gray, Turnbull, White and Jeffrey all had England at panic stations ...

... at least he showed some of the belligerence ...

England are still on short rations where tries are concerned ...

The similarities between the two domains are various – rival groups use tactics to obtain territorial advantage, for example – and so the metaphorical transformations *sport is war* or, in reports of armed conflict, *war is sport*, are understandable. Even so, they have different stylistic and ideological effects. Here, the excitement of a rugby game is heightened by the metaphor, whereas in reports of armed conflict we are encouraged to consider actual life-or-death situations in terms of game-playing. In sports journalism, war metaphors exaggerate the events described; in war reporting, sports metaphors 'domesticate' the events described.

Exaggeration of events accounts too for the metaphors *the English team is a large and fast vehicle* ('England's juggernaut forwards ... made life a joy ride') and *players are thieves* ('Armstrong robbed Hill ...'). The effect of the metaphors here is similar to the effect of the similes in the Linklater passage – to intensify the impact of the narrative. Unlike the Linklater passage, the source domains for the more fanciful metaphors seems to be topical events (such as joyriding) and popular culture (particularly other sports). An example of the latter transformation is *rugby is snooker* ('Chalmers ... potted four out of five ...'). The metaphor here stresses the accuracy demanded of a goal-kicker, whereas the common metaphor *rugby is boxing* (perhaps echoed in the sentence 'Lineen ... came at them swiftly and knew how to knock them down') foregrounds the physical aspects of the game.

It is unlikely that many readers would elaborate upon the metaphors found in economics texts or football reports, or even whisky appreciations, as far as they might elaborate upon the metaphors occurring in literature. Again, this tendency to focus upon the form of poems can be related to Jakobson's poetic function and the argument that it is a characteristic of literature that it communicates a message for its own (playful) sake. Jakobson's poetic function can be seen as the basis of Gerard Steen's four-part definition of literary texts – not so much by their textual characteristics as by what readers do with them (Steen 1994: 34):

1. Readers take maximal freedom for the subjective realisation of literary texts because they are not aiming at achieving practically important functions.
2. Readers treat literary texts as fictional because they do not take them as directly tied to factually relevant circumstances.
3. Readers realise literary texts in more than one way without thereby raising consequential interpersonal or social conflicts of interpretation.
4. Readers realise literary texts with special attention to form as contributing to, and indeed, partly determining, content.

Steen is arguing, in the first three points here, that the uniqueness of literary texts lies not so much in their linguistic features as in how readers process them. Since readers know that literature has no 'practical' function, they allow themselves the freedom to construct multiple interpretations (or 'subjective realisations') of such texts. In other words, the newspaper report of the rugby match discussed earlier, and the televised weather forecast discussed in Chapter 4, will be processed differently from the Eric Linklater passage or Kate Armstrong's poem, simply because the reader knows that the literary texts have no other purpose but to be inventive. Multiple interpretations of such texts are thereby 'legitimised' – no-one is going to argue that one interpretation of a literary text is 'truer' than another, although the validity of interpretations can be assessed in other ways – indeed, the discipline of literary studies is largely concerned with examining the claims of different interpretations of literary texts. The fourth characteristic, that readers know that they should pay attention to form in literary texts, is the closest to Jakobson's notion of a 'poetic function'. Readers of literature expect form to be important to literary texts, and, so Steen argues, they are likely to be particularly alert to the possibilities of metaphorical meaning within literary texts, since metaphor has such a well-established place in literary studies.

Steen thus makes a persuasive case for the importance of metaphor in linguistic approaches to literature. However, as this chapter has demonstrated, metaphor is also an everyday phenomenon, sometimes more evident in non-literary texts than in literary texts. It has a variety of functions, the basic one being to make sense of one domain of experience in terms of another. And so it can be used to familiarise the arcane, make public the subjective, exaggerate the everyday, or domesticate the awful. In literature, metaphor can have the magical effect of making us see the world in new and unfamiliar ways.

6

———— • ————

LANGUAGE IN USE

PRAGMATICS

For much of its history, the study of language has concentrated on the description of sentences. There is therefore a long tradition in the study of word-formation (morphology) and how words are ordered in sentences (syntax). More recently, attention has also been paid to the description of how language is organised above the level of the sentence (discourse analysis, a topic we shall turn to in Chapter 9). There are, however, other approaches to the study of language. An important one is the study of meaning (semantics). Semantics traditionally concerned itself with relations of sense and reference: that is, how words relate to each other (sense), and how they relate to the world, or, more precisely, to a 'universe of discourse' (reference). Not very much attention was paid to the way in which people use language to mean and understand certain things in certain contexts until the establishment of the field of pragmatics.

In his key work on the subject, Levinson (1983) devotes thirty-five pages merely to defining pragmatics. The present brief survey can therefore only present a simplification, but it is fair to say that the study of pragmatics is concerned with how people use language to mean what they want it to mean, and how others understand them. In other words, language is studied as part of human behaviour in context, rather than as decontextualised sentences in isolation. Thus, the study of pragmatics is an attempt to describe systematically not how language is structured, but how it is used.

We shall focus on two important areas of pragmatics in this chapter: speech act theory and conversational implicature. In stylistics, these theories probably find their most immediate application in the study of spoken language, so we shall concentrate mainly on drama. However, pragmatic analyses can equally well be applied to poetry and all types of written prose, particularly the representation of dialogue in novels and short stories (cf. Chapter 7).

SPEECH ACT THEORY

Speech act theory grew out of the work of the British linguist J. L. Austin, and the American linguist J. R. Searle, from the 1950s onwards (e.g. Austin 1962; Searle 1969). Austin's key concern was with certain types of utterance which could not be categorised as true or false. This observation was important because, at the time, a consideration of the truth value of utterances was fundamental to semantic analysis. Relationships of meaning were largely decided by determining whether, if utterance X was true, utterance Y was also true, or whether it was false. Consider the five utterances given below, and try to identify the type that caused Austin problems. Simply ask yourself, which could be true, and which could be false?

1. I see that you're losing your hair.
2. I warn you to keep away.
3. I hear that aliens have landed in Kelvinside.
4. I think this is a daft wee activity.
5. I now pronounce you man and wife.

You may have noticed that utterances (2) and (5) are different from the others. (1), (3) and (4) are all utterances which state propositions about the world (I see/hear/think something). These propositions can be true or false. Utterances (2) and (5) name actions (warn, pronounce) and, further, by naming them, perform them. They cannot be true or false in the same way as the others: they do not only assert something, they actually do something more. A small group of verbs functions in this way: when used with a first-person pronoun, they perform the act that they name. These verbs are called performatives.

TYPES OF SPEECH ACT

This observation – that it might be interesting to analyse what types of act are performed by utterances – led linguists and philosophers to attempt to classify speech acts. There is no consensus on the use of terminology – in linguistics there seldom is, since arguments within the discipline are largely concerned with how linguistic features should be classified. However, the following terms are fairly widely used.

Each utterance in context simultaneously performs several basic types of speech act. For example, in saying 'It's gey cauld the day', the speaker is performing both of the following acts:

1. a locutionary act (that is, forming sounds into connected speech in order to form a proposition);

2. an illocutionary act (that is, doing something by way of a proposition, such as making an assertion about the world: 'it's gey cauld the day').

An illocutionary act might be constative, that is, the speaker might be making an observation about the world. Such observations can be true or false. Alternatively, the illocutionary act might be performative – if the speaker were to say 'I warn you, it's gey cauld the day', the act of warning would be accomplished by the utterance. (A test which helps to identify performatives is the insertion of 'hereby' into the utterance: you can say 'I hereby promise to pay you £10' (performative), but not *'I hereby love you' (constative).)

Now if the speaker were a person of some authority, speaking to a subordinate in a room where the window is wide open, 'It's gey cauld the day' might be a type of speech act which results in a change in the hearer's behaviour: the hearer might well close the window. Speech acts which have an intentional or unintentional effect upon the hearer are labelled perlocutionary acts. Again it is important to note that a speech act might simultaneously be locutionary, illocutionary and perlocutionary.

Some illocutionary acts (such as complaining, ordering and recommending) are obviously intended to have perlocutionary effects, although in practice they might not – the intended act might fail to have any effect if the listener takes no note. Such acts are called directives, and their converse, commissives, commit the speaker to behaving in some way. Commissives include offering and promising.

TYPES OF ILLOCUTIONARY ACT

There is no rigorous taxonomy of illocutionary acts (or illocutions). The labels given to illocutions derive from the everyday system of social interaction. Hurford and Heasley (1983: 244) list the following as types of illocutionary act:

> accosting, accusing, admitting, apologising, challenging, complaining, condoling, congratulating, declining, deploring, giving permission, giving way, greeting, leavetaking, mocking, naming, offering, praising, promising, proposing marriage, protesting, recommending, surrendering, thanking, toasting.

The list is far from exhaustive (cf. Searle 1976), but it gives an idea of how to go about labelling illocutions in a rudimentary way: you simply ask yourself what the speaker is doing when he or she makes an utterance.

It is important to remember that an illocution might also perform a perlocutionary act, if the illocutionary act has an effect on a hearer. Proposing marriage to a mirror is different from proposing marriage to a hearer: one will have no perlocutionary effect, the other may well (for example, the hearer might swoon, scream or sue.) Illocutions are in the control of the speaker; perlocutions are not.

DIRECT AND INDIRECT ILLOCUTIONS

The relevance of speech act theory to literary analysis becomes clear when we begin to look more closely at how illocutions might actually be realised in utterances and how types of illocution are distributed among characters. Direct illocutions (which are not to be confused with directives, discussed above) match illocutionary acts to expected grammatical realisations, so:

Type of illocution	Expected grammatical form
asking	interrogative (e.g. 'Whit like's the wather?')
asserting	declarative (e.g. 'It's gey cauld.')
ordering	imperative (e.g. 'Pit oan yir woolly bunnet.')

Indirect illocutions, however, involve possible non-literal interpretations of the act being performed. For example, 'Wid ye mind closin the windae?' is not (literally) a request for information (although it might be taken literally and get the response 'Aye, I wid mind!'). The act is more like a polite command, especially if the speaker has some authority over the hearer. The degrees of directness of illocutions are a sensitive marker of the social and power relations between speakers and hearers (cf. R. Lakoff 1973). Since one of the main traditions in stylistics has been to consider the establishment and maintenance of power relations in society, the analysis of direct and indirect locutions can be extremely useful, as we shall shortly see in the discussions of a few illustrative texts.

FELICITY CONDITIONS

Another aspect of speech act theory which is directly relevant to stylistics is that of felicity conditions. These are statements of the conditions which must be in place if illocutions are to be carried out properly or felicitously. For example, if X gives an order to Y, then the felicity conditions state that X must be in a position to give orders, i.e. that X is superior in authority to Y. Similarly, if X asks Y for something, the felicity conditions state that X must believe that Y possesses something that X requires.

A special type of felicity condition is the sincerity condition, which states that for communication to function normally, you must be sincere in the acts carried out: i.e. the hearer must believe the speaker's assertions, and, for example, if you apologise for doing something, then you must believe that you are to blame. It would be insincere to apologise if you were not to blame. The sincerity condition, of course, does not mean that people are never insincere, or that they never lie – however, if people were routinely insincere, then communication would break down.

SPEECH ACTS AND STYLISTICS

The value in analysing communication in terms of speech acts is that the results can throw into relief the social relationships between interlocutors. Speakers who are powerful and who might wish to assert their power might use a high proportion of direct directives. Those who are more polite, or who are less comfortable with their authority, might use indirect directives. Those who are eager to please might use a lot of commissives. Knowledgeable people, like the writers of newspaper editorials or opinion columns, might use a lot of constative acts to assert propositions about the world; and those with defined social roles (such as ministers, spokespersons and toastmasters) may routinely use a predictable set of performatives (announcing, pronouncing, addressing, etc.). In drama, as we shall now see, character can be constructed and developed partly by the distribution of certain types of speech act.

My Way Home is the final part of Scots director Bill Douglas's largely autobiographical trilogy of childhood and young adulthood in Scotland and (during National Service) Egypt. The three short films are all sparse, minimalist and bleak. In the extract which follows, the hero, Jamie, is befriended by an Englishman, Robert.

> Jamie, a not too happy face, leaning on his hand.
>
> He is sitting at a table in the mess. He is staring mournfully at a kipper on his plate. Just then a bright and breezy Robert comes.
>
> ROBERT: Wotcha.
>
> He sits down, fetching his plate.
>
> On the tannoy, a woman's yearning voice is singing a song.
>
> ROBERT: Why aren't you eating?
> JAMIE: It's all bones.
> ROBERT: All kippers have bones. There is a way of coping.

He reflects on the situation for a moment, then he says at a more intimate level

ROBERT: Don't you know how?

Jamie shrugs.

ROBERT: Would you like me to show you?

Jamie stops leaning on the table. He inclines himself round to suggest that he is taking up the offer. Robert sets about his own kipper.

ROBERT: You set about it like so.

He frees the entire back bone with a slice of the knife and sets it neatly aside.

ROBERT: It's easy when you know how to get rid of the rubbish. Try it.

Jamie fumbles away for a bit but gives up.

Robert switches their plates. Jamie whispers.

JAMIE: Thanks.

Robert shrugs. Then there is just the two of them quietly eating.

This is a simple passage to analyse, yet it shows clearly the type of relationship which will develop between the two young men: Robert is competent, cheerful, the initiative-taker; Jamie by contrast is quiet and in some practical ways incompetent. The distribution of speech acts confirms such an interpretation:

Robert's utterances	*Type of speech act*
Wotcha	greeting
Why aren't you eating?	questioning
All kippers have bones.	asserting
There is a way of coping.	asserting
Don't you know how?	questioning
Would you like me to show you?	offering
You set about it like so.	instructing
It's easy when you know how to get rid of the rubbish.	asserting
Try it.	ordering

Jamie's utterances	*Type of speech act*
It's all bones.	answering
Thanks.	thanking

Robert's speech acts show him first of all as the authority: he asserts, instructs and orders. When he questions, it is to satisfy himself about the state of Jamie's ignorance. His is a benign authority – his instructions are a consequence of an offer to help. Robert is also the initiative-taker: he greets Jamie, Jamie fails to reply. His role as initiative-taker is also seen in the frequency of his illocutions as compared to Jamie's: he persists in the interaction despite getting little in the way of encouragement.

Jamie's speech acts show him in the subordinate position: he answers Robert's question, and thanks him when the plates are swapped. Otherwise, his communication is by way of shrugs and gestures.

This is the third scene in which Robert and Jamie's relationship is developed, and it contrasts markedly with the first scene. In their first encounter, it is Jamie who is the initiative-taker, and the authority of each is more delicately balanced:

> JAMIE: When was it you came out here?
> ROBERT: What?
> JAMIE: When was it you came out here?
> ROBERT: When what? Oh, about a month before joining up with you lot.
> JAMIE: I'll show you around if you like?
> ROBERT: What?
> JAMIE: Don't you speak English?
> ROBERT: I beg your pardon?
> JAMIE: What's your name?
> ROBERT: Robert. What's yours?
> JAMIE: What?
> ROBERT: What is your name?
> JAMIE: Jamie.

When we examine the illocutions in this scene, a different pattern emerges:

Robert

What?	requesting restatement
When what?	requesting restatement
Oh, about a month before joining up with you lot.	answering
What?	requesting restatement
I beg your pardon?	requesting restatement
Robert	answering
What's yours?	questioning
What is your name?	questioning

Jamie

When was it you came out here then?	questioning
When was it you came out here?	questioning
I'll show you around if you like.	offering
Don't you understand English?	questioning
What's your name?	questioning
What?	requesting restatement
Jamie.	answering

In this scene, Jamie has the authority and confidence to ask questions, although only twice does he receive an answer: there is some measure of mutual incomprehension. It is also Jamie who makes Robert an offer, although again this is not taken up. Towards the end of the scene it is Robert who is asking the questions, and Jamie who is answering – roles which they will settle into as the film progresses. An analysis of the film, scene by scene, would make explicit the relative authority of each character, and how their authority develops. This strength of speech act analysis is particularly evident in scenes where the respective authority of each character is a dramatic issue, as in Donald Campbell's *The Jesuit*.

The scene below is a prelude to an interrogation in 1614 by Archbishop Spottiswoode of the Jesuit priest (and, subsequently, martyr), John Ogilvie. Again, we can consider the illocutions particularly from the point of view of how each character tries to assert and establish his authority.

> SPOTTISWOODE: Captain Roderick Watson, is it no?
>
> OGILVIE (somewhat shakily): I think – perhaps it would be better to dispense with that name. It is a completely false one and to continue the pretence further would serve little purpose. My name is ...
>
> SPOTTISWOODE: Ogilvie. John Ogilvie. (Drops his cap on the table)
>
> OGILVIE (biting his lip): That is perfectly correct. You have the advantage of me, sir.
>
> SPOTTISWOODE (amused): Just so, Master Ogilvie. Just so. (Rubbing his hands together) Nou. Would ye take a dram? Ye look in sair need of it.
>
> OGILVIE: That is very kind of you. I would be most grateful.
>
> SPOTTISWOODE picks up the goblet that Andrew has used, examines it for a moment, purses his lips, and looks sceptically towards the door. He tosses the goblet in his hand, lays it aside, and pours OGILVIE drink into a fresh goblet.
>
> SPOTTISWOODE: Water?

OGILVIE: Please.

SPOTTISWOODE pours some water into the drink and hands it to OGILVIE.

OGILVIE: Thank you.

SPOTTISWOODE: And you are of noble bluid, I understand?

OGILVIE: I am – and all my people before me.

SPOTTISWOODE (conversationally): Sir Walter Ogilvie of Drum?

OGILVIE: My father.

SPOTTISWOODE smiles and, sitting down, turns his attention to the papers. He begins to read, then looks up solicitously.

SPOTTISWOODE: Sit ye doun, Master Ogilvie, sit ye doun. There is no need for you to stand.

OGILVIE: Thank you – but I prefer it.

SPOTTISWOODE (with a slight shrug): As ye please.

SPOTTISWOODE reads one paper, lays it aside with a sharp sniff of breath and frowns up at OGILVIE. He picks up the second paper and asks his next question casually as he spreads it out.

SPOTTISWOODE: And you have been saying masses in the City of Glasgow?

OGILVIE (mildly): If to do so is a crime, then it will be necessary to prove it – with witnesses.

SPOTTISWOODE leans back in his chair and regards OGILVIE with a kind of stern speculation before he speaks.

SPOTTISWOODE: To say the mass in His Majesty's Dominions – ye maun be maist siccarly assured – is a crime. (Leans forward and recommences his study of the paper.) And I have any amount of witnesses.

This is cat-and-mouse stuff, as a study of the illocutions – their realisations and distributions – makes clear. Spottiswoode begins with a question to which Ogilvie responds with answers which are realised as three assertions. The final assertion is interrupted and completed by Spottiswoode, with the effect that he answers his own question. His authority is thus established: he is the one who asks the questions, but he is also the one who knows the answers. Ogilvie is immediately put in the position of simply confirming what Spottiswoode already knows.

Ogilvie's subordinate position, his inability to be the questioner, is further established by the illocution 'You have the advantage of me, sir'. In isolation, this utterance might look like a simple assertion, but in context it is an indirect directive, a request for Spottiswoode to reveal his identity. That it is an indirect directive is a mark of politeness: Ogilvie either realises his subordinate position, or he might be seen as conforming to social niceties by distancing his request.

Spottiswoode has no desire or need to conform to the rules of etiquette. His confirmation ('Just so') treats Ogilivie's utterance as an assertion rather than a request, and leaves the priest in ignorance. In other words, he denies the power of Ogilvie to issue directives, indirect or not. More magnanimously, he then offers Ogilvie a drink. This hospitality token again positions Spottiswoode as the authority, since a felicity condition for the act would be that the Archbishop must have the power to give the priest something. The jailer thus presents himself as a host.

Ogilvie indirectly accepts the offer by making two polite assertions; Spottiswoode makes a further offer and Ogilvie directly thanks him. Having explicitly accepted Spottiswoode's authority, the priest has now accepted that he is in a subordinate position. The Archbishop now resumes his questioning, and this time Ogilvie provides direct answers. The realisation of the questions – as assertions with question-tags – suggests that once again the Archbishop is seeking confirmation of facts with which he is already acquainted.

The scene continues with what is on the surface a command ('Sit ye doun') which in context might be interpreted as another offer – the following assertion ('There is no need for you to stand') invites this interpretation. It is a curious linguistic paradox that speakers in authority (such as hosts to guests) politely express offers and suggestions as commands, while subordinate speakers politely express commands as suggestions and questions. Ogilvie, however, thanks him but declines the offer in this case, therefore attempting to re-establish his own independence and authority. Spottiswoode acknowledges the response, and the extract concludes with a further question to which we assume Spottiswoode again knows the answer. Ogilvie responds with an assertion which this time does not answer the question, but makes a general point. Spottiswoode reacts by confirming the general assertion and following this up with a further assertion which could be interpreted, indirectly, as a threat or a warning.

The scene as a whole shows Spottiswoode and Ogilvie engaging in some verbal sparring, a contest which it seems Spottiswoode is well equipped to win. He is the authority, in a position to question, offer and, indirectly, threaten. Ogilvie is in a position only to answer, confirm, accept or decline, thank and assert. When he does, indirectly, attempt a directive act, Spottiswoode simply refuses to recognise it as such. Ogilvie's only strategy during his interrogation is to substitute general assertions for specific answers, and Spottiswoode has little patience for this.

The characterisations of Spottiswoode and Ogilvie are largely achieved through the realisations and distributions of the speech acts. Spottiswoode's bluntness is partly a consequence of his issuing blunt directives (e.g. questions in the form of statements, or statement-plus-tag), and his blithe refusal to be directed himself. Ogilvie's vulnerability is part of his adherence to the kind of polite conventions which naturally put him in a subordinate position.

There are, of course other possible approaches to the analysis of this scene. For example, Spottiswoode's bluntness is accentuated by the fact that he speaks in Scots, whereas Ogilvie speaks in 'refined' English. Although, as discussed in Chapter 1, the difference in speech variety might not have been too great a social marker in the Scotland of 1614 (although the transferral of the Scottish court to England a decade earlier did begin to have some effect quite early), it is certainly a social marker today. For a present-day audience, the fact that the character in authority does not speak with the language now associated with authority (namely southern Standard English) adds to his threatening aspect. Nevertheless, an analysis of the illocutionary acts in this passage lays bare the power struggle between the two participants. The linguistic construction of politeness, of course, varies from culture to culture, and from language variety to language variety. Part of the drama of this extract lies in the fact that Ogilvie's politeness is part of his background and breeding, while Spottiswoode's bluntness is part of his. The cultural clash is dramatised here in the characters' use of language, as, in Robert Louis Stevenson's *Weir of Hermiston*, the generational clash between Hermiston, the father, and Archie, his gentrified son, is similarly dramatised:

'What's this I hear of ye?' he asked.

There was no answer possible to Archie.

'I'll have to tell ye, then,' pursued Hermiston. 'It seems ye've been skirling against the father that begot ye, and one of His Maijesty's Judges in this land; and that in the public street, and while an order of the Court was being executit. Forbye which, it would appear that ye've been airing your opeenions in a Coallege Debatin'.Society!' He paused a moment: and then, with extraordinary bitterness, added: 'Ye damned eediot!'

'I had meant to tell you,' stammered Archie. 'I see you are well informed.'

'Muckle obleeged to ye,' said his lordship, and took his usual seat. 'And so you disapprove of Caapital Punishment?'

> 'I am sorry, sir, I do,' said Archie.
> 'I am sorry, too,' said his lordship.

Here, Hermiston and Archie's use of language is comparable to that of Spottiswoode and Ogilvie's: Hermiston accuses and questions and insults his son in speech which is markedly Scots. Archie responds and apologises in a polite English form. The relative power of Hermiston is also evident in the realisations of speech acts which would otherwise put him in the 'inferior' position: when he 'thanks' his son ('Muckle obleeged to ye'), we can infer from both context and the use of Scots that the sincerity condition is not being observed; and when he echoes Archie's 'I am sorry', he is not apologising – but simply asserting a state of affairs. A common assumption is that Scots is a 'natural' medium for plain speaking and directness, whereas English is 'more polite', which means less direct. As the extracts from Campbell and Stevenson show, this assumption can find vivid dramatic expression in literary texts.

CONVERSATIONAL IMPLICATURE

So far, we have considered how dramatic texts might be analysed using a pragmatic theory which classifies utterances as different types of behavioural act. Now we shall turn our attention to a different pragmatic approach, one which considers how people comprehend utterances in conversation – when very often there is little or no linguistic link between utterances. What kind of 'rules' are people following in order to create coherence between utterances in context? This issue is covered in the study of conversational implicature. Consider this brief exchange between two young girls in Sharman Macdonald's *When I Was a Girl, I Used to Scream and Shout* (London: Faber and Faber, 1985). What are they talking about? And how do you know?

> 1955
> The bedroom.
> VARI: Willie games?
> FIONA: She'll see.
> VARI: Not down here.
> FIONA: Pencils?
> VARI: Pencils.

Apart from the repetition of the word 'pencils', there is little linguistically to link these utterances in meaning. And yet the utterances are coherent – the characters understand the utterances, and so (but perhaps to a lesser extent) does the audience. A linguist would ask how we make sense of apparently disconnected expressions.

One widely-accepted answer to this question is that we interpret utterances in accordance with certain socially-conditioned 'norms' of communicative behaviour. We assume that people who communicate with us are following these norms – they may not be following these norms, but if we began assuming that they weren't, then communication would break down, as it sometimes does. The norms of communicative behaviour have been formulated by the philosopher Paul Grice as a principle and four maxims, or 'rules' (Grice 1975). It is important to remember that people often deliberately and naturally 'break' these rules – and it is significant for a stylistic analysis to identify where and why these rules might have been broken. But in order for communication to proceed, we generally assume that these rules are not being broken. Grice's maxims are as follows:

The cooperative principle

For a conversation to succeed, the speakers must share the assumption that they are cooperating, i.e. that their contributions to the conversation will help it to go in the agreed or required direction. The speakers assume that cooperation takes the form of following four maxims:

1. Quantity: Give as much information as is required. Do not give too much information, and do not give too little.
2. Quality: Tell the truth. Do not say anything for which you lack evidence.
3. Relation: Make your contributions relevant.
4. Manner: Avoid obscurity, ambiguity and prolixity. Order your contributions in a reasonable manner.

How are these maxims related to the brief dialogue by Sharman Macdonald? Vari opens the topic with the suggestion that the girls play 'willie games'. Fiona replies: 'She'll see'. The first maxim to consider (and some would argue the most important maxim of all) is relation. The utterance 'She'll see' must somehow be relevant to the utterance 'willie games'. The link can be made if we assume that 'willie games' are somehow wrong, and therefore liable to punishment by authority. 'She' must then be a figure of authority, and if she 'sees' then punishment will follow. By restricting her utterance to 'She'll see' Fiona assumes that its relevance will be plain to Vari; her utterance therefore complies with the maxims of quantity and manner – she gives enough information, and she does so clearly and briefly.

And, of course, her assumption is justified: Vari responds appropriately with 'Not down here.' Again we assume that this utterance is relevant to the previous one – indeed that the unstated subject and verb are the same: '(She'll) not (see) us down here'. Vari also conforms to the maxim of relation: she gives enough information (quantity) and she does not bother to repeat items which are unnecessary (manner). Fiona similarly assumes that Vari is telling the truth (quality) because she tacitly withdraws her objection to the initial suggestion and begins to prepare for the game.

'Pencils?' As an audience, we assume that Fiona's request for confirmation is relevant to the given topic of 'willie games'. We therefore seek a connection, and probably find it in the shape of the 'willie', or penis. This is not perhaps a similarity which springs to mind when we contemplate pencils and penises outwith the context of Fiona and Vari's conversation; but that Fiona mentions pencils as part of a conversation about 'willie games' forces us to seek and find some kind of similarity. Again we assume that Fiona is being relevant to the topic, that she's giving Vari (and us) enough information, and that she is not being unnecessarily ambiguous or obscure. She is certainly not being prolix. So we think: 'Ah, she's checking whether they're going to use pencils as a penis substitute in a game in which girls pretend to be boys', and we'd be correct, as Vari's reply confirms. She knows what Fiona is talking about.

Stylistically, this is an interesting passage. Grice's maxims are concerned with accounting for the way in which interlocutors cooperate in the creation of shared meanings in conversation. In drama – as in literature generally – the communication patterns are more complex (Pratt 1977). In *When I Was a Girl, I Used to Scream and Shout*, we do not just have Fiona and Vari conversing with each other; we also have Sharman Macdonald communicating with an audience through these characters' conversations. Part of the humour of this passage is our surprised and perhaps shocked recreation of the knowledge which the playwright represents the characters as sharing. The connection between penises and pencils is relevant and straightforward to the small girls; it probably comes as a greater surprise to the audience.

FLOUTING THE MAXIMS: THE POLITENESS PRINCIPLE

The excerpt from Sharman Macdonald's play relies on our assumption that the characters are conforming to the cooperative principle. There are times, however, when we do not cooperate with our interlocutors. We lie, mislead or are economical with the truth. Irrelevance or ambiguity is employed to amuse or irritate. Similarly, we might cut short an unwanted conversation by being pointedly brief or obscure. Nervousness or the desire to ingratiate or impress might make us garrulous. In literature, an author might make the flouting of certain of the maxims a character trait. This happens in Tony Roper's *The Steamie* in the long, involved story that Mrs Culfeathers tells about Galloway's mince.

> DOLLY: Wait tae ye hear this. Tell them what ye telt me Mrs Culfeathers.
>
> MRS CULFEATHERS: Well I wis tellin' Dolly that I aye got ma mince oot o' Galloways because it is lovely mince ... there's hardly any fat in their mince Doreen ye know.
>
> DOREEN (slightly mystified): Aye, oh, it's good mince.
>
> MRS CULFEATHERS: D'ye no like their mince Magrit?
>
> MAGRIT: Aye ... it's awright. (Looks at DOLLY.)
>
> DOLLY: Tell them aboot whit Mr Culfeathers says aboot it.
>
> MRS CULFEATHERS: Well ... I wis tellin' Dolly aboot how I aye get ma mince oot o' Galloways, but sometimes I get it oot another butchers ... ye know just for a wee change, and I was saying that when I get it oot another butchers, Mr Culfeathers can always tell, even though I havenae said whit butcher's I got it oot o'. If I pit mince doon tae him, and I havenae got it oot o' Galloways, he aye says tae me, 'where did ye get that mince fae'?
>
> MAGRIT (slight sarcasm): Does he? ... (To DOREEN) D'ye hear that?
>
> DOREEN: Aye ... that's ... that's ... that's eh ... very interesting.
>
> MRS CULFEATHERS: That shows ye what good mince it is.
>
> DOLLY: Oh it is ... aye it is good mince, isn't it Magrit?
>
> MAGRIT: Oh ... second tae none.
>
> DOLLY: But that's no the end o' it. There's mair.
>
> DOREEN: Surely not.
>
> MAGRIT: Ye mean even mair interesting than that?
>
> DOLLY: Aye ... wait tae ye hear this.
>
> MAGRIT: Well I don't see how you can top that but do go on.

Tony Roper, *The Steamie*, in Alasdair Cameron (ed.), *Scot-Free: New Scottish Plays*, London: Nick Hearn Books, 1990

In this excerpt (the story continues for another two pages!), Mrs Culfeathers flouts at least three of Grice's maxims. Her story seems to have little relevance to the women's concerns, it contains too much information (for example, that the mince is lovely and contains little fat), and it is repetitive and prolix. Doreen and Magrit respond to the story by flouting the maxim of quality: they are lying when they say that it's an interesting story. Only Dolly is willing to cooperate in this conversation – and she cooperates to the point of insistence.

So far, an analysis of conversational implicature nicely points up the representation of Mrs Culfeathers as a slightly rambling old woman, and Dolly as an obsessively cooperative conversationalist. However, Magrit and Doreen cannot be simply represented as liars, and a careful reading of the text suggests that they are flouting the maxim of quality for quite different reasons. At this point, we have to pause and extend our model of conversational implicature. Since conversation is inherently a social activity, cooperation is obviously fundamental to its maintenance. And, as we have seen, conversation can only be sustained if all the participants assume that everyone is cooperating equally. Grice's maxims are an attempt to express the 'rules' that govern conversational cooperation. Also important, however, are certain maxims of politeness, which are formulated by Leech (1983, 1992) as follows (cf. Leech 1992: 261):

1. The *tact* maxim:
   (a) minimise the cost to others, e.g. 'This will hardly hurt at all'.
   (b) maximise the benefit to others, e.g. 'It's for your own good, after all'.

2. The *generosity* maxim:
   (a) minimise the benefit to self, e.g. 'I only ever thought of your future'.
   (b) maximise the cost to self, e.g. 'I've scrimped and saved for you'.

3. The *approbation* (or flattery) maxim:
   (a) minimise dispraise of others, 'Oh, she's not all bad'.
   (b) maximise praise of others, e.g. 'She's got a lovely personality'.

4. The *modesty* maxim:
   (a) minimise praise of self, e.g. 'This award is the result of many people's support'.
   (b) maximise dispraise of self, e.g. 'I was only ever a very minor cog in the machine'.

5. The *agreement* maxim:
   (a) minimise disagreement between self and others, e.g. 'Let's agree to differ.'
   (b) maximise agreement between self and others, e.g. 'I'm with you on that one'.

6. The *sympathy* maxim:
   (a) minimise antipathy between self and others, e.g. 'We're all in the same boat'.
   (b) maximise sympathy between self and others, e.g. 'We are one nation!'

The maxims which make up the politeness principle, like those which make up the cooperative principle, are better thought of as a set of assumed 'norms' rather than as prescriptive rules. People of course do not always conform to these norms, but generally we suppose that they will and tend to act accordingly. When we find that people are not conforming to the norms of cooperation or politeness, we make adjustments: we switch topics of conversation, get into arguments, leave the room, or even resort to physical violence.

Leech (1992) notes that the principle of politeness often comes into conflict with the principle of cooperation: to put it bluntly, it may not always be polite to tell the truth. Everyday conversation – and its literary representation – will therefore be an arena for negotiation and compromise between the sometimes conflicting principles of cooperation and politeness.

Returning, then, to the extract from *The Steamie*, we see in the frequent direct addresses and tag questions that characters continually seek agreement. Doreen is willing to conform to the maxim of agreement, as we see from her first response to Mrs Culfeathers: 'Aye, oh, it's good mince'. Her later flouting of the cooperative maxim of quality can therefore be seen to result from the greater weight which she puts on the maxim of agreement: 'Aye … that's … that's … that's eh … very interesting'. In both utterances, the hesitations suggest that the agreement is less than wholehearted. Compare Dolly's utterance, which conforms to both the maxim of agreement and quality: 'Oh it is … aye it is good mince, isn't it Magrit?' Dolly is sincere in her agreement, and seeks to extend the circle of conversational solidarity to Magrit. Magrit, however, shows by her hesitation followed by a pointed exaggeration that she is overtly flouting the maxim of quality: 'Oh … second tae none'. In other words, where Doreen is being polite, Magrit is being sarcastic. Dolly, blind to sarcasm, wrongly assumes that Magrit is conforming to the maxim of quality (Dolly is the cooperative principle personified), and so she promises 'mair'. This is too much for Doreen, and the politeness principle gives way: 'Surely not', she says. The final exchange in the extract shows Magrit continuing to flout the maxim of quality, and Dolly continuing to be unaware of this breach of cooperation.

Again, as in the case of Sharman Macdonald's play, we are not simply eavesdropping on a conversation here. The dialogue, which is constructed to represent characters, is a complex act of communication with an audience. By considering how each character in the extract negotiates the maxims of cooperation and politeness, we can articulate precisely why Doreen and Magrit fail to respond to Mrs Culfeathers' story (which flouts the maxims of relation, quantity and manner), and why Magrit is irritated by the over-cooperative Dolly. Magrit, whose sarcasm indicates an overt flouting of the maxim of quality, is also distinguished from Doreen, whose less overt flouting of the same maxim results from her giving greater weight to the politeness principle and the maxim of agreement.

Drama is not the only genre (literary or otherwise) which is open to pragmatic analysis. Consider the beginning of the following very short story by James Kelman.

> This man for fuck sake it was terrible seeing him walk down the edge of the pavement. If he'd wanted litter we would've given him it. The trouble is we didn't know it at the time. So all we could do was watch his progress and infer.

> James Kelman, 'This Man for Fuck Sake', in *Greyhound for Break-fast* London: Picador, 1987

The maxim being broken here – for literary effect – is the maxim of quantity. The reader is not told enough about the event to make sense of it in a straightforward way. At the beginning there is not enough information to explain why walking down the edge of the pavement was terrible, or why the reference to litter is relevant: is the man collecting litter, is he a down-and-out collecting cigarette ends? What was it that 'we' didn't know at the time? Like the speaker, all that the reader can do when the information is lacking is 'watch and infer'.

The overall effect of the story is like a jigsaw puzzle with many of the pieces missing. Part of the pleasure of reading a text like this – or the irritation, if the reader is unwilling to play the game – is in the 'creative reading' that is demanded. If too little information is given, then the reader has to supply the omitted pieces: why is the man collecting litter, what is it that 'we didn't know at the time'? The game is made possible by the deliberate – literary – uncooperativeness of this particular narrator.

In this chapter, we have considered two ways of approaching different aspects of language in use – namely, speech acts and conversational implicature. I have illustrated the kinds of description and interpretation of texts which can result when we pay attention to these aspects of language in use. The analysis of speech acts is particularly sensitive to the way in which the relationships between characters are established and developed: who takes the initiative, makes demands or requests, gives orders, promises, confirms, accuses or acquiesces in any particular situation or sequence of scenes? What does the realisation of these speech acts tell us about the characters' supposed relationships with each other (are they blunt, direct, cautious or rude)? The analysis of conversational implicatures tells us more about the shared world of the characters: what kind of information needs to be expressed, what do people think is relevant and what needs to be inferred? The conflict between the demands of truthfulness and of politeness can be used to establish characterisations across a range of literary genres.

7

———•———

SOUNDS AND STRUCTURES

In this chapter, we shall briefly consider a fascinating and complex area of stylistics: metrical form. As we saw in Chapter 2, the sound system and its relation to meaning was a subject of great interest to Jakobson: he was referring to sound patterning in poetry when he defined the poetic function of language as projecting the principle of equivalence from the axis of selection into the axis of combination (1960). Unfortunately, the systematic procedures and technical terminology used by stylisticians might give general readers the impression that the analysis of sounds in poetry is a soulless exercise, devoid of the creativity that draws them to literature in the first place. However, the analytical process is not nearly as mechanical as it may first appear.

There is a strong argument that most poets in the past were familiar with some form of metrical theory: it originated in classical literature, was adopted in modified form in Scots and English poetry, and survives from Barbour in the fourteenth century to the present day. As informed readers, we owe it to ourselves and to the poets whom we study to have some shared understanding of metrical composition. Therefore, in this chapter, we shall review in particular the rhythms and rhymes of poetry, with a particular view to Scottish literature.

THE RHYTHMS OF THE POETIC LINE

The metrical theory which we shall review is fairly simple and conventional. A much more thorough discussion can be found, for example, in Attridge (1982). One of Attridge's contentions is that there are two main rhythms in English poetry (and this applies equally to poetry in Scots): a four-beat line and a five-beat line. Of these, the more 'poetic sounding' is the four-beat line. And this is the line which forms the basis of much folk poetry in Scots – songs and ballads, for example.

PURE STRESS METRE

Folk poetry normally employs 'pure stress' metre: all that needs to be done is to count the number of primary stressed syllables (or 'beats') per line. Often the number of beats is four, as in the well-known traditional song, 'The Twa Corbies' (the primary stresses are marked by a dash above the appropriate syllables):

As I was walking all alane

I heard twa corbies making a mane

The tane unto the tither did say,

'Whaur sall we gang and dine the day?'

The pattern of four 'beats', or primary stressed syllables, per line is maintained throughout the song. There is a slightly irregular number of syllables in each line (eight or nine in the stanza above); but we can expect such irregularities in much folk poetry. The question to be asked here is simply: 'How many beats are there to the line?' If we have an irregular number of syllables per line and a regular pattern of beats, then we have pure stress metre.

Ballads have a distinctive metrical pattern: four-beat lines alternate with lines which have three beats plus a pause, as in 'Sir Patrick Spens':

The king sits in Dunfermline town

Drinking the bluid-red wine: (pause)

'Oh, where will I get a gude skipper

To sail this ship of mine? (pause)

Again, the number of syllables here is slightly irregular: eight, six, nine, six. Obviously, it is the third line which causes the problems: there is an extra syllable here which compromises syllabic regularity. But there is nearly a syllabic pattern, too. As we shall soon see, some pure stress metre merges easily into a form of poetry where there is not only a recurring pattern of stresses per line but also a recurring pattern of stresses and syllables.

TOWARDS STRESS-SYLLABIC POETRY

The folk tradition is obviously important to Scots poets: songs and ballads provided a continuity of literary tradition when the 'literary' poets largely decamped to London with the Scottish court in 1603, and it was to the folk tradition that the 'literary' poets of the eighteenth-century revival first turned when they wanted to raise the status of poetry in Scots. Moreover, the folk tradition can be said to have fulfilled a similar function in the twentieth century: witness the allusions to folk traditions in Hugh MacDiarmid's *A Drunk Man Looks at the Thistle*. MacDiarmid's borrowings of folk forms are part of his project to reinvigorate the Scottish literary tradition:

O wha's the bride that cairries the bunch

O' thistles blinterin' white?

Her cuckold bridegroom little dreids

What he sall ken this nicht.

As in 'Sir Patrick Spens', these lines from *A Drunk Man Looks at the Thistle* conform to a four-three-four-three stress pattern – and note that there is grammatical justification for a pause at the end of each three-beat line. The numbers of syllables per line are still irregular (nine, seven, eight, six), but the arrangement of primary stresses to un-stressed syllables is becoming even more regular than in the examples of folk poetry above. Compare the pattern of stressed and unstressed syllables in 'Sir Patrick Spens' and 'O wha's the bride?' (unstressed syl-lables are marked by an 'x'):

```
    x _  _ x  x _  x  _
The king sits in Dunfermline town

    _  x  x  _  x  _ (pause)
Drinking the bluid-red wine:

    x  _  x x _ x _  _ x
'Oh, where will I get a gude skipper

    x _  x  _ x  _   (pause)
To sail this ship of mine?

    x _  x _  x _  x x  _
O wha's the bride that cairries the bunch
```

```
x  _  x  _  x x     _    (pause)
O' thistles blinterin' white?
```

```
x  _  x  _    x  _  x  _
Her cuckold bridegroom little dreids
```

```
x  _  x  _  x  _    (pause)
What he sall ken this nicht.
```

MacDiarmid's poem is much more regular than the anonymous ballad: the later poem is composed largely of recurring units of two syllables, the first syllable being relatively unstressed, and the second being stressed – this is a pattern which is described as iambic (x_). There are two exceptions to this in the extract, but both exceptions are at similar points: the first and second line end with a unit of two unstressed syllables followed by one stressed syllable, namely anapaests (xx_).

The final line of 'Sir Patrick Spens' is also made up of regular iambs, and if we stressed the 'in' in the first line more than 'sits', the first line would be iambic too. (However, normally we stress lexical items rather than grammatical items.) The second line of 'Sir Patrick Spens' has two iambs out of three; it's the third line which causes most problems. Here we have an iamb, plus an anapaest plus another iamb plus a dactyl (that is, a foot with the pattern _xx); consequently there is not much of a basis for a recurring rhythmical pattern in this line!

However, there is still enough regularity in 'Sir Patrick Spens' to alert us to the fact that the boundaries separating pure stress from stress-syllabic metre are sometimes blurred. It is a mark of the 'literary' poet that the irregularities of much authentic folk poetry are smoothed out: early ballad- and song-collectors like Burns and Scott modified and often rewrote the versions which they heard, and modern poets who choose traditional folk forms can decide whether they want the irregular 'authentic' sound or a slightly more polished sound which has the advantage of appealing to both the folk tradition and the tradition of high-style poetry, the latter being conventionally associated with stress-syllabic metre.

STRESS-SYLLABIC METRE

Stress-syllabic metre adds a further level of sophistication to the traditional four-beat line of folk poetry. From classical models, medieval and Renaissance poets in Scotland and England borrowed the idea that lines should have a regular number of syllables, and, consciously or unconsciously, they furthermore introduced patterns whereby the sequence of stressed and unstressed syllables in each line should conform to certain patterns. It was not until the renaissance in England and Scotland that writers began to codify the rules of vernacular versification. Generally, in the poetry of the classical and Romance languages of the European continent, the syllabic pattern was not classified by a regular pattern of stressed and unstressed syllables, but rather by a pattern of syllables of a long and short duration. English and Scots, however, fall into the Germanic tradition of languages. Attridge (1982: 5) writes:

> George Gascoigne, the father of English metrical studies, is unusual in clearly perceiving the alternating stresses of English metre, but he identifies English stress with both 'grave' and 'long' syllables in Latin, thus combining the separate features of accent and quantity (1575, pp. 49–51).

The advice of Gascoigne and the French writer Du Bellay can be seen reflected in the *Reulis and Cautelis* ('Rules and Cautions'), published in 1585 by the young James VI of Scotland to guide Scottish poets. James's work is concerned to iron out the irregularities sometimes found in earlier poetry – he observes that older writers 'observit not Flowing' – and the brief text is a collection of 'arbitrary laws' governing rhythm, rhyme and versification (cf. Jack 1972: 55). James's laws are little different from Gascoigne's, despite the Scottish king's protestations about the separateness of the Scots and English languages. The description below follows the classical approach, whereby the rules of Latin verse were adapted to the medium of the vernacular languages.

In stress-syllabic poetry, lines are divided into units called feet. Each foot contains a set number of syllables (usually two, sometimes three), which have a recognised pattern based on the number and the sequence of strong and weak syllables. This recurring pattern is used to classify the line. The main types of feet are shown below. One word or phrase is given as an example of each pattern. You might try to add a few of your own to those given.

_ = stressed x = unstressed | = foot boundary

It is customary to put the symbols (_ and x) above the vowel, or above the syllabic consonant (that is, a consonant which has the duration of a syllable) if no vowel is present.

Type of foot	*Key word/phrase*
	x _
iamb	asleip
	_ x
trochee	thrissil

	| x x |
pyrrhic	whisky in a bottle
	_ _
spondee	Black Watch
	x x _
anapaest	unnerstaun
	_ x x
dactyl	Seturday

Of all these metrical patterns, the iambic foot is probably the most common. The others are more difficult to maintain. Spondees and pyrrhic feet are unlikely to be the organising principle of any poetic line: some syllables are bound to be relatively stronger or weaker than others in any given line.

Iambic and anapaestic feet (i.e. those that end on stressed syllables) are sometimes referred to as having rising rhythm; trochaic and dactylic feet (i.e. those that end on unstressed syllables) are referred to as having falling rhythm.

HOW TO SCAN STRESS-SYLLABIC POETRY

Determining the metrical pattern of the line is known as scanning it (the noun is 'scansion'). The following procedure is suggested:

1. Count the number of syllables in the line. Is there any regularity?
2. Look for the obviously stressed syllables. Is there a recurring pattern? Can you make the 'less obvious' syllables fit that pattern? If you can, do so. If not, look for a possible substitute foot and think of a possible reason for the deviation.
3. Once you have established the recurring pattern, you can count the number of feet in the line. Lines are labelled by referring to the type of foot which predominates (e.g. iambic), and the number of feet in the line (e.g. pentameter), to give a full classification: 'iambic pentameter'.

Number of feet per line:

1. monometer 2. dimeter 3. trimeter 4. tetrameter
5. pentameter 6. hexameter/Alexandrine
7. heptameter 8. octometer

Note that some lines might end on an extra unstressed syllable (i.e. they are feminine lines). This extra syllable does not alter the metrical classification of the line. Many trochaic or dactylic lines, on the other hand, omit the final unstressed syllable, such an omission being termed 'catalexis'. Alternatively, some lines, particularly of folk verse, have an extra syllable at the beginning, its presence being termed 'anacrusis'. Examples of each of these lines, all from the poems of Robert Burns, would be:

```
        x  _ x _ x _ x _ (x)
```
1. While we sit bousing at the nappy   feminine line

```
    _ x _ x _ x _ x
```
2. Brawlie kens our wanton chief (.)   catalexis

```
    (x) _ x _ x _ x
```
3. O lovely Polly Stewart   anacrusis

The following extracts 1–5 are examples of different types of metrical line. You might want to classify the lines before looking at the descriptions given below.

1. Pity one that bears love's anguish   Isabel Stewart; trans.
   Yet the cause that must conceal   by Nigel MacNeill

2. The first I'll name, they ca'd him   Robert Burns
      Cæsar,
   Was keepet for His Honour's pleasure.

3. It groans and shakes, contracts and   Edwin Morgan
      grows again,
   Its giant broken shoulders shrug off
      rain.

4. Bumpity doun in the corrie gaed   Robert Garioch
      whuddran he pitiless whun stane
   Sisyphus, pechan and sweitan, disjaskit,
      forfeuchan and broun'd aff

5. There's a hole i' the sky   Sheena Blackhall
   At the back o the day

6. 'Young Politician'   Alan Jackson
   What a lovely, lovely moon.
   And it's in the constituency too.

The first example is trochaic tetrameter with, in the second line, an omitted final unstressed syllable (catalexis). The second is an example of iambic tetrameter with an extra unstressed syllable at the end of each line (feminine lines). The third is an example of regular iambic pentameter; and the fourth is an example of dactylic hexameter, with the final foot of each line having a spondee substituted for a dactyl. The fifth extract is an example of anapaestic dimeter. The final example is a complete poem by Alan Jackson: the first line is trochaic tetrameter (with a catalectic final foot), and the concluding line is regular anapaestic trimeter. The change in metre can be said to reinforce the switch from enthusiastic outcry to cynical politicking:

```
_ x _ x _ x _ (x)
```
What a lovely, lovely moon.

```
x x _ x x _ x x _
```
And it's in the constituency too.

METRE AND RHYTHM

Attridge (1982) argues that the native, and most perceptibly poetic, rhythm in English – and, by extension, Scots – is a four-beat line. Five-beat lines, originally derived from continental poetry, are only found in the self-consciously 'literary' tradition. By adding an extra beat to the four-beat line, English and Scots poets move metre one step away from the obvious rhythm of poetry and closer to the subtler rhythms of every-day conversation. For this reason, a five-beat line, usually iambic pentameter, is used for dramatic verse and much 'literary' poetry. Poetry of this type relies on a counterpointing or tension between poetic metre and natural conversational rhythm.

Metre is best regarded as the abstract, underlying pattern in any stress-syllabic poetic line. It is often (but not always) established early, creating an expectation that the recurring pattern will be maintained. As we saw in the poem 'Young Politician', above, patterns are not always maintained: once expectations have been set up, they are often denied, for a variety of rhetorical reasons (e.g. to change the mood, foreground a word, or to represent emotional disturbance, etc.).

Rhythm is the pattern of stressed and unstressed syllables that we use when we actually say a line out loud. The rhythm given to a poem can be compared to the performance of a piece of music, while the metre can be compared to the musical notes on the page. The notes give the guide to the performance, but all performances are different inter-pretations of the musical notation, and there is scope for individual nuances and emphases. When reading a poem aloud, a reader might or might not choose to follow the metre closely. As noted above, a sequence of words sometimes departs from expected metrical norms deliberately, to suggest certain emphases at various points in the text. But even when the metre is regular, the content of the line might suggest a particular emphasis, or the reader might wish to highlight a particular point. Rhythm and metre can then part company.

SOUND EFFECTS

Most traditional Scottish poetry, then, has some kind of metrical pattern, whether it is the pure stress pattern of folk poetry or the stress-syllabic pattern of more 'literary' verse. Traditional poetry is also expected to rhyme (although there is a certain amount, particularly of dramatic verse, that does not). Rhyme has been a feature of Scottish poetry at least since the earliest written verse of the fourteenth century. In general, rhyme refers to the similarity in the final sounds of different words: there has to be an identical vowel sound in the final stressed syllable, and all succeeding consonants and vowels must also correspond, thus:

blaw	snaw
ingle	jingle
clatterin	watterin

Rhyme in Scottish poetry is complicated by the fact that there are many accents of Scots. Scots poets can use features from different accents to give rhymes that a single consistent pronunciation would not allow. This practice is evident in the poetry of Robert Burns, as the following lines show:

> Think, when your castigated pulse
>   Gies now and then a wallop,
> What ragings must his veins convulse,
>   That still eternal gallop.
>   ('Address to the Unco Guid', ll. 25–8)

> We think na on the lang Scots miles,
> The mosses, waters, slaps and styles,
> That lie between us and our hame,
> Whare sits our sulky, sullen dame,
> Gathering her brows like gathering storm,
> Nursing her wrath to keep it warm.
>   ('Tam o' Shanter', ll 7–12)

In Burns's Scots, and in the Scots pronunciations of many people today, the Older Scots vowel /a/ was retained after /w/. This pronunciation is evident in the lines from 'Address to the Unco Guid', in which 'wallop' is made to rhyme with 'gallop'. In 'Tam o' Shanter', we would likewise expect 'water' in line 8 to be pronounced 'watter', /watɪr/. However, the final two lines have the word 'warm' rhyming not with a word like 'harm' but with 'storm'. Later in the poem, we find the rhyme 'spread'/ 'shed':

> But pleasures are like poppies spread,
> You seize the flower, its bloom is shed
>   ('Tam o' Shanter', ll. 59–60)

Again, in Burns's Scots, 'spread' would be more likely to rhyme with 'speed', as 'speed', 'weed', 'greed', 'Tweed' and 'reed' rhyme with 'dead', 'dread' and 'bread' in 'Poor Mailie's Elegy'. Burns therefore took advantage of the variety of pronunciations available to him when writing poetry in Scots, particularly traditional Scots pronunciations and the more anglicised Scottish English pronunciations (cf. Smith 1996). It is interesting to note in passing that the kinds of strategies used by Burns in his rhymes find a modern analogy in the oral narrative styles of Ayrshire working-class speakers studied by Macaulay. He concludes his comparison of middle-class and working-class speech styles (1991: 262) by observing that:

> What seems to be clear from the interviews is that all the lower-class speakers have a stylistic choice available to them in a number of variables that is not available in the same way to the middle-class speakers.

Macaulay argues that the shifts between traditional Scots and Scottish English forms in working-class speech are less marked than a reverse 'drift' into traditional Scots by speakers of standard Scottish English (SSE). We expect working-class speakers to be able to modulate into the 'public repertoire' of SSE, but we do not expect middle-class speakers, whose speech tends to be closer to the standard dialect, to modulate into the more traditionally Scots working-class speech. The argument recalls Aitken's view that denser Scots is only used by SSE speakers on occasions when their Scottishness is at stake. Burns's use of rhyme prefigures this general dichotomy that Scots speakers have between a 'domestic repertoire' and a 'public repertoire'. As we have seen, he moves easily between rhymes in traditional Scots and rhymes in a more anglicised Scottish English. Burns's poetry in general gives evidence of a tension between traditional dialect and an anglicised Scots: lines 59–66 of 'Tam o' Shanter' are largely indistinguishable from the poetic English of their time, a fact that might itself encourage an ironic reading of these lines as a mock-homily amid what is essentially a Scots comic narrative. However, Burns's use of rhyme in general cannot be categorised according to content: Scots and English pronunciations are not confined to 'high' or 'low' styles, and many lines offer the opportunity for either type of realisation (again, see Smith 1996).

There is no space here to develop further a discussion of rhymes in Scots (for detailed descriptions of Scots pronunciations, see, for example, Aitken 1984; Aitken and McArthur 1979; Murison 1977; Robinson 1985; Wells 1982). The main point to note here is that the different varieties of Scots, alluded to in Chapter 1, give rise to a range of possible pronunciations that can be utilised by poets. Neither should we expect poets to be entirely consistent in their rhyming policy: where a useful rhyme can be found in another variety of Scots, many poets will take the opportunity to use it. As Burns cautions the over-serious critic:

> Some rhyme a neebor's name to lash;
> Some rhyme, (vain thought!) for needfu' cash;
> Some rhyme to court the countra clash,
>   An' raise a din;
> For me, an *aim* I never fash;
>   I rhyme for *fun*.
>   ('To J. S[mith]', ll. 25–30; original emphasis)

Rhyme and metre, are, of course, not the only ways of patterning sound. Alliteration is a common device and can be an organising principle of poetry, as in Dunbar's *Tretis of the Twa Mariit Wemen and the Wedo*. In this poem, the lines are determined neither by metre nor rhyme but by recurring initial consonants:

> Apon the Midsummer evin, mirriest of nichtis,
> I muvit furth allane, neir as midnicht wes past …

The recurring initial /m/ phoneme here links together corresponding half-lines and, as here, occasionally sets up links between lines (cf. McFadyen 1975). The poem is a Scottish throwback to an older native tradition of alliterative poetry which gives us the Old English poem *Beowulf* and the fourteenth-century, northern Middle English poem *Sir Gawain and the Green Knight*. In metrical poetry, alliteration is used more for local effect, perhaps to link two or more important words, or for extravagant ornamentation, as in the sonnet by John Stewart of Baldynneis discussed in Chapter 2.

Consonance and assonance are also common means of sound patterning in poetry. Neither tends to be used as an organising principle in a poem, but they can add to the pleasure taken in the sounds of a poem. Consonance refers to the repetition of consonant sounds in different words, while assonance refers to the repetition of vowel sounds. Each, therefore, like rhyme, has an echoic effect, as is evident in the following lines, taken from Hugh MacDiarmid's *A Drunk Man Looks at the Thistle*: the echoing /b/ and /l/ sounds are an example of consonance, while the echoing /a/, /ɪ / and /e/ sounds are an example of assonance (although, again, different accents might realise the vowel sounds differently):

         /b/   /l /   /b/ /b/

Consonance Beauty and Love that are bobbin' there

         /b/   /l / /b/

Syne the breengin' growth that alane I bear

                                 (ll. 464–5)

         /a/   /ɪ/   /ɪ/ /ɪ/ /a/   /ɪ//ɪ/

Assonance But I'll dance the nicht wi' the stars o' Heaven

  /ɪ / /ɪ /e/ /ɪ / /e/   /e/   /ɪ//ɪ /

In the Mairket Place as shair's I'm livin'

                                 (ll. 471–2)

RHYME SCHEMES

Rhyme, alliteration, consonance and assonance can be considered as different types of sound effect in poetry. As mentioned above, of these effects, only rhyme and alliteration have been used as organising principles in the construction of poems, and, of the two, rhyme is by far the more common organising principle, at least in traditional poems.

We considered earlier the two traditions which feed into Scottish poetry: the 'literary' tradition (based on models taken from classical and continental sources, and implicitly 'learned' and 'serious'); and, increasingly important since the end of the Union of the Crowns, the 'folk' tradition (based on native ballads and songs – implicitly Scottish but often comic, heroic or fantastic rather than serious, philosophical and learned). Scottish poets, not surprisingly, have wanted both to be distinctively Scottish and to be taken seriously, at times, and so there is an intermixing of the two traditions. By paying attention to the rhyme schemes, we can often see when this is occurring.

A list of stanzas commonly used in Scots poems follows the final chapter of this book. Generally speaking, the more difficult the stanza form is to sustain, the more 'literary' the poem is. Dunbar, for example, is astonishingly versatile in his range of stanzas, as is John Stewart of Baldynneis. After events such as the removal of the Scottish court to London, the failure of the '45, and the eighteenth-century Enlightenment, poets who wish to be classed as 'Scottish' generally favour folk forms – although there are notable exceptions: Fergusson and Burns used the Spenserian stanza (in 'The Farmer's Ingle' and 'The Cottar's Saturday Night' respectively) in order to 'raise' the subject matter of their poems (Scottish peasantry) to the elevated plateau of serious literature.

THREE SCOTTISH SONNETS

By far the most enduring and popular of European 'literary' verse forms is the sonnet, and its popularity is also evident in Scotland. The endurance, attraction and flexibility of the sonnet can be seen in the three examples given below. The first, written in the sixteenth century, is a Spenserian sonnet, with the form *abab bcbc cdcd ee* (the letters refer to the end-rhyme of each line). This form allows, for example, a problem to be set up in the three quatrains (that is, the four-line units, *abab* + *bcbc* + *cdcd*), which the concluding couplet (*ee*) can suddenly solve: here the speaker imagines that his stolen kiss has encouraged his life, his spirit and his heart to desert him in order to be in the presence of his mistress. However, the consequent threat of death is abated by the mistress giving the speaker her breath to sustain him. The three quatrains roughly correspond to the three vital 'parts' which are taken from the speaker, while the concluding couplet reverses his mock-anxiety by providing an appropriate resolution to his seeming predicament.

Alexander Montgomerie, 'To his Mistress'

	So suete a kis yistrene fra thee I reft	last night
	In bouing doun thy body on the bed	
	That evin my lyfe within thy lippis I left;	
4	Sensyne from thee my spirits wald neuer shed;	since then
	To folou thee it from my body fled,	
	And left my corps als cold as ony kie.	key
	But vhen the danger of my death I dred,	
8	To seik my spreit I sent my harte to thee;	
	But it wes so enamoured with thyn ee	eye
	With thee it myndit lykuyse to remane:	
	So thou hes keepit captive all the thrie,	
12	More glaid to byde then to returne agane.	
	Except thy breath thare places had suppleit,	
	Euen in thyn armes thair doutles had I deit.	

Montgomerie's sonnet is metrically regular, its regularity itself a meaningful signal of the poet's stylish virtuosity and polished wit. At this point in history, a sonnet whose metre was irregular would probably have been considered the product of an incompetent versifier. The aesthetic of the period demanded that poets in the vernacular show themselves equal to the skills demonstrated by the revered continental poets. Half a millennium later, poets are still writing sonnets, but their impact is quite different. Edwin Morgan's *Glasgow Sonnets* are poems as polemics, social observations which provoke anger at the poverty and deprivation which they portray. Here, the most prestigious of verse forms is used to describe people and conditions sometimes considered of little worth. In the example given, the most traditional of sonnet forms is used to 'zoom in on' a modern Glaswegian family:

From *Glasgow Sonnets* by Edwin Morgan

A mean wind wanders through the backcourt trash.
Hackles on puddles rise, old mattresses
puff briefly and subside. Play-fortresses
4   of brick and bric-à-brac spill out some ash.
Four storeys have no windows left to smash,
but in the fifth a chipped sill buttresses
mother and daughter, the last mistresses
8   of that black block condemned to stand, not crash.
Around them, the cracks deepen, the rats crawl.
The kettle whimpers on a crazy hob.
Roses of mould grow from ceiling to wall.
12 The man lies late since he has lost his job,
smokes on one elbow, letting his coughs fall
thinly into an air too poor to rob.

The rhyme scheme is *abbaabba cdcdcd*: a Petrarchan sonnet. The first eight lines (or the 'octave') correspond to the panoramic, external view of the crumbling housing scheme, gradually focusing on one window in one block. The sestet then takes us inside the flat, giving detail after detail of the living conditions. The subject is society's underclass and the social injustices that it is exposed to. In this context, the choice of the sonnet is a political one: the form is a traditional signal of high-style subject matter of weight and value, and here it is applied to those often neglected by the more privileged in society.

The final example is another modern sonnet which utilises the traditional meanings of the sonnet, but in a different way. It is in fact debatable whether Edwin Muir's poem 'The Late Wasp' is a sonnet at all; however, it does have fourteen lines, there is some rhyme, albeit irregular, and some lines are iambic pentameter, or nearly so (lines 2, 5, 6, 8, 11, 14). However, the rhyme scheme is far from what we would expect from a sonnet (*aba cdc efef ghgh*), and many lines are extremely short and metrically irregular.

The 'destruction' of the sonnet form in this poem can be taken as a symbol of the 'destruction' of the summer: the 'familar avenues' are crumbling indeed. What rhyme scheme there is suggests an inversion of the Petrarchan sonnet, a six-line sestet preceding an eight-line octave, and there is just enough of a recurrence of iambic pentameter to remind us of what has been lost. The poignance of the poem is heightened by this implicit sense that the tradition is coming to an end.

Edwin Muir, 'The Late Wasp'

> You that through all the dying summer
> Came every morning to our breakfast table,
> A lonely bachelor mummer,
> And fed on the marmalade,
> So deeply, all your strength was scarcely able,
> 6 To prise you from the sweet pit you had made, –
> You and the earth have now grown older,
> And your blue thoroughfares have felt a change;
> They have grown colder;
> And it is strange
> How the familiar avenues of the air
> 12 Crumble now, crumble; the good air will not hold,
> All cracked and perished with the cold;
> And down you dive through nothing and through despair.

In this chapter, we have looked most closely at traditional poetry because it has certain linguistic features that distinguish it from prose – in particular, a greater degree of sound patterning. Free-verse poetry often contains attenuated echoes of these patterns, as well as a great sensitivity to the interplay of poetic line and grammatical sentence. A brief example of a free verse poem is Liz Lochhead's 'Inventory':

> you left me
>   nothing but nail
>   parings orange peel
>   empty nutshells half filled
>   ashtrays dirty
>   cups with dregs of
>   nightcaps an odd hair
>   or two of yours on my
>   comb gap toothed
>   bookshelves and a
>   you shaped
>   depression in my pillow

Here, the tension between the line divisions and the grammatical units of phrase structure creates puzzling and amusing ambiguities (is the comb or the bookshelf 'gap-toothed'? what is the nature of the 'depression'? is the depression 'you' or 'U'-shaped?). In the twentieth century, poets have increasingly turned towards non-traditional means of creating poetic language. As a result, traditional verse may have lost its position of pre-eminence in the literary world, but many poets still practise it, many readers still read it, and any announcement of the long tradition ending is certainly premature.

8

·

NARRATIVE (1): ADDRESS, DEIXIS AND SPEECH

NARRATIVE

The next two chapters turn from poetry to focus on narrative, fictional and non-fictional. Narrative might be thought of, most simply, as story-telling, and it is important at the outset to stress that story-telling is not confined to novels and shorter prose: many poems tell stories, most jokes tell stories, and non-fictional genres, such as press reports, television and radio commercials, and even the experimental passages of scientific papers, also tell stories – stories which make an additional claim to veracity. As John Barbour says, in his introduction to *The Brus* (1375):

> Storyss to rede are delitabill,
> Supposs that thai be nocht but fabill;
> Than suld storyss that suthfast wer,
> And thai wer said on gud maner
> Have doubill plesance in the heryng.

Stories which are true, and well told, should give double the pleasure that we find in fables. Assuming that Barbour is correct, the analytical tools explored here in order to investigate narrative techniques in literary prose should easily be extended to investigate different genres which have a narrative component. First of all, we shall look at the way in which a writer creates a space for the reader to inhabit. This is sometimes referred to as 'positioning the reader' (cf. Montgomery et al. 1992; Mills 1995). We shall consider two linguistic means by which this 'positioning' is achieved: modes of address, and the use of so-called 'deictic' terms, that is, terms which can only be interpreted if the context of items to which they refer are already known to the reader (e.g. the context-dependent phrases 'over there' and 'right now' are deictic in 'She's standing over there right now, looking at me'). Then, in the following sections of this chapter and the next, we shall consider the representation of speech and thought, the presentation of a particular point of view, and typical underlying discourse structures in narrative.

Our focus will be on the linguistic forms and functions which are used, for example, to construct an implied reader or to realise a particular point of view.

FORMS OF ADDRESS

It might seem strange to argue that texts construct readers. What is meant by this is that in obvious or subtle ways, a writer will create a role for an intended or idealised reader. The 'actual' reader might happily slip into this role, or, for different reasons, the reader might 'resist' the role foisted upon her. Or him. Resisting readers are associated primarily with feminist readings of texts (e.g. Fetterley 1978), but in principle a resisting reader is any reader who 'does not accept the knowledges which the text presents in the dominant reading' (Montgomery et al. 1992: 228). Whether the reader is acquiescent or resisting, he or she will be addressed directly or indirectly by a text.

DIRECT ADDRESS

The positioning of the reader is perhaps most obvious when the narrator addresses him or her as 'dear reader' or 'you'. Another possibility is for the narrator to give the reader instructions, such as 'Picture this ...' or 'Look over here and you'll see ...'. This form of address is one which directly engages the reader – the narrative gives the appearance of direct interaction between reader and narrator. Various questions can usefully be asked about the role so explicitly allocated for the reader in such texts:

1. Is the address general ('all readers') or specific (i.e. a certain group of readers, or an individual)?
2. If the address is specific, do you naturally fit into the group or individual role created?
3. If you 'accept' the role, how do you interpret the text?
4. If you 'resist' the role, how do you interpret the text?

Consider the following passage from Muriel Spark's short story 'The House of the Famous Poet', paying particular attention to the use which she makes of direct address in this extract. The story is about a woman who, in wartime Britain, meets a young soldier who sells her an 'abstract' funeral.

'What's that?' I said.

'A funeral,' said the soldier. 'I've got it here.'

This alarmed me, and I went to the window. No hearse, no coffin stood below. I saw only the avenue of trees.

The soldier smiled. 'It's an abstract funeral,' he explained, opening the parcel.

He took it out and I examined it carefully, greatly comforted. It was very much the sort of thing I had wanted – rather more purple in parts than I would have liked, for I was not in favour of this colour of mourning. Still, I thought I could tone it down a bit.

Delighted with the bargain, I handed over the eight shillings and sixpence. There was a great deal of this abstract funeral. Hastily, I packed some of it into the holdall. Some I stuffed in my pockets, and there was still some left over. Elise had returned with a cab and I hadn't much time. So I ran for it, out of the door and out of the gate of the house of the famous poet, with the rest of my funeral trailing behind me.

You will complain that I am withholding evidence. Indeed, you may wonder if there is any evidence at all. 'An abstract funeral,' you will say, 'is neither here nor there. It is only a notion. You cannot pack a notion into your bag. You cannot see the colour of a notion.'

You will insinuate that what I have just told you is pure fiction. Hear me to the end.

I caught the train. Imagine my surprise when I found, sitting opposite me, my friend the soldier, of whose existence you are so sceptical.

'As a matter of interest,' I said, 'how would you describe all this funeral you sold me?'

Muriel Spark is playing interesting games with the reader in this extract (and indeed in the story as a whole). The fictional quality of the narrative is explicit insofar as the lines are blurred between abstractions and concrete entities, incredible coincidences occur, and the dialogue is highly mannered. This obvious fictionality is unexpected, given that prose fiction is usually based on the simulation of 'reality'. We might be expected to become irritated with fiction that is so obviously incredible.

The narrator anticipates such an objection, and the direct address to the reader creates a role in which he/she is sceptical, irritated and just about at the point of giving up. The 'you' of the address is specific, individual rather than general; and, given the ridiculousness of the story, we may well find ourselves aligning ourselves with the implied reader. In accepting the role, possibly with relief, we find ourselves back on the narrator's side: she knows that we are sceptical, indeed she expects us to be. Thus reassured, we are both more likely to hear this strange story to its end and more likely to work at trying to understand and account for its stranger elements.

Direct address, then, can be used to create a particular 'space' for the reader to inhabit. The reader can then decide whether or not to occupy that space – indeed, in ironic narratives, the reader may be expected not to occupy the space created, but to question the narrator's reliability.

INDIRECT ADDRESS

Most texts do not address the reader directly. However, the vast majority of texts engage the reader insofar as they assume shared background knowledge and a shared system of values. The reader is then in a position either to accept or to resist the values which are being presented as shared. The reader might (or might not) be willing to use inferencing skills to 'fill in the gaps' where knowledge which is presented by the text as shared is in fact not shared by the reader. Again, those texts which withhold necessary information, or deliberately subvert the reader's system of values, might be labelled as avant-garde or ironic (an example of a text which withholds necessary information and demands a high degree of inferencing is James Kelman's 'This Man for Fuck Sake', discussed in Chapter 6).

Consider the following narrative, embedded in John Knox's *The Historie of the Reformatioun of Religioun within the Realm of Scotland*. The anecdote recounts the rivalry between the Archbishop of Glasgow and Cardinal Beaton, plus their respective youthful followers. This rivalry erupts into open violence when each group tries to take precedence in a religious procession in Glasgow.

> Cuming furth (or going in, all is on) att the qweir doore of Glasgow Kirk, begynnes stryving for state betwix the two croce beraris, so that from glowmyng thei come to schouldering; frome schouldering thei go to buffettis, and from dry blawes, by neffis and neffelling; and then for cheriteis saik, thei crye, '*Dispersit dedit pauperibus*,' and assayis quhilk of the croces was fynast mettall, which staff was strongast, and which berar could best defend his maisteris preeminence; and that thare should be no superioritie in that behalf, to the ground gois boyth the croces. And then began no littil fray, but yeat a meary game; for rockettis war rent, typettis war torne, crounis war knapped, and syd gounis mycht have bein sein wantonly wag from the one wall to the other. Many of thame lacked beardis, and that was the more pitie; and therefore could not bukkill other by the byrse, as bold men wold haif doune. Butt fy on the jackmen that did not thare dewitie, for had the one part of thame reacontred the other, then had all gone rycht. But the sanctuarye, we suppose, saved the lyves of many. How mearelye

that ever this be writtin, it was bittir bourding to the cardinall and
his courte. It was more then irregularitie; yea, it mycht weall have
bene judged lease majestie to the sone of perdition, the Papes awin
persone; and yitt the other in his foly, as proud as a packocke, wold
lett the cardinall know that he was a bischop, when the other was
butt Betoun, befoir he gat Abirbrothok. This inemitie was judged
mortall and without all hope of reconsiliatioun.

Here, Knox has broken off from his serious task of giving an account of
the history of the Reformation in Scotland in order to tell an anecdote
at the expense of local Catholic dignitaries, particularly Cardinal
Beaton, whose later murder he is about to relate and justify. This anecdote is laboriously signalled as being 'merry' in a direct address to the
reader: 'Yf we enterlase merynes with earnest materis, pardon us, good
readar, for the fact is so notable that it deservith long memorye'. The
direct address, therefore, positions the 'good reader' as a serious student of history, critical of trivial or amusing asides. The anecdote itself
assumes certain kinds of shared knowledge and values: the narrator assumes that the reader will be sympathetic to the slapstick characterisation of the Cardinal and Archbishop's followers, and that he or she will
enjoy the satirical comparisons between 'bold men' in battle and the
feuding of choirboys. Presumably the reader is also expected to agree
with the passing description of the Pope as 'the sone of perdition'.

The actual reader is of course free to 'resist' what is sometimes
termed the 'dominant' reading, that is, the one which appears to be
most obvious, given what we know of the author, the ideologies of the
time, and his or her relation to them. A contemporary Catholic reader
might well have resisted Knox's characterisation of the story as 'merry'
– indeed, Knox himself recognises that Beaton would regard the inci-
dent as 'bitter bourding'. The point is that Knox creates a space for the
reader to inhabit: in this case, the space is for a Protestant reader who is
willing to laugh at the follies of Catholic dignitaries and who is willing
to share a contempt for the Catholic hierarchy. Any contrary reading
will need to be established in relation to the dominant reading. A resisting reading of the Knox text would critically examine his use of heavily-
signalled humour, his appeal to the mock-heroic style in order to serve
the purpose of character assassination – in general, it would make explicit the ideological bias of his 'history'. This resisting or oppositional
reading would cease to view the narrative as a merry little anecdote
illustrating the pettiness of Catholics, and view it as a carefully-con-
structed piece of propaganda designed to subvert one type of authority
(Catholicism) while maintaining another (Protestantism).

In general, dominant readings can be probed, and even 'resisted', by asking various questions:

1. Which values does the text assume you share? (e.g. are you expected to approve or ridicule certain groups; are you asked to agree with the descriptions of certain individuals or groups?)
2. What power structures underlie the narrative? (does the dominant reading favour a particular sex, class, race or religious orientation?)
3. Are alternative readings possible? (rather than regarding Catholics as petty, we might regard Knox as being petty for laying so much stress on so trivial an occurrence as choirboys fighting.)
4. What ideologies (systems of value and belief) underpin different readings? To which reading/ideology do you align yourself? Importantly, are there clues in or outside the text which suggest that you are expected to align yourself in opposition to the (apparent) implied reader – in other words, are you expected to read the text ironically?
5. What does the process of answering all these questions tell you about the way that the readers in general construct meaning from texts?

DEIXIS

We have seen that the reader can be 'positioned' in relation to a narrative by direct address (an explicit reader–narrator relationship is occasionally evoked), and by indirect address (complicity in a shared set of values and beliefs is usually assumed). We shall turn now to a consideration of deixis, the name given to the different linguistic means by which readers are 'positioned' in a narrative in relation to place and time.

Traditionally, deixis is considered in terms of person, place and time. Deictic terms require some understanding of the context in order to be interpreted. For example, in order to understand 'I gave that book to him, there and then', the interpreter needs three types of contextual information:

1. person   who is referred to by 'I' and 'him'?
2. place   which place is referred to by 'there'? which book is 'that' book?
3. time   which time is referred to by 'then'? (the tense gives us the information that it is sometime in the past; but the specific time, 'then' ought to be known to the interpreter.)

Person Deixis

The personal pronoun system is the most obvious way of linking personal reference to context. The table below is an adaptation of Quirk and Greenbaum (1973: 102) to include modern Scots items, in *italics*, where different (cf. Macafee 1992–3: 12–13 for a description of Older Scots equivalents):

Table 8:1: Personal, reflexive and possessive pronouns

			Personal pronouns		*Reflexive pronouns*		*Possessive pronouns*	
			subj.	*obj.*			*det.*	*nominal*
1st pers.	sing.		I *Ah*	me	myself *masel*		my *ma*	mine *mines*
	pl.		we	us	ourselves *wursels* *oorsels*		our *wur* *oor*	ours *oors*
2nd pers.	sing.		you *ye*	you *ye*	yourself *yirsel*		your *yir*	yours
	pl.		you	*youse*	your-selves *yirsels*		your *yir*	yours
3rd	sing.	masc.	he	him	himself *himsel*		his	his
		fem.	she	her *hur*	herself *hersel*		her *hur*	hers *hurs*
		non-pers.	it		itself *itsel*		its	–
	pl.		they	them *thum*	them-selves *themsels* *thumsels*		their *thai*	theirs

The value of analysing the personal pronoun system can be illustrated by considering Janet Paisley's short story 'Vices', a good example of narrative style in modern Scots. A first-person narrative (see Chapter 9), it relates its story from the point of view of the main character:

> So ah phone the polis. Ah've done it afore. They come, they go. Nuthin ever happens. This time we're roon aboot question number seventeen an ma patience is strung oot that ticht ye could play tap C oan it whin somethin bumps against ma front door. Ah dive ower tae open it an Netta faws in against me. She's a mess, bleedin, an a wee ruckle o bones in ma airms. So ah draw hur in, loack the door an sit hur doon oan the sofa. Ah dinnae ken whither tae greet ur sweer. Ah go back tae the phone.
>
> 'Oaficer,' ah say. 'That surmise you sayd ah wis surmisin jist fell in ma door hauf deid. Ah need tae phone an ambulence noo.'

The personal pronouns here are linked to the context of the story: 'ah' refers to the narrator; 'she' and 'hur' to Netta, and 'they' to the police. The referent of 'ye' is not to the specific reader, but to a generalised 'you'. Although never directly referred to, the individual reader here is put in the position of someone who is in the physical presence of the narrator, and being directly addressed – it is as if the story is being told face-to-face. The question of point of view is related to person deixis and also to modality, a topic which will be discussed more fully in Chapter 9.

Place Deixis

Place deixis concerns linguistic items which express location relative to the speech event. The most obvious items to consider are certain adverbs of location (here and there; and in Scots, *heir, thair,* and remote *yonder/thonder*) and the demonstratives shown below (cf. Macafee 1992–3: 17–18):

Table 8:2: Demonstratives

		singular		plural	
				Traditional Scots	*Urban Scots*
near	reference	this	these	*thir*	*them*
distant	reference	that	those	*thae*	*they*
remote	reference	*thon/yon*		*thon/yon*	

The Scots demonstratives 'thon' and 'yon' survive as remote forms, signifying objects which are further away than 'this'/'thir'/'them' or 'that'/'thae'/'they'. The form 'yon' derives from the Old English 'ȝeon', which was later conflated with the 'th-' forms to produce 'thon' (cf. *CSD*). An example of the use of place deixis in the opening of a Scottish novel, *The Dear Green Place,* is discussed shortly.

Time Deixis

Time deixis concerns those linguistic items which express time relative to the speech event. Again, adverbs are an obvious category to consider (now/noo; soon/sune/suin etc.; today/the day; tomorrow/the morn; yesterday evening/yestreen etc.). Note that, like the person and place deictics mentioned above, these items can only be interpreted by referring to the speech event (thus 'Ah'll see ye the morn's mornin' has a different time reference on different days).

Tense can also be considered an aspect of deixis, although it is too complex a subject to deal with fully here. One of the functions of tense is to relate the proposition in time to the speech event. Thus, in a similar way to the demonstrative category above, we can make the crude distinction:

I'm going	near reference (now)
I went	distant reference (then)
I had gone	remote reference (remote past)

As Macafee (1981), Milroy (1981) and Macaulay (1991) demonstrate, the verb system is simplified in working-class Scots speech. This can result in paradigms such as the following:

ah'm gaun	ah see it	near reference (now)
ah've went	ah seen it	distant reference (then)
ah'd went	ah'd seen it	remote reference (remote past)

Milroy (1981) and Macaulay (1991) report occasional 'flip-flop' paradigms, where the SSE preterite and past participle are reversed, which would give:

ah see it	near reference
ah seen it	distant reference
ah'd saw it	remote reference

The verb system and its meanings are, of course, quite complex. The point to remember is that the use of tense, in a narrative, with other deictic items, can serve to position the narrator and/or the reader in a certain time and place, and in relation to other people.

Consider the deictic items in the following extract, from the opening of Archie Hind's *The Dear Green Place* (1966), and how they are used, in conjunction with the non-deictic items, to 'position' the reader.

In every city you find these neighbourhoods. They are defined by accident – by a railway yard, a factory, a main road, a park. This particular district was reached from the town by a main road. On your left as you approached it was a public park; on your right, back from the road, was a railway embankment. Beyond the railway embankment lay stretches of derelict land of the kind seen on the edges of big cities. Broken down furnaces and kilns were still crumbling around where the claypits had once been worked. This derelict area was divided in part by brick walls, in part by some bits of drystane dyke, in part by some straggly hawthorn. Further on than this, slag heaps and dumps for industrial refuse – here in Glasgow they are called coups – stretched down to the Clyde. The main road curved round the south end of the park, then entered abruptly into the neighbourhood. If you left the tram here and continued along the main road you pass the brownstone tenement, the ground floor of which contains the shops, the surgery, the pub. On the corner opposite the pub there is an old two-storey tenement, a newspaper shop, a telephone booth. Turning to the left here, you come into a street with rows of council houses. Further down the road is the school.

The first line directly addresses the reader ('you') and places him or her in close proximity to the neighbourhoods ('these neighbourhoods'). It is unclear at first whether the reader addressed is general or particular – the general nature of the proposition ('in every city' + simple present tense) suggests a generalised 'you' but, as we shall see as the passage continues, the degree of generalisation is ambiguous. In the third sentence, the proximity of the area is again expressed ('this particular district'), the second-person pronoun is also repeated, but the tense shifts to past simple ('as you approached it') suggesting more of a particular personal reference, although it is unlikely that a single individual is meant. The role created for the reader here is rather one of general visitor, one who does not know the area and who is being introduced to it by one who does – thus the necessity to translate 'slag heaps and dumps for industrial refuse' ('here in Glasgow they are called coups'). It is the combination of deictic positioning and second-person address that is primarily responsible for constructing the narrator–reader role of guide-and-visitor in the opening passage: 'Turning to the left here, you come into a street with a row of council houses'. The assumption from the start is that we will be unfamiliar with this district, this city, these people. The contract which the novel is offering is to introduce us to an aspect of life with which we are unfamiliar. Obviously, if we are familiar with the situations and people that the novel is describing, we will read it in a different way from those for whom the role offered is an appropriate one – we might be more interested, for example, in the accuracy of the depiction. But we might well still align ourselves with the role offered, and read the novel as if we were new to the city being described.

POSITIONING THE READER

This chapter so far has focused on three ways of positioning the reader: in a personal relationship with the narrator; in relation to a set of (shared?) beliefs and attitudes; in time and place. Consider how all three ways of positioning the reader function in the following two extracts.

Jean M'Farlane, in the *Weekly News*, 13 January 1906

> There's a wumman I am unco weel aquaint wi' whase husband ackually drank himsel' intae his grave, leavin' his weedie wi' a helpless femmily o' seven, a rickety coal cairt an' an auld horse the same as gin it had been made in a cooper's shop.

That puir wumman took up the management o' a business whilk wis scarcely worth a docken, but, bein' a contractor's dochter, she kent a' aboot horses an' cairts, and to manage an' a' the rest o't.

Weel, settin a stoot he'rt till a stey brae, she stairted wi' that auld coal cairt an' the dune auld horse, an' she stack in till she gat a new horse an' cairt. Syne she got twa horses, an' syne she got three. She gat employment an' guid wages tae men, keepin their wives an' weans in comfort an' independence, an' at this present mamment she has atween thretty and forty horses, an' abune a score o' men workin' till her, an' dependin' on her tae find wark for them tae gie them their weekly wages.

The mere men buddie governors o' oor nation hae decreed that a' thae men are entitled tae hae a vote in the government (guid or bad) o' oor country, but they likewise hae decreed that their employer – because she is a wumman – shall hae nae vote.

Oh, wives, did ye ever hear o' sich nonsensical tomfoolery, eh? I'm thinkin' no'. That wumman gies over a hunner pounds a year tae the sae-ca'd Government o' this country in rates an' taxes, an' yet hasna a single say in whaur it is tae gang or hoo it is tae be spent or squandered.

I ken anither wumman what is the heid proprietor o' a big millinery, dressmakin' and haberdashery bisness. In her lassie-hood days she wis cruelly jilted an' deserted within a week o' her waddin' by a worthless scamp o' a mere man buddie. Sae she was never merrit – no, nor never will be, the sensible wumman.

She had a graun' heid an' clever fingers, hooever. Sae she stairted in busness for hersel' in a sma' wey, an' has noo a great big braw warehoose. She has aboot forty weemen an' lassies workin' till her, an' only twa men – wan tae clean the windaes an' the bress name-plates, an' the ither tae look after the pownie an' trap whilk tak's hame the braw dresses an' bannets tae the gentry.

Thae twa men hae votes for Paurliament, but their ain mistress an' breedwinner canna be trusted wi' wan.

Noo, wives, is there no' something far wrang wi' oor system o' government, whan sich managin' weemen are not only refused a vote, but are shut oot frae renderin' service tae their country in oor great Hoose o' Commons? My conscience, whan I think o' the busness abeelities o' some weemen o' my ain acquaintance and think o' some o' the mere men poleetical candidates wha are cuttin' sich sorry figures on the platform at the praisent mament, it fairly puzzles me tae ken whare the sense o' the thing comes in.

This is a fascinating passage in a number of respects, not least in its easy assumption of a literate and politicised female readership, in the Aberdeen of 1906. The reader is strongly positioned as one of the group of 'wives' directly addressed, and the narrator assumes the role of spokeswoman for her peers. The rhetorical questions asked of the 'wives' and answered by the narrator also set 'Jean M'Farlane' up as an opinion-former. Obviously, males do read articles such as these, and they do make sense of them, but in order to do so they must position themselves, as 'actual readers', in relation to the role of implied female reader that the text constructs. This positioning of actual reader in relation to implied reader occurs every time a text is read. The repositioning of male as female is relatively unusual – it is more likely that females have to reposition themselves as males in order to make sense of most texts (Mills 1995: 75ff.).

The reader is also positioned with respect to 'Jean M'Farlane's' attitudes to the sexes. Several times, males are referred to as 'mere men buddies' or 'mere men poleetical candidates', and the general impression given is of men as inferior and unreliable creatures, compared to their resourceful and reliable sisters. The unmarried career woman is singled out for particular praise, which is again perhaps surprising given the place and time of writing. The favouring of one group at the expense of another is comparable to Knox's strategy in the passage quoted earlier, and again the reader is invited to share the narrator's ideological position: in short that men are worthless, shiftless and undeserving of political power, while women are hard-working, self-reliant and unjustly deprived of the right to vote.

Place and time deixis are not so evident in this text. It is a piece of topical journalism in a local newspaper, and it is assumed that the readers share the knowledge of the locality, the contemporary political situation and current events with the narrator. Again, as readers of this text, male or female, almost one century on, we are distanced from the 'implied' reader by time, but we can still align ourselves with the implied reader, or resist, depending on our inclination and our own ideological positions.

If time and place are of least importance to the Jean M'Farlane text, then they are arguably of most importance to the next extract, taken from Naomi Mitchison's science-fiction novel, *Memoirs of a Spacewoman* (1962):

There was more danger on this expedition than I had anticipated; much more. It turned out to be the disastrous expedition to Jones 97, as everyone called it. You will remember about that. I was one of the lucky ones. As a matter of fact, I can remember very little: it all becomes dreamlike in my recollection. I have only a vague feeling of the dark Jonesian landscape shimmering and crumbling. The blast which deafened me for some days does not exist in my memory. I can only begin to recollect clearly when Vly was in contact with me, communicating reassurance and affection with all that was in him. He was the Martian communications expert, my opposite number on this expedition. As you know, of course, Martians rarely speak and only indeed in what they consider embarrassing situations. They communicate through the highly educated tactile senses. This started in their subterranean days, in the original darkness in which they lived for so many millennia; they have gradually learnt to communicate at a distance, their long-distance sight improving at the same time, but tactile communication is the quick and natural thing.

Dear Vly was communicating all over with his tongue, fingers, toes and sexual organs. I felt so grateful; it was so kind, so kind of him. More especially when one realises that on a mixed expedition the Martians never wish to communicate with the humans except for strictly technical and scientific purposes. It was with this feeling of gratitude towards him, of tensions easing, that I came to waveringly. Or was it only gratitude? Might it have been something more physiological, less ethereal? Difficult to ascertain.

Here, as in many science-fiction narratives, the reader is positioned in a possible future: he or she is someone who can remember the ill-fated expedition to Jones 97, and furthermore is familiar with the physiology of Martians. For many 'actual' readers, the process of aligning oneself with a 'future reader' gives a pleasurable sense of escapism; others might find it irritating, especially when the narrator notes that the implied reader will know something that the actual reader obviously cannot know (for example, how Martians communicate), and then is required to inform him or her of it. My experience of using this text with students suggests that some readers are happy to adopt certain reading positions, while others resist, partly on the basis of their tolerance of certain fictional conventions.

Ideologically, this text is also an interesting one, although it is less overtly so than the 'Jean M'Farlane' article. The Martian, Vly's, communication with the human narrator is described as 'so kind', and the human female's reaction is to be 'grateful'. Yet, as our growing understanding of Martian communication informs us, these aliens communicate via sexual intercourse. For a novel written in the early 1960s, when much popular science fiction was still concerned with square-jawed heroes saving helpless heroines from the clutches of bug-eyed monsters, a narrative which places the reader in a position of regarding sex with aliens as both natural and generous (on the alien's part) is remarkably daring (see Ash 1977: 212–20 for a brief survey of sexual themes in science fiction). It is important to note that while the 'actual' reader may be shocked by the narrative (and perhaps is meant to be), the implied readers are, by dint of their knowledge of Martians and the relation of the narrator's reaction, expected to accept the interspecies intercourse as being a natural and positive occurrence. The narrative therefore prefigures the era of sexual experimentation and the liberalisation of sexual attitudes which were to characterise the decade.

This narrative, too, directly addresses the reader as 'you' in such phrases as 'you will remember' and 'as you know'. This gives the narrator–reader relationship the character of an immediate and direct personal relationship, without specifying the reader too precisely. The degree of specificity is greater than that found in the beginning of *The Dear Green Place* although the characterisation of the reader is still vague. Neither is the gender of the implied reader(s) as specific as the 'wives' of 'Jean M'Farlane's' text. The role of future reader is therefore fuzzy enough to accommodate a wide variety of actual readers, male and female, who are thus encouraged to rethink their sexual attitudes.

REPRESENTATIONS OF SPEECH AND THOUGHT

So far in this chapter, we have considered different ways in which an author 'positions' an implied reader: namely, in relation to a narrator, in relation to a belief system, and in time and space. In the following sections, we shall look at some ways in which a writer can represent the speech and thought of the characters in a narrative. This related topic is important because, by representing different characters' speech and thought, the narrator can offer the reader a plurality of voices and beliefs. These might ironically undermine the dominant reading offered by the voice of the narrator. Also, in Scottish literary studies, it has long been a cliché (challenged by Donaldson 1986) that the use of Scots in fiction has been largely confined to the representation of some characters' speech. We can therefore consider what happens when the shift from narrative voice to characters' voice involves code-switching.

FRAMEWORK FOR ANALYSIS

The framework for analysis of speech is adapted (with some terminological additions) from a simple model presented in Fowler's *Linguistics and the Novel* (1977, revised 1983: 102ff.). We can identify five ways of presenting speech in narrative:

1. Bound Direct Speech (BDS): 'I'm worried sick about you doing this', he said.
2. Free Direct Speech (FDS): 'I'm worried sick about you doing this'.
3. Bound Indirect Speech (BIS): He said that he was worried sick about her doing that.
4. Free Indirect Speech (FIS): And he was worried *sick* about her doing this.
5. Narrative Report of a Speech Act (NRSA): He voiced his anxiety about her action.

Bound representations contain explicit markers of a speech act (e.g. 'he said', 'she remarked', etc.); free representations give no explicit signals. Direct speech presents the exact words spoken by the character; indirect, or reported, speech involves some narratorial intervention. In bound indirect speech, for example, there is a shift in deixis: 'I' becomes 'he', 'this' becomes 'that' and present tense 'backshifts' to past tense. In free indirect speech, there is a combination of deictic shift with maintenance of the character's point of view: because the explicit marker ('he said') is omitted, the character's point of view can only be preserved by, for example, italicising *'sick'* to indicate the character's tone of voice, and by maintaining the deictic 'this'. A narrative report of a speech act is just that: the narrator paraphrases the character's words and presents them in the context of a reporting verb such as 'voiced'.

A parallel framework can be devised for characters' thoughts:

1. Bound Direct Thought (BDT): I'm not going to do this, he thought.
2. Free Direct Thought (FDt): I'm not going to do this.
3. Bound Indirect Thought (BIT): He thought that he wasn't going to do that.
4. Free Indirect Thought (FIT): He was *not* going to do that.
5. Narrative Report of a Thought Act (NRTA): He decided not to embark on that course of action.

Notice that, out of context, (2) and (4) above ('I'm not going to do this' and 'He was *not* going to do that') could be an example of free direct or indirect speech or thought: in other words, they could correspond either to 'He said, "I'm not going to do this"', or 'He thought, I'm not going to do this'. The context, however, usually indicates whether the character is speaking or thinking.

As noted, Fowler's model for the analysis of speech and thought is very simple, and it is sometimes difficult to apply simple models to actual texts. If we consider, for example, the opening of Muriel Spark's *Loitering with Intent* (Bodley Head, 1981) and try to categorise each example of speech and thought, a number of interesting problems immediately arise.

One day in the middle of the twentieth century I sat in an old graveyard which had not yet been demolished, in the Kensington area of London, when a young policeman stepped off the path and came over to me. He was shy and smiling, he might have been coming over the grass to ask me for a game of tennis. He only wanted to know what I was doing, but plainly he didn't like to ask. I told him I was writing a poem, and offered him a sandwich which he refused as he had just had his dinner himself. He stopped to talk awhile, then he said goodbye, the graves must be very old, and that he wished me good luck and that it was nice to speak to somebody.

This was the last day of a whole chunk of my life but I didn't know that at the time.

Like many novels, this one blurs the boundaries between narrative voice and character voice. The blurring here is compounded by the fact that the narrator is one of the characters, a novelist called Fleur. The thoughts and speech of the other characters are largely reported by Fleur, but at times these reports shift towards free indirect speech or thought.

Narrative reports of a thought act include: 'He only wanted to know what I was doing, but plainly he didn't like to ask'. Narrative reports of a speech act include: '[I] offered him a sandwich which he refused' and 'He stopped to talk awhile' (and, possibly, 'then he said goodbye').

Although 'he refused' is a narrative report (it is unlikely that we are meant to think that the policeman would have said 'I refuse'), the following clause of reason shifts into bound indirect speech, with its suggestion of the character's own words, mediated by a deictic shift ('I've just had my dinner myself' becomes 'as he had just had his dinner himself'). In this single sentence, then, an NRSA and a BIS are joined together, and the NRSA functions as a 'frame' for the subsequent mediation of the policeman's own words.

The problem with categorising 'Then he said goodbye' is that 'goodbye' might be considered a paraphrase of the character's farewell (NRSA) or it might be considered his exact words (bound indirect speech). The continuation of the clause is also a mixture of NRSA and BIS. The narrator apparently echoes the character's own words using bound indirect speech ('then he said ... the graves must be very old ... and that it was nice to speak to somebody'); but this is interpolated with what is possibly an NRSA ('that he wished me good luck'). The problem here is that the clause is structured in such a way as to say 'he said that ... he wished me ...'. Unless we are to understand that the policeman used the formal expression 'I wish you good luck', this would have to be interpreted as an NRSA rather than BIS.

Arguably, the stylistic interest of the opening passage lies partly in the ambiguous status of the voices we hear: we are not given direct access to the speech or thoughts of the secondary character, the police-man – his words are reported by Fleur, the narrator, who offers tantalis-ing suggestions of his own phrasing in BIS, sometimes blurring into NRSA. One of the effects of this opening is to give us a strong sense of Fleur as having a dominant narrative voice: we only hear the secondary character's voice through the voice of the dominant narrator. This duality of voices, and the issue of dominance, may be considered appropriate in a novel which is about a novelist and her fight to gain control of a manuscript which has been stolen. Narrative control and its usurpation are major themes of the novel.

The passage could, of course, be analysed from a slightly different perspective, using the theory of speech acts discussed in Chapter 6. Because we do not know the exact words of the policeman, it is difficult to give a precise analysis, but it is clear, again, that Fleur is a dominant character. The policeman is not the stereotypical figure of authority, but 'young' and 'shy' – he wishes to know what Fleur is doing, but does not 'like to ask'. It is Fleur who is the figure of greater authority – offering information and even food. The policeman's refusal of the of-fer of food is qualified by a token of politeness: 'he had just had his dinner himself', to mitigate the loss of face entailed by an authority-figure having an offer refused.

An analysis of the realisation of speech acts supports the reading con-structed from an analysis of the representation of speech in the opening passage. Neither form of analysis is without its problems, but each leads to a systematic consideration of the linguistic construction of the text – and such a consideration may give valuable insight into the themes of a text.

SCOTS SPEECH, ENGLISH THOUGHT?

It has been a convention in much Scottish literature of the past two centuries, at least that which was published in book form for a reader-ship within and beyond Scotland, to confine Scots largely to the dia-logue of all or some of the characters. This Scots dialogue is embedded in a Standard English narrative framework. One ideological assump-tion of a mediating narrative voice in Standard English is obviously that mediation is necessary – that the preferred code used by the reader is also Standard English, even if the variety of Standard English is a Scot-tish one. The implied reader, therefore, is not one who speaks Scots, although the reader presumably understands and enjoys the code used in the direct speech of the characters. The author often does not gloss the dialect of his characters; however, the relationship between narrator, implied reader and characters is a significant one: the anglophone narrator and reader are linguistically bonded in a discourse community which is different from that of the Scots-speaking characters. We observe the characters from an external perspective, even though they speak for themselves.

That this should be so is not surprising. Books which have such characteristics, such as John Galt's *The Entail*, were written for both the Scottish and the lucrative English market: in a letter to his publisher, Blackwood, Galt pronounced the early London sales 'very satisfactory and flattering' (Introduction to *The Entail*, p. xiv). The Scots content of many novels was partly constrained by the dual market. Understandably, the most widely-published novels will tend to have a mediating element, a narrator who 'goes between' the Scottish characters and the possibly non-Scottish readers. However, it would be a mistake to believe that all Scots writing needs to construct a mediator who will explain it to a wider readership. Donaldson (1986, 1989) suggests that prose written in Victorian times for a more localised readership, and mainly published in Scottish regional newspapers, used Scots for a wider range of purposes. It is interesting to compare the strategies of two of the writers whom Donaldson champions: the columnist W. D. Latto, and the novelist William Alexander. The latter's novel *Johnny Gibb of Gushetneuk* was originally serialised in the *Aberdeen Free Press* before making the transition to hardback. Its dialogue is written in extremely dense Scots, although the dominant narrative voice is still English. Latto, however, uses Scots throughout. He wrote social and political satires for the Dundee *People's Journal* under the pseudonym of 'Tammas Bodkin'; these were later the basis of three anthologies, *Tammas Bodkin: or the Humours of a Scottish Tailor* (1864), *The Bodkin Papers* (1883) and *Tammas Bodkin: Swatches o Hodden Grey* (1894). Donaldson has noted substantial changes to the material as it is reformulated for the geographically wider, predominantly middle-class book-buying readership (Donaldson 1989: 46–7).

Donaldson's argument gains support from a comparison of the language of the book version of *Johnny Gibb of Gushetneuk* with a local newspaper version of the 'Tammas Bodkin' stories:

From William Alexander, *Johnny Gibb of Gushetneuk* (hardback, 1871)

Tam pursued his work industriously afield through the day, along with the 'orra man', Willie M'Aul, a youth of sixteen or seventeen, and son of the soutar of Smiddyward. When six o' clock had come,

Tam incontinently 'lows't.' Then came supper of kale and kale brose, of which the three partook in company, amid no little badinage, consisting mainly of equivocal compliments to Jinse on her housekeeping capabilities, from Willie M'Aul, or as he was more commonly designated, 'the loon,' who was of that particular character fitly described as 'a roy't nickum.' Tam next lighted his pipe and blew clouds of smoke to the kitchen roof, as he watched Jinse 'washing up' her dishes, an operation which Jinse invariably perfomed with an amount of clattering and noise that made the beholder marvel how it happened that she did not break at least one half of the crockery as it passed through her hands. Whether Tam was admiring Jinse's dexterity and vigour in going through her work or not, I cannot say; I rather think, at any rate, that Jinse was not altogether unconscious that she was making a considerable display of those qualities before the new ploughman. At last she had finished, when, addressing 'the loon', she said –

'Gae 'wa', ye haveril, an' fesh hame the kye, till I get them milket.'

'An' fat'll aw get for that, Jinse?'

'Gin ye get fat ye deserve, ye winna braig aboot it.'

'Wud ye gi'e's a kiss gin aw war to dee't?'

'Ye're a bonny ablich to seek a kiss. I'se rug yer lugs t'ye gin ye dinna gae this minit.'

'Hoot, man, ye've nae pluck ava,' exclaimed Tam, as 'the loon' retreated towards the door to escape from Jinse, who had shown a distinct intention of suiting the action to the word. 'Canna ye tak' a grip o' 'er?'

'I wudna advise you to dee that, Tam, or ye'll maybe fin''t she's a sauter,' replied Willie, as he marched off for the cows.

From W. D. Latto, in *People's Journal* [1867; reprinted in Donaldson 1986: 48]

Havin' dressed oorsels, we ordered breakfast, or a *déjeuner* as the Frenchies ca' their mornin' meal, never dreamin' nor anticipatin' but we wad get tea an' toast an' maybe a couple o' eggs, or a bit gude ham or cauld meat, but judge o' oor disappointment when the garçon brocht in twa cups o' *café au lait* – that is to say, coffee an' milk in't – wi' twa wee rolls, or *petits pains* as he ca'd them, an feint foondit besides!

'My man,' quo' I, 'is there no sic a thing as tea an' toast to be gotten in this pairt o' the ceeveleezed warld?'

But I micht as weel have addressed mysel' to the stanes o' the wa' – the puir creature did not understand a single syllable o' what I said till him.

'Parle voos Anglais?' quo' I.

'Nong, Monsieur!' quo' he, an' he shook his head dubiously. I was wae for him.

'Parle voo Français?' quo' he.

'Nong, Monsieur,' quo' I, an' I also shook my head dubiously while he seemed wae for me. Oor pity was, therefore, mutual ...

The narrator of *Johnny Gibb of Gushetneuk* delights in the use of Scots, importing it into the dominant narrative (albeit in inverted commas) and assuming that his readers will be familiar with it (again, no immediate gloss is given for the long passages of direct speech, although there is a glossary of Scots vocabulary items at the end of the book). Scots is the 'other' language for the reader, confined to the direct speech of the characters and occasional, marked-off, importations into the narrative. The use of English by the dominant narrator again positions the implied reader as a fellow English speaker: from this perspective they can together enjoy and even empathise with the Scots-speakers, whose language brands them as being from a different place or class or educational background.

The Latto passage, in contrast, assumes that the reader is a Scots speaker (even if this 'Scots' is described as 'Anglais' to the French waiter). The direct speech is in Scots but so too is the narrative, including narrative reports of thought acts (such as 'I was wae for him').

Latto, then, appears to be writing for Scots in Scots: the narrative is presented to the community of readers in their own language. However, it is significant that the narrative here is in the first person: Latto's strategy is possibly to distinguish clearly between the author and his narrative alter-ego, Tammas Bodkin, a Dundee tailor. The working-class readership of the newspaper might be expected to occupy a position of identification with the working-class Scots speaker; meanwhile, the middle-class readership might enjoy the essays, knowing that it was all a fiction, the representation of working-class speech by an 'educated man'. It would be an interesting stylistic exercise to compare the 'newspaper Bodkin' with the 'book Bodkin' as part of a wider exploration of whether the change in readership between newspaper-buyers and book-buyers is paralleled by a change in the presentation of working-class Scots characters. There is not sufficient space to explore such a complex but intriguing issue here.

INTERNAL AND EXTERNAL PERSPECTIVES

We can ask a final question about the representation of speech and thought in narrative: to what extent does the writer give or withhold information about his or her 'creations' – in other words, to what extent are the characters treated as creatures who are independent of the narrator, their secrets effectively 'hidden' from the narrator?

The relationship between characters and narrators can be seen in terms of focalisation (Rimmon-Kenan 1983; Mills 1995; see also Chapter 9). Is the focus of the narrative the consciousness of the narrator or the consciousness of the characters in the narrative? A related question is how much of the characters' 'inner lives', their thoughts, feelings and motivations are made explicit to us. Fowler (1977; 1983: 89) writes:

> A basic distinction can be drawn between 'internal' and 'external' perspectives on the thoughts and desires of characters. The *internal* view opens to us characters' states of mind, reactions and motives, either by narrative report (and judgement, inescapably), by the telling of what in real life would be hidden from an observer, or by one of the more dramatized, soliloquy-like, 'stream-of-consciousness' or 'interior monologue' techniques. The *external* perspective accepts the privacy of other people's experience: the writer constructs, for himself and for us, the role of an unprivileged observer coming to partial understanding of the fictional figures in a fragmentary way.

Fowler goes on to state that there are many ways of moving between these poles of internal and external perspective – and we shall return more generally to this question in the next chapter, when we consider point of view. But it is also relevant to the discussion of speech and thought – indeed, we have already begun to address the issue in our consideration of the Muriel Spark extract earlier, where the narrator – the character Fleur – is a mediator of the other characters' words and thoughts. She reports them to us, but she does not have privileged access to them: that is, all that she knows of the words and thoughts of the young policeman is what he reveals to her. What we have, then, is an external perspective on the policeman, mediated by the narrator (Fleur), on whom we have an internal perspective. It is the use of free indirect speech – or at least the suggestion of free indirect speech – by which a secondary character is mediated through a dominant narrative voice. In contrast, the narrator of *Johnny Gibb of Gushetneuk* does have privileged access to the characters' thoughts, and he expresses these thoughts in formal English. The internal perspective of a member of a different community is here mediated by a narratorial 'go-between'. In these narratives, the characters only represent themselves in direct speech (and very occasionally in indirect speech).

The word 'free' in 'free direct speech' and 'free indirect speech' suggests freedom from the dominant narrator's intrusion: characters are allowed to speak for themselves, and our understanding of them is based largely on what they say and how they say it. This mode of representation is related to Fowler's 'external' representation. 'Bound' direct and indirect speech implies a degree of narrative intrusion: the presence of a narrator is evident, and the possibility of the narrator's evaluation is always present. Bound direct and indirect speech, along with narrative reports of a speech act, are associated more with 'internal' perspectives: the dominant narrator has the opportunity to rephrase, 'translate' and comment on the characters' motivations – whether or not this opportunity is taken up.

As explorations of the narrative possibilities in urban Scots, James Kelman's novels and stories reward close study. Like Latto, Kelman adopts the language of his specific community in his narratives as well as in his dialogue. Kelman's third-person narrator is typically an external one: as we saw in Chapter 3, and shall see again in Chapter 9, it is a voice which constructs the role of observer, who does not have privileged access to characters' thoughts but who tends to focus on physical activity, and is seldom, if ever, privy even to the emotions of the characters described. Even so, the third-person narrative voice is sometimes fused with that of the main protagonist, and the perspectives of narrator and character are merged.

From James Kelman, *A Disaffection* (Picador, 1989)

Alison was already there. It was ten to twelve. She was standing in from the corner of the junction, next door to the cafe, which seemed to be shut, the outside door closed. Alison there, she was looking good; she had on eh clothes. She had spotted him in the car but made no sign. She stared in the direction of the schoolgates which were locked and bolted.

He slowed, winding the window down, and he waved to her and drove on into a U-turn and parked for her. She walked round to the driver's door. The owner's inside, she said, he must be opening soon. Do you want to wait?

Eh

We could go somewhere else I suppose.

Aye. He smiled and looked away.

Do you think we should?

Eh, I think eh aye maybe it would be best.
She nodded.
Fancy it?
Yeh, she said and returned round to the passenger's side. He leaned to open the door for her. When she was adjusting the seatbelt across her shoulders she spoke; she asked, Have you had a nice weekend, then?
Eh okay I suppose, the usual ... He smiled, letting the hand-brake off and manoeuvering the car out into the centre of the road. What about yourself?

In this novel, the dominant narrator is not one of the characters in the story; however, the voice of the protagonist, Patrick, spills into the narrative in unsignalled free indirect thought: 'Alison there, she was looking good; she had on eh clothes'. It is partly the fragmented syntax and the hesitation 'eh' which suggests that these are Patrick's perceptions. The deictic shift in tense ('is' to 'was'; 'has' to 'had') signals that these are indirect rather than direct thoughts. The conversation which follows is largely unpunctuated free direct speech ('We could go somewhere else I suppose'), with some bound direct speech ('Yeh, she said').

The lack of punctuation is significant because it denies the reader a 'signal' that the narrative voice is changing from that of the dominant narrator to that of the characters: this adds to the fluidity of perspectives. Patrick is distanced from us because he is not the dominant narrator (compare Muriel Spark's Fleur); yet, in free direct and indirect speech and thought, his is the voice we suddenly hear. We also have privileged access to his perceptions (although not his thoughts or emotions – Kelman avoids stating those directly). Alison is more externalised: her speech is presented as bound and free direct speech, and we see her from Patrick's point of view. The overall effect is to alternate the distanced observations of the detached third-person narrator with the perceptions of a particular character. The focalisation shifts; the external and internal perspectives are not fixed, but fluid.

9

—————— • ——————

NARRATIVE (2): POINTS OF VIEW, COHESION AND COHERENCE

POINTS OF VIEW

It has long been recognised in literary studies that stories have been narrated from different points of view, ranging from the godlike 'omniscient narrator' outside the story, to the perhaps unreliable narrator who is situated as a character within the story (cf. Booth 1961). The selection of a narrative voice – or voices – in which to tell a story is one of the most important stylistic choices that an author makes. Crucially, it affects the attitude of the reader to the events related in the story: we might be more inclined to trust an omniscient narrator, whereas we would be on the lookout for distortion in a story told by an unreliable narrator. Sometimes, as in James Hogg's *The Private Memoirs and Confessions of a Justified Sinner*, a story is told from more than one point of view: an editor tries to piece together the events of the story, and then the main character, the justified sinner himself, tells the story from his own point of view. Both accounts in Hogg's narrative are unreliable in different ways. Our subject for the beginning of this chapter is, then, the range of narrative voices open to a writer. As a descriptive framework, we will look at an adaptation of a scheme devised by Simpson (1993). Simpson's framework is based very much on a consideration of the modality of the narrative voice (cf. Chapter 3). I have changed the abbreviations used by Simpson largely in order to make them easier to remember.

TYPES OF NARRATIVE VOICE

Narrative voices can be divided broadly into two general types: first person (1P) and third person (3P). (Very occasionally we find second-person (2P) narrators; these fall outside the scheme described by Simpson, although we shall consider a Scottish example later.) First-person narratives are usually told by a character participating in the story; third-person narratives are told by a non-participating, 'invisible' narrator. Of the two general

151

types, third-person narratives are more complex, as we shall see. However, let us first consider first-person narratives.

First-person Narratives (1P)

First-person narratives are usually told by a participating character in the story. The degree of participation might vary: the 'Editor' of *The Private Memoirs and Confessions of a Justified Sinner* is a clearly-defined character in his own right, even if he 'participates' in the story to a much lesser extent than the main protagonist and narrator of the second half of the novel, Wringhim. Both parts of the *Confessions* are first-person narratives, even when the Editor is telling the story of Wringhim. It is particularly common in nineteenth-century fiction for the narrator of the story to be a visible but unnamed character, who only 'intrudes' upon the story at key moments, perhaps to comment or evaluate the events told so far. At other points in the narrative, such stories might as well have an invisible and omniscient third-person narrator. Simpson's categories are therefore best regarded as fluid: as we saw, particularly in the discussion of James Kelman's novel at the end of Chapter 8, many narratives switch quickly back and forth from different types of voice.

Simpson categorises 1P narratives according to how certain the narrator is about the events which he or she is relating. It is a useful categorisation, if only because the reader might be inclined to doubt the reliability of a narrator who is explicitly uncertain (or even perhaps too certain) about the events which he or she is relating. Simpson's categories are as follows:

First-person narratives

Label	Meaning	Characteristics
1P+	First-person narrator Positive shading	Certainty about events, indicated by positive generalisations; evaluative vocabulary; use of adjuncts such as 'naturally', 'of course'; absence of features characterising 1P- mode.
1P-	First-person narrator Negative shading	Uncertainty about events, indicated by generalisations qualified either by epistemic modals such as 'maybe', 'perhaps' or by verbs of perception such as 'I think', 'I suppose', 'I imagine' etc.

1Pn First-person narrator   Categorical assertions, made
Neutral shading   without any explicit markers of
certainty or uncertainty; focus on
physical description; avoidance of
psychological analysis or evaluation

Examples of each type of narrative voice are given below:

A: From Margaret Oliphant, 'The Secret Chamber', in *Selected Short Stories of the Supernatural* (Scottish Academic Press, 1985)

I was about to say that no ghost-story I ever heard of has been so steadily and long believed. But this would be a mistake, for nobody knew even with any certainty that there was a ghost connected with it. A secret chamber was nothing wonderful in so old a house. No doubt they exist in many such old houses, and are always curious and interesting – strange relics, more moving than any history, of the time when a man was not safe in his own house, and when it might be necessary to secure a refuge beyond the reach of spies or traitors at a moment's notice. Such a refuge was a necessity of life to a great medieval noble. The peculiarity about this secret chamber, however, was that some secret connected with the very existence of the family was always understood to be involved in it. It was not only the secret hiding-place for an emergency, a kind of historical possession presupposing the importance of his race, of which a man might honestly be proud; but there was something hidden in it of which assuredly the race could not be proud. It is wonderful how easily a family learns to pique itself upon any distinctive possession. A ghost is a sign of importance not to be despised; a haunted room is worth a small farm to the complacency of the family that owns it.

Margaret Oliphant has here selected a 1P+ narrator: the narrator addresses the reader as a character involved in the story, yet with much of the confident knowledge of the omniscient narrator: the shading is very positive, as seen in the grasp of historical background, the detailed knowledge and the easy generalisations: 'It is wonderful how easily a family learns to pique itself upon any distinctive possession. A ghost is a sign of importance not to be despised; a haunted room is worth a small farm to the complacency of the family that owns it.' In this ghost story, the degree to which we trust the narrator (and she has an air of authority which is easy to trust) helps in the willing suspension of disbelief necessary for tales of the supernatural. However, it is not the only narratorial option available for the telling of a fantastic story, as we shall now see.

B: From Carl MacDougall, 'A Small Hotel', in *Elvis is Dead* (Mariscat Press 1986)

I don't know why I drove up the avenue. I'd passed dozens of hotel signs, so why I picked that one is something of a mystery. If I was a Buddhist I'd believe the hotel picked me. I am not even sure there was a sign at the foot of the driveway, but I suppose there must have been something.

The building wasn't special, hundreds like it are scattered across the country, houses that used to be a place out of town for a Dundee jute baron, an Edinburgh banker, an Aberdeen fish merchant or a Glasgow bailie – a two-storeyed sandstone square with a turret on each corner, steps to the front door, which was made of oak and a carved lintel, all closely modelled on Balmoral.

I remember a drystone dyke, then a cluster of trees and bushes. The drive swept upwards from the roadside, with a grass verge in the middle marking the way. There was a verge where I imagined daffodils and bluebells in the spring and beyond the ridge rhododendrons, laurel and gorse.

This is an example of a first-person narrator, negative shading (1P-). The opening of the story establishes the narrator as much more tentative than Margaret Oliphant's narrator: he 'doesn't know' his own motivations, he is 'not sure' of details, he 'supposes' some things and he 'imagines' others. In the 'small hotel', thus situated on the border of everyday reality and half-remembered dream, the narrator will encounter a host of forgotten, fictionalised icons of Scotland's recent past – as much ghosts as Margaret Oliphant's spirits. The effect of the two narrative voices is, however, very different: where Margaret Oliphant's authoritative narrator invites you to treat the story as fact (which is part of the supernatural thrill of this particular fiction), Carl MacDougall's tentative narrator invites you to share a dream.

The first-person neutral narrator (1Pn) is used in Janice Galloway's more 'realistic' love story:

C: From Janice Galloway 'Love in a Changing Environment', in *Blood* (Minerva, 1992)

The bakery was how we found it. They gave us the address and the bakery was right underneath the window, under where we were moving in. Neither of us had much to bring. We ferried clothes and a radio, two big cushions, cooking things and our bed linen along a tunnel of lukewarm pie, gingerbread hearts, the sweet fat reek of doughnuts. The bed last, mattress jamming up in the closemouth, shutting him in the dark and me on the other side, trapped in the light and crusty smell of split rolls. Lunchtime. Tuna wholemeal and his laughter on the other side of the foam, the mattress wresting from his unseen grip.

The narrative voice here is partly responsible for constructing what Fowler refers to as an 'external' viewpoint (see Chapter 8): the narrator is involved in the action, yet we are told little or nothing about her internal state or emotions, nor does she venture general views or opinions about her world. Instead, we are given specific detail after specific detail from which to infer emotional states and build up a general picture. The joint construction of meaning and significance is a deliberate contract which the narrator offers to the reader.

The three types of narrative voice described above are reasonably easy to illustrate, as long as we use short extracts. However, it is debatable how much one particular narrative voice can be maintained without tedium setting in: as mentioned above, normally there will be switches from more or less 'authoritative' voices, or from a greater to lesser degree of explicit evaluation. Still, the 1P+, 1P- and 1Pn categories prompt us to pay attention to these constructions of authority and evaluation – and it is important to pay attention to them, because as readers we may wish to (and even might be expected to) challenge the authority assumed and the values expressed. Where the narrative voice does not assume authority and avoids the expression of value, then we as readers might be expected to infer where authority and value lie in the narrative related: how much can we trust the teller of the tale? What are we to think of the events related? Does the first-person narrator assume common ground with the reader? How, linguistically, is this achieved (e.g. by direct or indirect address)? Is any assumption of common ground justified?

Third-person Narratives

Third-person narratives are even more subtle in their distinctions. Simpson divides them initially into two broad categories, the 'narratorial mode' and the 'reflector mode', depending on the type of focalisation involved (cf. Chapter 8):

Narratorial mode (3PN): the third-person narrative is related from a point of view outside the consciousness of any of the characters.

Reflector mode (3PR): the third-person narrative is related from the point of view of one (or, over the course of the entire narrative, more than one) of the characters, even though the narrative is ostensibly 'external'.

Like the 1P narratives, the 3PN and 3PR narratives can then be subcategorised into positive, negative and neutral modalities, based on the type of modality realised in the text.

Third-person narratives (narrative mode)

Label	Meaning	Characteristics
3PN+	Third-person narrative Narrative mode Positive shading	'External' viewpoint: evaluative adjectives and adverbs; 'strong' generalisations; use of phrases such as 'certainly', 'naturally', 'of course' etc.
3PN-	Third-person narrative Narrative mode Negative shading	'External' viewpoint: vague language, e.g. 'someone', 'a kind of' etc.; language of uncertainty, e.g. 'perhaps', 'possibly', 'seemed' etc.
3PNn	Third-person narrative Narrative mode Neutral shading	'External' viewpoint: avoidance of modal features, certain or uncertain; avoidance of description of characters' thoughts and feelings; preference for statements of fact, often linked by 'and' or 'but'.

The following extracts illustrate these types of narrative voice:

A: From Nigel Tranter, *The Price of the King's Peace: Robert the Bruce Vol. III* (Coronet, 1972: 142)

It was not all just what Edward had asked for, of course. There was a considerable array of knights and captains, yes; some heavy chivalry, some bowmen, and much light cavalry; in all, perhaps 7,000. Also many spare horses, largely captured from England, grain, forage and money. All went under King Robert's personal command. Edward indeed was not present, having returned to Ireland weeks before, with his court of kinglets and chiefs, and in a very uncertain frame of mind. He was getting men and aid – but scarcely as he had visualised. Although he could hardly object to his brother's attendance he was obviously less than overjoyed. But at least it had already had one excellent result; for Edward, put out and concerned to prove his prowess, had managed to reduce the important English base at Carrickfergus, which had so long been a thorn in Ulster's side, in a great flurry of activity on his return.

Oddly enough, though Ireland's new monarch would have been the last to admit it, he had to thank his brother's father-in-law mainly for this.

In its authoritative tone, this passage very much resembles the 1P+ extract quoted earlier. The narrator has easy and privileged access to a wealth of information about what people do and what people think – the narrator's authority is realised by confident assertions, bolstered by such adverbial phrases as 'of course' and 'obviously'. The main difference between the 1P+ and the 3P+ narrator is that the latter is invisible, outside the action – he or she is not just authoritative, but completely or very nearly omniscient. This narrator has to be trusted, not just with the narrative of a single supernatural event, but with the sweep of historical events which shaped Scotland's destiny half a millennium ago. As a fast-paced historical thriller, Nigel Tranter's novel needs a narrative voice that is unobtrusive and reliable: the 3PN+ voice is ideal for his needs.

In contrast, the 3PN- voice which begins R. B. Cunninghame-Graham's short story 'Mirahuano' is less confident in its grasp of facts:

B: From R. B. Cunninghame-Graham, 'Mirahuano' in *The Penguin Book of Scottish Short Stories* (Penguin, 1970)

Why Silvio Sanchez got the name of Mirahuano was difficult to say. Perhaps for the same reason that the Arabs call lead 'the light', for certainly he was the blackest of his race, a tall, lop-sided negro, with elephantine ears, thick lips, teeth like a narwhal's tusks, and Mirahuano is a cottony, white stuff used to fill cushions, and light as thistledown. Although he was so black and so uncouth, he had the sweetest smile imaginable, and through his eyes, which at first sight looked hideous, with their saffron-coloured whites, there shone a light, as if a spirit chained in the dungeon of his flesh was struggling to be free.

There is some alternation of narrative voice even within this short extract: the narrator is unsure why Mirahuano was given his nickname, but he is sure about the fact that he was 'the blackest of his race'. This shifting from 3PN- to 3PN+ constructs the impression of a narrator who is careful with his facts, one who sifts through available information, sorting the speculation from the hard truths. In his own way, the narrator is as trustworthy as the supremely authoritative narrator of Tranter's tale, because he is seen to discriminate between fact and fancy. The extract demonstrates that an uncertain narrator is not necessarily equivalent to an unreliable one – here, certainty and uncertainty combine to create a narrator who might best be described as 'careful'. Further examples of switches in narratorial perspective are considered shortly.

Another narrative by James Kelman illustrates one of his preferred styles: neutral third-person narrator:

> C: From James Kelman, 'The Wean and That', in *Greyhound for Breakfast* (Picador 1987)
>
> Brian yawned; he had shifted his stance, taking the weight of his body onto the other foot. He squinted at the clock on the far wall then turned slightly to look at those queuing behind. And reaching into his jerkin pocket he brought out a cigarette packet and opened it, but put it back again, thrusting his hands into his jeans pockets. He was whistling; he stopped it. He took the UB40 from his back pocket and gazed at the information on it. Then the man in front was preparing to step to the counter. Brian started whistling again and he followed him forward. And while the man was crouching to sign the receipt he peered over his shoulder, as though trying to read his signature. Then he too had signed and was walking quite quickly out through the door and onto the pavement. He strolled along, on the edge of the kerb, gazing to there and into the gutter.

Like the other 3PN narratives considered above, the neutrally-shaded option is similar to the 1P equivalent: there is the focus on detail rather than generalisation, the external view of the characters, the reluctance to evaluate (even to the extent, here, of avoiding adjectives). The third-person perspective further distances the action by disengaging the narrator and the protagonist: we are left observing the character and his actions in a detached, almost clinical fashion.

The final set of categories are those of the third-person narrator in reflector mode (3PR). The reflector mode is the fusion of a third-person narrative with the perspective of an individual character.

Third-person narratives (reflector mode)

Label	Meaning	Characteristics
3PR+	Third-person narrator Reflector mode Positive shading	Limited third-person perspective; language of certainty and assurance as found in 1P+ and 3PN+.
3PR-	Third-person narrator Reflector mode Negative shading	Limited third-person perspective; language of uncertainty and vagueness as found in 1P- and 3PN-.

3PRn	Third-person narrator	Limited third-person perspec-
	Reflector mode	tive; language of categorical
	Neutral shading	assertion and physical descrip-
		tion without positive or nega-
		tive shading (as 1PN and
		3PNn).

These narrative styles can be illustrated by the extracts below.

A: From William McIlvanney, *The Papers of Tony Veitch* (Hodder and Stoughton, 1983)

It was the moment when Mickey arrived in Glasgow, in a city that was about proximity, not anonymity, a place that in spite of its wide vistas and areas of dereliction often seemed as spacious as a rush-hour bus. He understood again the expectancy that overtook him every time he arrived. You never knew where the next invasion of your privateness was coming from. He remembered, too, why he found Birmingham easier. This place was full of enthusiastic amateurs, Sunday punchers. You were as likely to get yours from a bus-conductor or a quiet man in a queue, especially at night. He remembered the words of a song about Glasgow that he liked:

> Going to start a revolution with a powder-keg of booze,
> The next or next one that I take is going to light the fuse –
> Two drinks from jail, I'm two drinks from jail.

Still, it was good to be home, if only for a short trip, and knowing you would be leaving holding a lot more money than you came with. But there was no sign of Paddy Collins.

Here, the third-person narrative is fused with that of Mickey, to the extent that it is sometimes unclear which sentences represent narrative, and which represent free indirect thought – for example, it is uncertain whether the opinion that Glasgow is 'full of enthusiastic amateurs, Sunday punchers' is Mickey's or the narrator's. Whichever it is, it is a positively-shaded generalisation that is authoritative, and demands to be considered as fact. The 3PR+ mode, then, combines the features that we saw in the Nigel Tranter passage – the near-omniscient knowledge of a wide range of matters – and those seen in the Margaret Oliphant passage – the engagement with a single, authoritative perspective. Verbs expressing mental processes, such as 'He under-stood … He remembered … He remembered …' frame the third-person narrative from Mickey's point of view. McIlvanney uses this fusion of narrative voices to elevate the observations of one character, Mickey, into generalisations and aphorisms. Like Kelman, McIlvanney is concerned to give voice to the inarticulate; but his narrative strategy is very different: he constructs a third-person narrative in reflector mode to articulate their experience. The result is not unlike a series of NRTAS (as in Chapter 8); however, the reporting of the thoughts of the character seems here to be a thinly-disguised vehicle for the expression of the thoughts of the invisible third-person narrator.

The uncertain or negatively-shaded 3PR narrator is again very difficult to sustain, as is evident from Giles Gordon's short story 'Liberated People':

> B: From Giles Gordon, 'Liberated People', in *Modern Scottish Short Stories* (Faber and Faber, 1982)
>
> What had he at home? A wife, three kids? In-laws to look after, or at least keep in victuals? A mother, or a father? Did he work in the Civil Service, in a clerking capacity, or on the rigs? He wasn't a fisherman, she was sure of that. The government, somehow or other, she thought, a blue collar job, though his clothes were better than a disguise. A nationalised man. Perhaps he was a widower, not that he was *old* – he was between ages. He wasn't too old to change the world if that was his ambition, or his inclination. If he lived near the Cocker Spaniel it must either be in a block of flats or in a terrace house. Which again gave away nothing. He might have had a basement or a couple of rooms in an attic, or a room and a stove.

Here, the 3PR- voice is created very largely by free and bound direct and indirect Thought, sprinkled with modal adverbs and auxiliary verbs ('perhaps', 'might'), primary verbs of cognition ('thought'), conditional clauses ('If ...') and questions. The questions and uncertainties are mitigated, as in 'Mirahuano', by assertions of what the character does know – here, that another character is not a fisherman, and that he is neither old nor young. Again, the narrator/ character's uncertainties are not necessarily an indication that she is untrustworthy, but rather that her perspective is a limited one. The limitations of her knowledge are here exacerbated by the enigmatic qualities of another character.

James Kelman is again taken as an example of a neutral perspective, this time in a third-person reflector mode. The point of view in the novel *A Chancer* is similar in many respects to that of *A Disaffection* considered earlier.

C: From James Kelman, *A Chancer* (Picador, 1987)

The gaming room was still crowded, every chair was occupied and a line of men behind. He had decided to bet only with the bank. If it won he would allow it to go the five coups, then he would withdraw all the winnings and just let it pass.

When the opportunity arose he threw in £5 and it lost on the first round. The next in line put in £2 for the bank and Tammas threw in £5 alongside it. It lost. He had suspected he would lose that one too but all he needed was one winning bank. One winning bank would return him the losses plus a fair profit. In fact, he could afford to lose seven straight £5 bets with the bank and still be £40 ahead on one winning 4 timer.

By the time the bank had travelled round the table and arrived back with him, he had £10 left in his pocket; he leaned across and put it on the baize. He lost again. Soon afterwards he was walking home.

There are similarities here too with the first-person neutral mode: the concentration on physical detail, and the privileging of external, observable states rather than internal states. At no time are we given any indication of Tammas's excitement or disappointment at the run of the cards. We are mainly told what happens, although at certain points we are given access to unemotional mental processes: 'He had decided ... He had suspected ...'. Given the neutrality of the modes, 3PRn is very difficult to distinguish from 3PNn. However, if we compare the extract from 'The Wean and That' with the extract from *A Chancer*, it is possible to argue that the latter narrative brings us closer to the perspective of the protagonist, in this case Tammas. None of the expressions in 'The Wean and That' could be considered free indirect thought; however, in *A Chancer* it is difficult to know whether the following expressions are meant to reflect the thoughts of the invisible third-person narrator or of Tammas himself: 'One winning bank would return him the losses plus a fair profit. In fact, he could afford to lose seven straight £5 bets with the bank and still be £40 ahead on one winning 4 timer.' Rimmon-Kenan (1983: 75) suggests that, as a test of external focalisation (narrative mode) or internal focalisation (reflector mode) passages might be rewritten in the first-person. If this is easy to accomplish, then the focalisation is internal (reflector). If it is more difficult, the focalisation is external (narrative). Kelman's *A Chancer* is certainly easier to rewrite in the first person than 'The Wean and That', and it is this fusion of third-person narrative and the point of view of the protagonist that is the defining feature of the reflector mode.

As with the first-person narratives, it is unusual for any particular third-person point of view to be maintained over a very long stretch of text: the short story 'Liberated People' in fact switches from perspective to perspective in almost every paragraph. A single extract, then, can give a misleading impression of a whole text.

Second-person Narratives

As stated earlier, second-person (2P) narratives are comparatively rare, probably because they can seem extremely mannered. We shall consider here only one example, an extract from Ron Butlin's *The Sound of My Voice* (Canongate, 1987):

> Seveno one with sunlight seeping through the curtains. A beautiful summer's day. A radiant green lawn. Red, yellow and pink flowers.
>
> You get dressed: underwear, socks, shirt, waistcoat, trousers, jacket and very shiny shoes.
>
> In the mirror: a twenty-a-year man if ever there was one, and well worth your weight in biscuits. You straighten your tie, smooth down your hair and leave, closing the door behind you. Half way down the stairs you stop and go back to open the bedroom door a little. You will be calling Mary to breakfast in a very short time – so, no need to strain the vocal chords.
>
> Down the stairs again, across the hall and into the kitchen. Locatelli and a very quick Courvoisier to keep the morning mud at bay. Water on for tea, bread under the grill. A glimpse of the outside world. A breath of fresh air. Then back into the kitchen for Courvoisier number two. Next: the plates, the cups, the saucers, the spoons and bowls. A Rossini overture. Make the tea and butter the toast. A last Courvoisier, then call the family down. What timing! Masterful as always.

Here, the ambiguity of the deictic pronoun 'you' is utilised for a range of effects. First of all, the narrator, Morris Magellan, seems to be talking to himself: he is simultaneously acting and providing a commentary on his actions, and the reader is put in the position of eavesdropper on this private commentary. At this level, the focalisation is internal: we are privy to the internal dialogue of a man experiencing alcoholism and a mental breakdown. The verbless clauses are also indicative of 'stream-of-consciousness' perceptions, noted as the character registers them. The modality is positive insofar as there is no doubt that the events are happening and that the perceptions are accurate. The narrative here might be labelled 2PR+.

On another level, the second-person narrative also implicates the reader in the story. Given the content of this narrative, the effect is even more accusatory than the use of 'we' to include the reader in the events described in Janice Galloway's 'Fearless', discussed later in this chapter. The 'you' of this narrative positions the implied reader as the principal protagonist: when the reader looks in the 'mirror' of the text, it is Morris Magellan who peers back. This narrative option is an extreme example of the construction of a specific implied reader, and in this case it might be resisted by actual readers, especially if they are not male, thirty-five years old, alcoholic, and managers of biscuit factories. But part of the novel's unsettling power lies in its insistence that the events described in the narrative are happening to the reader, an effect that probably only the 'double reference' achieved by an effective second-person narrative voice can accomplish.

DISCOURSE UNITS

We turn now to a consideration of narrative, not from the perspective of narrators and readers, but as a sequence of structured units, that is, units of discourse. The analysis of 'discourse' is an attempt to describe principles of linguistic organisation beyond the level of the individual clause or utterance (clause organisation, or 'grammar', was considered in Chapter 3). In other words, discourse analysis looks at two or more written clauses and spoken utterances, and asks: how are these items related? How is their relationship signalled and understood?

The main difference between discourse analysis and grammatical analysis is that grammatical analysis is concerned with the level of the clause. Most theories of grammar share the common ground that clauses exist, and, in slightly different ways, grammatical theories will break clauses down into constituent components: each main clause will have a predicator (a verb phrase), probably a subject (usually a noun phrase or clause), possibly an object (again usually a noun phrase or clause) and perhaps a number of adjuncts (usually prepositional phrases or adverb phrases). Discourse analysis goes 'up' from the level of the clause, and asks: how can we describe the organising principles of the whole that the clause is part of?

Theories of discourse attempt to devise answers to this question. However, where most grammatical theories share substantial common ground (for example, that the clause is an important unit), theories of discourse are much more diverse. In particular, ways of describing spoken discourse are often quite different from ways of describing written discourse. Indeed, some discourse analysts reserve the label

'discourse' for spoken language only, emphasising the differences between it and its written counterpart, 'text'. Such a distinction is not
made here. Here, since we are concerned largely with literary texts, we
shall concentrate on the analysis of written discourse and survey several
possible ways in which discourse analysis can be applied to stylistics.

WAYS OF DESCRIBING TEXTUAL STRUCTURES

The following list is not exhaustive, but it indicates the variety of
approaches to discourse analysis. Discourse can be analysed with
reference to:

grammatical models	The units of discourse are modelled on the units of grammar: thus, as the clause can be broken into units such as Subject, Predicator, Object, Adverbial, so the narrative can be broken into constituent parts too.
cohesion	Linguists look for those features of language which explicitly create 'links' between clauses. Such items are pro-forms (i.e. pronouns or substitute verbs, such as 'do'), conjunctions and conjunctive adverbs (e.g. 'moreover'), repetition of semantically-related items, and the omission, or ellipsis, of items which have appeared previously in the text and are therefore 'understood'.
coherence	Linguists look for underlying semantic relationships between different clauses or sets of clauses: e.g. cause–effect, general–particular, sequence in time. Unlike cohesion, coherence does not presuppose that the semantic relations are explicitly realised by items in the text (although some argue that there is always some kind of signal).
knowledge (e.g. schema theory)	Some linguists relate discourse to the mental structures of discourse users: speakers expect their interlocutors to be cooperative, for example; and they know from experience that certain texts (especially generic texts like business letters) have certain characteristics. Certain types of discourse are therefore more likely to exhibit these routine characteristics.

Discourse analysts are interested in discovering the organisational
principles of discourse; it is not their principal goal to account for the

ways in which we interpret texts. However, in stylistics, that is one of our main intentions. As ever, we have to remember what we are doing and why: discourse analysts attempt to construct economic and powerful descriptions of textual structure, while in stylistics we are attempting to use these descriptions of how language works to aid us in our understanding of how we interpret texts.

We have only enough space to consider a few brief applications of discourse analysis to stylistics here. We shall focus on prose narrative, although there is every reason to extend the principles of discourse analysis to poetry: Chapter 7 touched on the relationship of a sonnet's rhyme scheme to its discourse structure (e.g. a general statement in an octave might be followed by a particular example in the sestet). The sound effects of traditional poetry (rhyme and alliteration especially) are often considered as a cohesive 'linking' device: Jakobson, for example, argued that words which were linked by rhyme or alliteration should be scrutinised for some kind of semantic relation too. In this chapter, we shall pay attention to prose structures.

GRAMMATICAL MODELS

There is a tradition in literary theory, going back to Propp and the Russian Formalists in the 1920s, and culminating in the work of Todorov, of analysing narrative by analogy to grammar (see Wales 1989 and Cook 1994 for an overview). In such a scheme, the protagonist of a story is compared to the Subject; the events or actions are compared to the Predicator (or Verb); 'receivers' of the action are compared to the Object, and so on. Thus texts can be reduced to a set of 'narremes' or micro-structures which can then be compared. One assumption behind this procedure is that a finite set of features will generate a wide variety of narratives. Another assumption is that narrative structure works in a way that is directly comparable to grammatical structure – and this assumption, although important in the early days of discourse analysis, when linguists were engaged in seeking some kind of rigorous descriptive framework for discourse, is questionable. There is no guarantee that discourse is structured in similar ways to grammar – the variety of spoken and written genres would suggest that it is not. The descriptive frameworks that we shall consider here, therefore, do not assume that discourse structure and grammatical structure are similarly patterned. We shall consider two main topics: cohesion and coherence. The final approach to discourse, schema theory, will be considered in the following chapter.

COHESION

Since the publication of Halliday and Hasan's *Cohesion in English* (1976), linguists have been concerned with those features of language which serve to 'link' stretches of discourse to each other. Cohesive 'ties' are of various types, discussed below.

Reference

Certain items in a text (such as pronouns and deictic terms) can only be interpreted by referring to information which is available elsewhere, within or outwith the text. Such information might be given by words or phrases which precede the item in the text (anaphoric reference), or – less commonly – by words or phrases which come after the item in the text (cataphoric reference). Sometimes the reader/hearer has to refer to information outside the text in order to interpret the item (exophoric reference). For example:

1. Gie *it* tae me. *Thon buik*'s mines.   Cataphoric reference
2. *Thon buik*'s mines. Gie *it* tae me.   Anaphoric reference
3. Gie *it* tae me. [*Pynts at a buik*]   Exophoric reference

Lexical Cohesion

Any reasonable text of any length will contain items which are related in meaning, that is, they belong to the same semantic field or they enter into a sense relation. We can also expect a high degree of repetition of certain lexical items (cf. the discussion of 'weather words' in Chapter 4). Consider, for example, the repeated and related lexical items in the following extract from 'Hillsborough' by Gordon Legge, in *In Between Talking About the Football* (Polygon, 1991):

> I could talk football for hours on end. When I phone up friends in London we spend most of our time talking about football. When I go round to my dad we talk about football. When I meet new people I usually end up judging them by how much they know about football. I could go on. But not just now. Cause just now I'm watching the goals from the Falkirk game. The commentator says, 'Alec Rae. Oh, goal of the season' and the camera cuts to a jubilant section of the crowd. When I freeze-frame I can see my pal from school, the lad from work, the bloke that looks like my dad, and me and my two friends. There's a lot of faces there that I recognize.

Here, the repeated word 'football' in conjunction with related words (goals, game, season) collocates with words which express (implicitly or explicitly male) relationships: 'friends', 'dad', 'new people', 'pal from school', 'lad from work', 'the bloke that looks like my dad', 'faces that I recognize'. The role of sport in bonding the male community is evident in the lexical cohesion here.

Substitution

Substitution is the replacement of a word or phrase by a 'pro-form'. The pronouns 'he'/'she'/'it' do not only refer to entities elsewhere in the text, or outside the text in the context of situation; they also prevent unnecessary repetition of longer phrases. Similar substituting functions are performed by 'do' and 'so'.

> Examples:
> A: Do you wrestle bulls?
> B: Yes, I do. (cf. Yes, I wrestle bulls.)
> A: That's amazing. But isn't it cruel to animals?
> B: I don't think so. (cf. I don't think it's cruel to animals.)

Ellipsis

In certain contexts, no substitute word or phrase is necessary, and a repeated item can simply be omitted. For example, if the subject (plus the following auxiliary and/or main verb) remain the same in two coordinate clauses, the second instance can be omitted, as in the following extract from James Miller's story 'The Hamecomin' in the anthology *A Tongue in Yer Heid* (B&W, 1994):

> For he wid tak doon his muckle leathern boots frae the peg an [he wid] pit them on ower the thick lang socks at her mither left hingin til warm afore the lowes o the fire.

Conjunction

Conjunctions, and certain types of adverb, make the relationship between clauses explicit. Addition can be expressed by the conjunction 'and' and the adverbs 'moreover' and 'furthermore'. An adversative relation can be expressed by the coordinating conjunction 'but', the subordinating conjunction 'although' or the adverb 'however'. Relations of cause and effect can be expressed by the subordinating conjunction 'because' or adverbs such as 'thus', 'therefore' or 'consequently'.

As an example, consider the function of the italicised cohesive markers in the following extract from William J. Rae's 'Antic Disposition' in *A Tongue in Yer Heid* (B&W, 1994):

> Fowk wha gaed tae the schule wi him tellt me he wis gey dwaiblt as a loon, mair aften awa nor present, *though* some'll say he wis plunkin maist o the time. *Gin* the Attendance Officer had taen a thocht, *and* had socht him wi mair fusion, he micht hae fund him mony a day sittin by the burnie near Fowlie's fairm. *But* the Attendance Officer for that district wis a piner himsel.

The first cohesive conjunction, 'though', indicates that the following subordinate clause ('some'll say he wis plunkin maist o the time') is a qualification of the clause that precedes it. 'Gin' introduces a clause which is a condition of a later clause, and 'and' indicates that the clause which follows that conjunction gives additional information to the clause which precedes it. 'But' also gives additional information – information which is in some way contradictory to that which has gone before. Thus the conjunctions 'though', 'gin', 'and' and 'but' function as signals of the relationships between the different clauses in the passage.

COHESION AND COHERENCE

The boundaries of what is meant by the terms 'cohesion' and 'coherence' are sometimes blurred. It is simplest to think of cohesive items as explicit markers of certain underlying semantic relations which might exist between clauses or longer stretches of discourse. We might not actually need the explicit markers in order to recover the underlying semantic relation. For example, what would you say was the relationship between the following two clauses?

(1) It cam doon cats an dugs.   (2) I got fair drookit.

The relationship is one of cause and result. This is fairly obvious given our general knowledge of Scotland's weather and its consequences; however, we could make explicit the semantic relationship – the relationship which makes this a short but coherent text – by adding a cohesive marker of cause and result, for example:

> I got fair drookit, cause it cam doon cats an dugs.
> It cam doon cats an dugs, sae I got fair drookit.

The cause–result relation between the two clauses (whether explicitly marked or not) is the semantic relation that gives this text coherence. Incoherent texts are those which have no recoverable semantic relation, for example:

(1) It cam doon cats an dugs.   (2) I went the messages.

Here, the relationship between the utterances is more obscure: why should shopping be related to rainfall? Because of the cooperative principle, we might work hard to make this text coherent (perhaps I have some allergy to sunlight that allows me only to shop in bad weather); but here we would probably need some kind of cohesive marker to reassure us that our interpretation is feasible:

It cam doon cats an dugs, sae I went the messages.

More likely, in this instance, would be an adversative signal, showing that the shopping was done despite the weather:

It cam doon, cats an dugs; however, I still went the messages.

MATCHING RELATIONS AND LOGICAL SEQUENCES

Working independently of Halliday and Hasan, Winter (1977, 1982) developed a framework for identifying semantic relations between clauses that included many of the features of cohesion discussed above. Winter's major innovation was to include lexical items as well as conjunctions and adverbs as signals of underlying semantic relations. Thus, as well as the conjunction 'cause' and the adverb 'sae' signalling a cause–result relationship in the examples above, nouns such as 'result' can be used to indicate the relation:

It rained cat an dugs. The result wis I got fair drookit.

Hoey (1983) developed the ideas of Halliday and Hasan, but particularly Winter, in a study of patterns of coherence in longer stretches of text. These, he claimed, fell into a fairly small set of disourse patterns which he classified as 'matching relations' and 'logical sequences'. A summary of these is given below, based on Hoey (1983):

Matching relations	*Characteristics*	*Typical lexical signal*
compatibility	stretches of text are semantically similar or equivalent	likewise, similarly, equally, etc.
contrast	stretches of text are semantically dissimilar or indeed opposed	in contrast, the opposite is true of ..., etc.

Logical relations	*Typical lexical signal*
condition–consequence	if ... then; a condition of this is ...
cause–consequence	because; thus; therefore

generalisation–example	for example; for instance
preview–detail	A occurs in X ways; the 1st/2nd/ nth … kind/type/etc. is …
hypothetical–real	in fact; actually
instrument–achievement	by; thereby; was instrumental in …
instrument–purpose	in order to
denial–correction	indeed; set the record straight
time sequence	then; next; afterwards
problem–solution (i.e. situation + problem; response + results/evaluation + basis)	problem; in response; solve; the result was; fortunately/sadly; etc.

The above tables are not exhaustive: in particular, other types (or subcategories) of logical relation are possible. However, the examples give an idea of some of the kinds of semantic relation which we expect texts to exhibit if we are to find them coherent, and they also show some of the cohesive ties which might signal this coherence.

In the examples below, we shall select two texts to consider what makes them coherent, and how certain writers might disrupt patterns of coherence, or our expectations of cohesion, for stylistic effect.

COHESION AND STYLE

Consider the opening sentences of Janice Galloway's 'Fearless' and identify some examples of the following cohesive 'ties'. To what extent is cohesion used for stylistic effect?

reference; substitution; conjunction; lexical cohesion; ellipsis

From Janice Galloway, 'Fearless', in *Blood* (Minerva)

There would be days when you didn't see him and then days when you did. He just appeared suddenly, shouting threats up the main street, then went away again. You didn't question it. Nobody said anything to Fearless. You just averted your eyes when he was there and laughed about him when he wasn't. Behind his back. It was what you did.

Fearless was a very wee man in a greasy gaberdine coat meant for a much bigger specimen altogether. Grey-green sleeves dripped over permanent fists so just a row of yellow knuckles, like stained teeth, showed below the cuffs. One of these fisted hands carried a black, waxed canvas bag with an inept burst up one seam. He had a gammy leg as well, so every second step the bag clinked, a noise like a rusty tap, regular as a heartbeat.

The first point to note is that this opening section employs a common fictional strategy, namely that of delaying the naming of the character 'Fearless' by using cataphoric reference. (Arguably the character is named in the story's title, but since 'Fearless' there might well be understood as a characteristic rather than a character, its use probably does not trigger anaphoric reference.) The use of cataphoric reference in the opening passage creates a degree of engagement: the reader is intrigued by the information denied – who is this person, and what is he like? To gauge the effect, try reading the two paragraphs in reverse order (that is, beginning the story with 'Fearless was a very wee man ...'). They make perfect sense, but the strong sense of immediate engagement disappears.

The other example of pronominal reference – 'you' – is equally interesting. Here the pronoun refers – exophorically – to an impersonal everyone, a group that includes both narrator and reader. Again, to gauge the effect of inclusion in the events, try substituting the pronoun 'we' (which would include the narrator but exclude the reader) for 'you' in the opening sentences:

> There would be days when we didn't see him and then days when we did. He just appeared suddenly, shouting threats up the main street, then went away again. We didn't question it. Nobody said anything to Fearless. We just averted our eyes when he was there and laughed about him when he wasn't. Behind his back. It was what we did.

Cohesive reference, then, can account for two of the ways in which the reader is drawn into this narrative: by withholding information about the main character until the second paragraph, and by including the reader in the events described.

The first paragraph is also characterised by a great deal of substitution and ellipsis. A fuller realisation of the paragraph would look something like this:

> There would be days when you didn't see him and then (there would be) days when you did (see him). He just appeared suddenly, shouting threats up the main street, then (he) went away again. You didn't question it (= his sudden appearances, his shouted threats, his departures?). Nobody said anything to Fearless. You just averted your eyes when he was there and laughed about him when he wasn't (there). (You laughed at him) behind his back. It (= laughing at him behind his back) was what you did.

The high degree of implicit, unspoken components in the first paragraph also serves to draw the reader into the narrative. The substitutions and ellipses, like the repetitions, mimic conversational discourse (in which a great deal of shared knowledge and a relationship of familiarity between speaker and hearer are assumed). The reader is addressed by the narrator as if they are in conversational interaction, which again increases the sense of immediate engagement with the text.

The lexical cohesion in the text is fairly straightforward and serves to build up an initial impression of Fearless. The occurrence in close proximity of the items 'greasy'-'waxed'-'dripped'-'tap' gives a general impression of viscous sliminess; the presence of 'grey'-'green'-'yellow'-'black'-'stained'-'rusty' gives a general impression of discoloration and dirtiness; while the words 'gammy'-'inept burst'-'rusty tap'-'stained teeth' give a general impression of disrepair; and the focus on the body parts, 'knuckles'-'teeth'-'permanent fists'-'fisted hands', gives a sense of animal aggression – these are, after all, the parts used in fighting. Note that not all these words are used of Fearless himself: it is, for example, the noise that his bag makes which is compared to the drip of a rusty tap. Even so, the combination of the words in proximity, and the distant association with the character, add to the general feeling that the text evokes.

Conjunction is not a major feature of this text. There is a range of types of conjunctive cohesion – additive, temporal, causal and comparative – but there is no obvious pattern in the occurrences. These explicit signals of the underlying coherence of the text can be usefully compared with those in the following example.

COHERENCE AND STYLE

Consider the patterns of coherence in the extract below from A. L. Kennedy's 'A Perfect Possession' in the collection *Now That You're Back* (Jonathan Cape, 1994). The main relationships of coherence between the clauses of the two paragraphs are shown. The terminology is based on Hoey's classification, given in the tables earlier:

1 If we let the child know our rules — condition (1)
2 and what happens — condition (2)
3 when he breaks them, — time
4 it's only a matter of time — consequence
5 until everything falls into place. — time
6 More people should understand that — matching–
7 and keep the incoming flood of modern and imported attitudes out of their homes. — contrast
8 Today we all suffer at the hands of criminals created by sloppy care. — problem 1/result cause

9 A good child will be a good citizen	matching–
10 and a bad child will not,	contrast
11 as anyone can appreciate.	(= basis of claim)
12 Upbringing has to be just that –	response to
13 bringing up from the animal level	problem
to something higher, better,	result of
closer to God.	response
14 Obviously, some races will always be nearer	negative evaluation
the animal than others,	(= problem 2)
15 we must accept this as God's will,	response (1)
16 but if everyone would simply do their best	response (2)
17 then how much more pleasant	result + positive
the world would soon become.	evaluation
	(contrasts with)
18 As it is,	situation +
19 we are almost afraid	problem 3
to go out.	

The patterns of coherence in this text are more complex even than those shown here. The main development of the text can be analysed as a logical sequence, a problem–solution pattern, which begins with a statement of the parent's childrearing practice, expressed as a condition + consequence sequence (1–5). The first problem is implicit in the contrast between other parents' carelessness and this parent's principled approach to childrearing (6–8), and the problem is stated explicitly in (8). Problems are equivalent to negative evaluations of preceding problem–solution patterns, and there is a realisation that this problem has been caused by poor upbringing, as we see in the basis of the negative evaluation (i.e. the matching contrast in 9–11). A general response to the first problem is then defined (12) which would yield the result of a more godly creature (13). This hypothetical result is qualified by the negative evaluation that some people – some races – are beyond any form of improvement (14). The main response to this negative evaluation/second problem is to accept it as 'God's will' (15). But a secondary response, 'doing one's best' (16), would result in a (positively evaluated) 'more pleasant' world (17). This hypothetical result is in matching contrast with the restated present situation and problem (18–19), which is in matching compatibility with its earlier realisation (8).

The logic of the passage, in sum, is that these parents know the key to good upbringing and that others do not. As a result, the world is a violent and ungodly place. If only others followed the parents' practice of strict and moral upbringing, the world would be a better place – at least for the civilised races. But it isn't.

   The first paragraph as a whole relates to the second paragraph in a
General–Detail sequence. That is, the first paragraph states the principles of good childrearing, and the second paragraph goes into detail
about the practice.

20	He never goes out with us, of course,	situation (1)
21	and we can't trust him to strangers.	
22	This means	
23	we must be with him always	
24	which takes time and effort,	problem (1)
25	but we would rather do a good job now	evaluation (contrasts with)
26	than reap the sour rewards of slacking and idleness later.	potential problem (2)
27	We tell him this	matching–compatability
28	and expect him to feel the same.	equivalence
29	Equally, we wouldn't leave him to the tender mercies of the television.	situation (2)
30	If we sat him in front of an endless stream of filthy music and filthy talk, filthy actions,	condition/
31	what would we get?	question
32	We would get a filthy boy.	consequence/answer (= problem)
33	He may listen to some radio,	responses
34	look at his picture book	
35	or amuse himself	
36	in any way he likes	
37	and enjoy the haven we have made for him.	
38	Our home is a clean home, free from tabloid sewage and the cheap and foreign pollution most people seem content to have wash around them all the day.	result

matching contrast |
39	We are not like that,	matching contrast
40	we even sing hymns	
41	to keep the air sweet in our rooms.	
42	It's such a pity	negative evaluation
43	we can't take him out to church.	

The thread of a problem–solution pattern is again the coherent tie which unites this paragraph, although many other minor patterns of coherence are evident (again, not all of them accounted for in this summary). The situations (20–21) and (29), which are in a matching equivalence relationship, are all to do with keeping the child uncontaminated by outside influences. The first set of situations (20–21) gives rise to the practical problem that looking after the child takes considerable 'time and effort'. This problem is not solved, but is evaluated (25) in relation to a potentially worse problem (26), which would be that the child grows into a bad citizen. The matching equivalence relationship is one of mutual expectation: the child is expected to share the parents' views on this.

The second situation (29) is to do with contamination by television programmes. The problem is stated as a hypothetical condition–consequence sequence in the form of a question and answer, but the basic assumption is that television corrupts. The responses to this threat lie in restricting the child's activities to 'some' radio and picture books, presumably under parental control. The result of these restrictions is that the family home is uncorrupted, which puts it in matching contrast with the homes of other parents. However, there is a qualifying negative evaluation at the end of the paragraph – the child cannot be taken to church, for fear of corruption.

'A Perfect Possession' is an interesting text to look at in terms of coherence, and particularly in terms of logical sequences, because the 'logic' of the narrative is so terrrifyingly warped. The apparatus of objective, 'scientific' argumentation is put to the service of the strict indoctrination of a young child into religious fanaticism – an indoctrination that has nothing to do with religious values but everything to do with xenophobia, racism, jealousy and, at times, simple snobbery.

Looking beyond this text, however, all coherent texts will display different kinds of semantic relationships between the clauses. The schemes devised by different discourse analysts are attempts to describe and explain these relationships. Winter and Hoey's scheme is the framework for an analysis of the text as a series of overlapping and sometimes curtailed matching relations and logical sequences, but it is well to remember that the apparent logic is always in part a rhetorical construction, and we would do well to examine the motives behind the arguments.

SUMMARY

Chapters 8 and 9 have considered narrative from a range of perspectives: address, deixis, representation of speech and thought, point of view, and textual structure. These perspectives can be distinguished, although they frequently overlap, and it is difficult to talk about, for example, the representation of speech and thought without considering narrative focalisation. All the perspectives considered in these chapters share the assumption that narrative structure can be accounted for by textual analysis; in other words, that an analysis of the linguistic features of a narrative (such as deixis, modality and cohesion) can reveal its main points of interest. This is only true to a degree. To reveal other points of interest, we must change our own focus from the text to the reader.

10

BEYOND THE TEXT:
SCOTTISH STEREOTYPES

COHERENCE RECONSIDERED

The previous chapter introduced the concepts of cohesion and coherence, with the implicit assumption that both are in some way inherent in the text. Coherence, in this view, would refer to a set of semantic relations between stretches of discourse (such as matching compatibility, or condition + consequence), and cohesion would refer to the optional signalling of such relations on the surface of the discourse (for example, by subordinating conjunctions such as if ... then). This view of coherence, as being somehow located within the text, is reconsidered in the present chapter. Recent approaches to discourse studies argue that coherence is not so much inherent in a text as constructed by readers in interaction with texts. Cook (1994: 35) states:

> Coherence, then, while reinforced by cohesion, is also created by elements which have no textual realization, but can be provided by someone processing the text when necessary. Given the human predilection to perceive coherence whenever possible, there may well be instances where the links will be different when provided by different individuals.

In other words, the relationships between clauses, suggested by Hoey and tabulated in Chapter 9, should be seen as provisional, and my account of the relationship between successive clauses in the two paragraphs of A. L. Kennedy's 'A Perfect Possession' should be considered an individual interpretation: my construction of meaning from the 'blueprint' available on the page. Others might well follow the blueprint but come up with a slightly different construction, and so disagree with at least some of the details of my account of the coherence of the passage.

This chapter considers how to investigate those 'elements which have no textual realization', in Cook's words, quoted above – that is, those elements which the reader brings to the text when he or she reads it. These elements correspond to structures of expectation, otherwise known as schemata. Readers bring to texts different types of knowledge, and they use that knowledge, in interaction with the textual elements, to interpret the texts (see Brown and Yule 1983; and Davies 1995, for an overview of reading theories). In the process of interpretation, the readers' knowledge might well be modified or changed altogether. The thesis of Cook (1994) is that the gratuitous, pleasureful modification of schemata is the major motive for reading literary texts in the first place. Whether or not this is the case (and it is difficult if not impossible to substantiate directly), the question of the role of schemata in Scottish literature is a pertinent one, particularly when the expectations of Scottish characters, and their regressive or progressive qualities, have long fuelled a heated debate (cf. McArthur 1983a, 1983b; Beveridge and Turnbull 1989; McCrone 1992).

SCHEMA THEORY AND STEREOTYPES

Schema theory has already been mentioned in the discussion of conceptual metaphors in Chapter 5, and also in Chapter 9, alongside rival approaches to discourse analysis. According to schema theory, the structure of discourses (including narratives) is partly determined by our expectations. Through experience of language and the world, we develop 'mental structures' by which we recognise and produce at least certain types of text, generic texts such as business letters, lectures, sports reports, obituaries and Kailyard novels. As discourse producers, we can depart from the discourse structures which we suppose our readers' mental structures or 'schemata' would lead them to expect; but if we do so, then we run the risk of confusing or alienating our audience. At the very least, unexpected types of discourse demand a greater degree of effort for receivers to process – some may enjoy this effort, others may not.

The nature of these mental structures is understandably a matter of considerable debate. The human mind is inaccessible to direct observation, and research on schemata has focused either on secondary data – namely, the observable ways in which people seem to process and produce discourse – or on artificial intelligence. An interesting synthesis of the two approaches can be found in Cook (1994). Following work done in computer studies (e.g. Schank and Abelson 1977), Cook presents the argument that schemata are non-linguistic representations of knowledge and expectation, ordered as Scripts, Plans, Goals and Themes. Scripts would be ordered structures of knowledge, for example, the knowledge that Scottish landscape consists of:

mountains
glens
lochs
vegetation (heather, a few trees)
birds (grouse, osprey, golden eagles etc.)
animals (e.g. red deer, hares, sheep etc.)
a few people (crofters, gamekeepers, shepherds)

This 'knowledge', or mental representation, might or might not correspond with the actuality of Scottish landscape. It is certainly the image promoted by the Scottish Tourist Board (cf. McCrone et al., 1995), and those whose knowledge comes from such media-produced images are likely to structure their 'script' of Scottish landscape in such a fashion.

Plans come into action when a script for a situation or event is not in place. For example, someone with no experience of a ceilidh might follow a plan. Plans are non-specific types of schemata which enable us to create coherence from unfamiliar verbal or non-verbal data: novices at a ceilidh might make sense of the dances by attributing ritualistic significance to flailing arms and cries of 'Heuch!' What is happening here is that, in the absence of a specific script for ceilidhs, the novice follows a different kind of schema, namely a plan which leads him or her to expect that, in the context of gregarious social activities such as dances, extravagant motions and occasional exclamations are important. If this expectation is borne out enough times or with enough impact, a ceilidh script will be established.

Plans serve goals and themes. Returning to the ceilidh, the novice might pay attention to the significant behaviour of the 'experts' in order to join in, or perhaps to avoid joining in. The immediate goal of 'joining in' can be explained by the more general theme, of wishing to be seen to be part of the community, effectively adopting the role of an 'Honorary Scot' (or perhaps an 'Honorary Highlander'). Equally, the significant behaviours could be noted and avoided, if the individual wishes to adhere to the goal of 'not joining in' which would serve his or her theme of wishing to maintain some distance from the dancing community.

Scripts, plans, goals and themes, then, are all different types of non-linguistic schemata. Plans come into play when scripts are insufficient, and they can be explained with reference to goals and themes. All vary from individual to individual, although there will usually be some form of overlap, some shared cultural references. In the following discussion, we shall initially consider scripts in most detail, since we are less concerned here with how readers make sense of unfamiliar data than with the established structures of expectation which lend coherence to a text.

Controversies arise when those scripts which individuals and groups have of a particular community and place – let us say the Scots and Scotland – are perceived by some members of that group to be flawed or regressive. Given the simplified, partial nature of schemata in general, this is not a rare event. Fowler (1990: 92) makes the following point about schemata (which he refers to as stereotypes) in the British press:

> We manage the world, make sense of it, by categorizing phenomena, including people. Having established a person as an example of a type, our relationship with that person is simplified: we think about that person in terms of the qualities which we attribute to the category already pre-existing in our minds.
>
> In so far as we regard the category of person as displaying strongly predictable attributes or behaviour, the category may harden into a stereotype, an extremely simplified mental model which fails to see individual features, only the values that are believed to be appropriate to the type. This is, of course, a basic ideological process at work. A socially constructed model of the world is projected on to the objects of perception and cognition, so that essentially the things we see and think about are constructed according to a scheme of values, not entities directly perceived.

In other words, we construct mental categories, or stereotypes, which we project onto the world as we perceive it. The stereotype is socially created, and, once it is in place, we see people as, for example, an Islamic fundamentalist, an Irish Catholic, a schoolteacher or a university student, and we attribute to individuals the characteristics associated with the type.

The shape of discourse is also partly determined by shared expectations between discourse producer and discourse processor about how events in the world are routinely expressed. Similarly, the roles and attributes of certain groups of people in society are allotted particular characteristics because we share knowledge of how certain groups are commonly represented and how they are expected to behave. The degree to which we participate in this systematic stereotyping of certain groups in society might vary – and some people will take stronger exception to stereotyping than others. Some groups in society certainly suffer more from stereotyping than others. In this chapter, we consider some of the ways in which stereotypes are supported or subverted by language use, and some of the implications of stereotyping for certain groups in society. There are various groups whose representation has prompted study and excited controversy, among them women, ethnic groups, different social classes and, particularly in Scotland, urban and rural groups, lowland and Highland groups. Let us consider first of all the representation of women in various texts.

THE REPRESENTATION OF WOMEN

The linguistic representation of women has been a keen topic of debate for the last quarter of a century at least, and it still causes feelings to run high. There are good reasons for considering the stereotyping of women as an initial example: feminist linguistics has been studied extensively (e.g. by Cameron 1990, 1992; Coates 1986; and Mills 1995), women are obviously a very large group in any society, and their stereotyping can have profound and negative social consequences. One reason for the interest in women and language is that speakers and writers have systematically represented women as powerless. This is done in a number of ways. Fowler (1990) discusses some of the ways in which the press represents women as powerless: the language conspires with the press to portray women as irrational, powerless, dependent on their families (especially their husbands) and sexually avaricious.

Linguistic discrimination may take some of the following forms:

1. the use of male expressions to refer to males and females, e.g. 'mankind', 'chairman', 'postman', etc.
2. the generic use of the pronoun 'he' (e.g. 'Anyone may apply as long as he is over 18 years old') except when the context conventionally suggests a female (e.g. 'A cook must keep her kitchen clean').
3. the use of marked expressions to refer to female workers, implying that the example is deviant or abnormal (e.g. 'girl soldier', 'lady doctor'). The use of male markers is less common (e.g. 'male nurse').
4. the use of diminutive or juvenile forms to refer to women: e.g. 'Maggie' (i.e. Lady Thatcher), 'girl', 'doll', etc.
5. the fact that there are more words referring to women than to men; for example, words expressing:

   dehumanisation: 'bit of skirt'; 'bit of stuff' etc.
   trivialisation: 'pet', 'chick', 'bird', 'hen' etc.
   male possession: 'wife', 'mistress' etc.
   women as edible: 'honey', 'sweetie' etc.

6. the tendency (now declining) to indicate the marital status of women in their titles ('Miss' or 'Mrs'), whereas the male form ('Mr') is unmarked. Women are thus 'titled' with respect to their marital status, men are not.

As well as the discriminatory practices illustrated above, it is equally important to look at the processes that women and men are shown to participate in: are women or men the initiators or the beneficiaries of action; are they agents of change or are they affected by change (cf. Chapter 3)? If women are the initiators or agents, what kind of action do they undertake: for example do they repeal laws or do they model clothes? In other words, are women represented as being active or decorative?

Sexist representations of women are not, of course, confined to journalism. Various of the above examples of discriminatory language are evident in the following advice to speakers at Burns Suppers, taken from Hugh Douglas, *Johnnie Walker's Burns Supper Companion* (2nd edn, Alloway Publishing, 1983):

THE LASSIES

If there is a joker in the pack, play him now! The Toast to the Lassies should be the most amusing speech of the evening.

I notice that some programmes say 'Lassies' and others 'Lasses'. Which is correct? Both in fact, and the only explanation of the difference which I can offer is the 'Lasses' is the plural of the word 'lass' which is a standard English word. 'Lassie', on the other hand, is purely Scottish. For that reason I prefer the programme to say, 'The Lassies'.

If you cannot make up your mind which you prefer, you can entitle the toast 'Bonnie Jean' and associate it with the Poet's wife and wifely virtue in general.

The toast varies according to whether the Dinner is all-male or mixed company. If there are women present, then it is a speech teasing womenfolk for their shortcoming as pointed out by Burns. There are plenty of examples from which to choose – from Tam o' Shanter's wife to the strong-minded landlady with whom the Poet lodged on his first visit to Edinburgh; from Maria Riddell's teasing of his emotions to Willie Wastle's harridan at Linkumdoddie.

> Willie Wastle dwells on Tweed,
>   The spot they ca' it Linkumdoddie,
> A creeshie* webster till his trade,   *greasy/filthy
>   Can steal a clue wi' any body;
> He has a wife that's dour and din,
>   Tinkler Madgie was her mither,
> Sic a wife as Willie's wife,
>   I wadna gie a button for her.

This should be a racy speech, with plenty of jokes and fun to be poked at womankind in our society. There's a lot of scope in these days of 'Women's Lib' and laws which forbid one from advertising for a charwoman or even a chairwoman.

Gentle fun is the key to this speech, and it must always end on a complimentary note, again referring to Burns, his patient, understanding wife, and his basic respect for the female sex.

At the end of the speech the proposer will ask the men to rise and join him in drinking the toast to the Lassies.

Many of the discriminatory practices which routinely represent women as powerless are evident here: for example, 'womenfolk' are represented as 'the lassies', that is, women of all ages are represented (a) as young women to which (b) a further 'purely Scottish' diminutive tag is added. The positive characteristics of women are seen almost exclusively in terms of 'wifely virtue', which consists largely in 'patient understanding' of a wayward husband. Negative characteristics of women include strong-mindedness (or independence?), teasing of men, and – most especially – being a poor wife, such as Tam o' Shanter's or Willie Wastle's. There is a word in the language for such a creature – 'harridan' – where a male equivalent does not exist. A diminutive form of a woman's name ('Tinkler Madgie') is also used in the song; but it is a comic song, and so we would expect diminutives to be used for men and women (e.g. 'Willie' is equally an object of amusement). Ridicule is in fact a common and effective disempowering strategy: we are told that this speech should be the most amusing of the evening, 'with plenty of jokes and fun poked at womankind in our society'. Women are there to be laughed at; and presumably if those women who might be present decline to laugh, then they might well stand accused of being humourless 'Women's Libbers'. Typically, attempts to redress the linguistic discrimination of the language are ridiculed as extremist and fanatical – a strategy found today in the blackening of the phrase 'politically correct' (cf. Cameron 1995).

I could well be accused of humourless political correctness in the foregoing analysis. I could also be accused of selective quotation: after all, in his discussion of 'The Response', Douglas does point out:

In cold print, the Toast to the Lassies may sound an outdated, chauvinist display, out of tune with modern life. In practice, it is a highly enjoyable part of the evening, which still goes down well.

The 'Toast to the Lassies' and 'The Response' may well be about stereotypes: the traditional context of a Burns Supper may well demand discourses in which stereotyped representations of women and men are held up for ridicule. Many women may see the practice as harmless fun, even as part of the long Scottish tradition of 'flyting', or the ritual exchange of insults, while others may take mild or serious offence. These divergent reactions can be analysed in terms of differing schematic themes, that is, the general goals that different people have in the expression of their own sense of identity. Some women might wish to participate in a ritualistic male–female 'flyting' as part of a traditional 'Scottish' celebration; others might wish to distance themselves from a tradition that involves gender-based insults of any kind. A possible feminist argument, and it is a powerful one, would be that the stereotyping of women as decorative, domestic creatures is not confined to Burns Suppers, or indeed Burns Supper Companions. It runs right through our discourse practices, sustaining a social attitude whereby it seems only 'common sense' that women in society should display certain characteristics and are confined to certain roles.

A whole range of media, then, plays an important part in establishing and maintaining stereotypes, or schematic scripts. These structures of knowledge can, if the social processes are pervasive enough, discriminate against certain communities, even if that community is at least half of the world's population. Scots are, of course, a much smaller proportion of the global populace, but their representation is as controversial as that of women. Principally, it has been argued that the representations of the Scots and Scotland fostered by various media, particularly powerful media such as film and television, tend to have their origin outside Scotland (mainly in England and in America), and therefore an inaccurate set of schemata is kindled in most non-Scots. Worse, it benefits Scots economically to participate in this systematic misrepresentation of their culture. In the following sections, we shall consider the arguments for and against the stereotyping of the Scots.

STEREOTYPING SCOTS

In the twentieth century, it has been a recurring argument that 'deformed' representations run through Scottish culture, especially popular culture, locking Scots into an 'inferiorist' mentality. The complaint gains eloquent expression in the protagonist's contemptuous exclamation in Hugh McDiarmid's *A Drunk Man Looks at the Thistle* (line 29):

Heifetz in tartan and Sir Harry Lauder!

Buthlay's edition of the poem notes that 'The alleged phoneyness of art in Scotland is represented by the cosmopolitan violinist, Jascha

Heifetz, camouflaged in tartan alongside Sir Harry Lauder, who in MacD's view prostituted his talents by exploiting a music-hall caricature of the Scotsman' (MacDiarmid 1987: 7n). The demonising of Sir Harry Lauder and his associated characteristics of tartanry and couthy humour resurfaces in the work of such critics as Colin McArthur, for example, whose articles such as 'Breaking the Signs' (1981–2), and book on Scottish cinema, *Scotch Reels* (1983a), argue that certain stereotypes of Scottishness are more regressive than others, insofar as they restrict images of Scotland and its people to a narrow set of images from a largely mythologised past. In contrast, critics such as Cairns Craig (1983), John Caughie (1990) and David McCrone (1992, 1995) take a more relaxed view of the process of national stereotyping. It is worth reviewing the main points of the controversy.

The argument is not usually couched in terms of schemata, but it is possible to see it as a debate about the merits of three dominant stereotypes of Scottishness: 'Kailyard' and the closely-associated 'tartanry', versus 'Clydesideism'.

Kailyard

Kailyard is usually associated with sentimental post-Burnsian representations of rural, lowland Scots in literature by such authors as J. M. Barrie. Adapting critics such as McCrone (1992: 178ff.). we can extract and tabulate some of the characteristics of the Kailyard Scot. The Kailyard Scot amounts to a potential script, which might be based on such 'key works' as those suggested below – in other words, by consuming these types of cultural product, certain structures of knowledge about the 'typical Scot' will be established.

Kailyard Scots

Attributes	Representatives	Key works
domesticity	the minister	*A Window in Thrums*
rusticity	Sir Harry Lauder	Scottish music hall
humour	Dr Finlay	*Dr Finlay's Casebook*
humility	the dominie	etc.
modesty	the crofter	
decency	etc.	
piety		
poverty		
canniness		
etc.		

Kailyard representations of Scotland, sometimes ironic, sometimes not, are now most usually found in television programmes and films, such as *Hamish Macbeth* and *Local Hero*.

Tartanry

Tartanry does not have literary origins, but is a set of visual signs which has as its origin the middle-class lowland yearning for a romantic Highland past. Its central sign is the kilt, which was banned in 1747 except for those serving in Highland regiments of the British army, then reinvented in the nineteenth century following the repeal of the Proscription Act and tartan's subsequent adoption by George IV and Queen Victoria. In the words of McCrone (1992: 184):

> A form of dress and design which had some real but haphazard significance in the Highlands of Scotland was taken over by a lowland population anxious to claim some distinctive aspect of culture at a time – the late nineteenth century – when its economic, social and cultural identity was ebbing away.

Tartanry complements and reinforces the elements which contribute to the Kailyard script of rusticity. It makes the rustic exotic by dressing it up in bright colours, setting it to strange music and associating it with particular food, drink and social pastimes. Moreover, it elevates the exotic, rustic Highlander by stressing his nobility, and it makes his image relevant to lowlanders by claiming a common ancestry: the implication, strongly supported by the commercialisation of Scottish culture, is that there is a tartan out there with your clan name on it too (cf. McCrone et al. 1995).

Tartan Scots

Attributes	Representatives	Key products
patriotism	Highland soldier	kilt
nobility	'noble savage'	tourist shops/souvenirs
romanticism	football fans	international football team
Highland ancestry	Sir Harry Lauder	genealogical research
sentimental	Andy Stewart	Wallace Monument
Jacobitism	etc.	Scotch whisky
etc.		bagpipes
		Braveheart
		Rob Roy
		etc.

Tartanry and Kailyard are closely related: as McCrone (1992: 180–1) comments, 'Harry Lauder represented the fusion of both tartanry and Kailyard – the jokes and mores from the latter, the wrapping from the former'. Both tartanry and Kailyard are strongly in evidence in the opening passages of Lauder's autobiography, discussed later in this chapter.

In the 1970s and 1980s, a group of Scottish critics resumed a strong attack on Kailyard and tartanry, dismissing them as 'Scotch Myths' (see C. McArthur 1981–2). In their place, an alternative stereotype was promoted, one which was (so it is claimed) more rooted in the 'real' Scotland of today: Clydesideism.

Clydeside Scots

Attributes	Representatives	Key works/products
working-class	shipyard workers	*The Ship*
heroic	the young Jimmy Reid	*Docherty*
male	Billy Connolly	Irn Bru ads (c. 1980s)
sensitive	Rab C. Nesbitt(?)	*Swing Hammer Swing*
skilled	Jimmy Maxton	domestic football
socialist		
poor		
alcoholic		
violent		
trapped		
oppressed		
etc.		

Commentators who follow McArthur's reasoning have argued that a Scottish national culture should be based on 'progressive' images such as those deriving from Clydesideism. The claim is that such images are 'real', that they accurately portray the actuality of Scottish life. Cairns Craig, on the other hand, argues that such arguments about 'real' Scottishness versus 'mythical' Scottishness are futile: 'The identity we construct will be an essentialising, an idealising, a reduction to paradigmatic features, of Scotland as home , a counterbalance to the "home counties" as core of English/British culture' (1983: 8). The basic argument here can be reconfigured as the psychological and political validation of the schemata induced by stereotypical representations of certain communities. On the one hand, it is argued that the representation of the community should be in the hands of the community, otherwise psychological damage can be inflicted by others' misrepresentations. On the other, it is argued that if all representations are constructions, then simplifications and idealisations will occur anyway, and it does not matter who is responsible. On the political side, the idealised view of tartanry and Kailyard is considered to be inauthentic, an avoidance of the problems and claims of a 'real' Scotland often associated with urban, working-class communities. Yet this supposed 'reality' is also a simplification, which in its own turn avoids the experiences and claims of those Scots working in agriculture, in white-collar jobs, in the electronics industry, in small businesses, in the service industries, in tourism and so on.

STEREOTYPES, STYLISTICS AND SCOTS

Kailyard, tartanry and Clydesideism can indeed be seen as the products of essentialising, idealising processes: effectively, they are stereotypical representations of Scottish people which might give rise to individual scripts whereby knowledge of the Scots and Scotland is simplified and so seriously flawed. Stereotypical representations are socially constructed, but they are also dynamic: as we have seen, they can be challenged and they do evolve. The friction between different stereotypes of Scottishness can be traced back to complex social relations and frictions: Highland and lowland, rural and urban, middle- and working-class. It is interesting to note that the dominant stereotypes of Scottishness are exclusively male: there is as yet no female equivalent of Dr Finlay, Harry Lauder or Rab C. Nesbitt. Scottish feminists have lamented this point, commenting that 'the most dominant symbol for which women are used in Scottish culture is "mother of the earth" – the Peggy of "The Gorbals Story", the Ma Broon [sic] of that long-running "Sunday Post" strip cartoon' (Skirrow 1983). The point of all this for the stylistics of Scots is that stereotypical representations occur in discourses again and again, particularly in the area of popular culture. If Rab C. Nesbitt is the negative image of Clydesideism, then Mrs Nesbitt can also perhaps be seen as the negative image of Maw in 'The Broons'. 'The Tales of Para Handy', in its various literary and television incarnations, is a testament to the endurance of Kailyard, although there is an interesting hint of Clydesideism, particularly in the television series' characterisations of the engineer, MacPhail. What we are seeing is the structure of discourses determined by structures of expectation as well as structures of language: the 'ingredients' which make up discourses can derive in part from the culturally-constructed elements of scripts or stereotypes.

THE USE OF STEREOTYPES

The debate reviewed above can easily be seen in simplistic terms: positive versus negative stereotypes. Certain stereotypes can and should be challenged, particularly when representations seem to lock individuals into powerless roles: woman as domestic worker, working-class male as helpless victim of social forces, etc. However, it has been argued (e.g.

Caughie 1990) that those who complain about the regressive stereotyping of Kailyardism and tartanry underestimate the uses which people
make of stereotypes; for example, the use of shared representations (however far removed from 'reality') as a form of shared culture, to bond
communities together. These shared representations can be celebrated
(as on Burns Night or at social events such as weddings), and they can
be questioned, subverted and denied. Indeed, the possibility of parody
and pastiche rely on shared knowledge of stereotypes, their attributes
and icons. It is salutary to remember that stereotypes can work for people as well as against them: the Kailyard association of canniness can be
invoked by those who wish to present a view of careful economic planning to the wider community – the North American chain store
'Thrifty's' uses a cartoon figure in Highland dress as its logo. This representation might be offensive to a Scot who feels that the logo simpli-
fies national characteristics and sustains an image of meanness. But in a
North American context, where Scottish ancestry is often valued, the
association of a cartoon Scot and a corporate image of thriftiness might
be considered positive. Similarly, Scots abroad might appropriate stereotypical attributes to mark themselves out as a distinctive group – fans of
the Scottish international football team have been known to wear tartan
dress, at least partly to distinguish themselves from English fans, whose
reputation overseas has been sullied by well-publicised hooliganism.
Authentic or not, stereotypical representations have a complex set of
social functions and give rise to very different individual responses.

ANALYSING STEREOPTYPES

For our present purposes, we shall confine the notion of stereotypes to
shared expectations to do with the representation of people or things (rather
than, say, events, which are extensively covered in Cook 1994). How do
we go about analysing their linguistic maintenance and/or subversion?

1. *Names*: What are the individuals/things called? There is, for
   example, a great range of names referring to women (e.g. 'harridan'). Is there any semantic relationship between the names
   used for a particular group? Do equivalent names exist for
   other groups? (e.g. what is the male equivalent of 'harridan'?)
2. *Descriptive vocabulary*: How are individuals/things described
   (e.g. 'bonnie', 'couthie', 'worthie' etc.)? Looking at the semantic relationship between descriptive items and the names used
   to represent individuals/things should give you the key attributes
   of the stereotype.

3. *Producers and receivers*: As well as looking at the representation of groups, it is important to consider who is producing these considerations and for whom. William Donaldson (1986) has challenged the view that Victorian fiction in Scotland was dominated by Kailyardism, by arguing that the Kailyard writers were middle-class exiles writing for a book market largely outwith Scotland itself. Donaldson focuses on the hitherto neglected newspaper literature of Scotland, where, he claims, Kailyardism is conspicuous by its absence. Questions of the representation of the culture of a small country become even more pointed in cost-intensive media like television and cinema: producers of popular programmes tend to fall back on familiar stereotypical images if the target audience is English or American. It is therefore important to ask:

> Who is producing this representation?
> At whom is it targeted?
> What kind of stereotypes can they be expected to share?
> Why is the representation being produced? (e.g. to inform, amuse, challenge or obtain profit?)

The first extract is taken from a successful one-man stage play by W. Gordon Smith about a semi-retired Scottish soldier, given the eponymous name, Jock. *Jock* is partly about representations of Scottish history, and their 'distortion' by vested interests. In *Jock*, we have one embodiment of the Scottish Everyman, familiar from the tartanry script, but his function is to modify our stereotypes, to purge our Scotland script of false information. In the scene below, Jock demonstrates how to wear the kilt:

From W. Gordon Smith, *Jock* (Cacciatore Fabbro, 1977)

When I started with the Seaforths it was the kilt or nothing. Or rather it was the kilt *and* nothing. They had a mirror set in the concrete at the guardroom. You had to pass over it and do a wee kind of a … one, two, three, and a chassis over it before you could get out of the barracks. The briefest flash of a pair of knickers and you were peeling tatties for a week.

When the good Lord made the Jocks he did not design them to go upstairs in tramcars.

He sits on stool, slips off shoes, rises, goes upstage and fetches a very large bundle of cloth and a brass-knuckled leather belt.

There's no mystery, nowadays, about what the modern Jock wears under his kilt. He either does or he doesn't.

JOCK has surreptitiously loosened the zip on his flies. By releasing one button or clip his trousers should clatter to the floor with the weight of things in his pockets. The more the fat women guffaw the longer he should stare them out, taking no part in the hee-hawing but maintaining his considerable dignity – which should prolong the laughter rather than reduce it. When he is good and ready he clears a big space on the floor and sets the kilt down carefully.

The kilt is a corruption of the Highlanders' original feilidh-Mor, the big blanket or plaid.

He picks up the bundle of cloth and teases it out over his arms, yard by yard.

The blanket is made of wool and roughly dyed. The colours and patterns or setts didn't emerge for a long time. The blanket should be two yards wide and six yards long.

He lays the entire length of the blanket across the width of the belt, leaving about three feet of cloth below one end of the belt.

There's only one way to get into it – and the secret baffled the Sassenachs for centuries. First of all, you've got to lay it out, across the belt, then pleat it like this, reducing the width of the blanket.

He pleats the blanket

Then …

He lies down on the blanket, the belt under his waist, the short end of the blanket under his thighs, the long end stretching out behind his head.

You buckle the belt and …

He sits up, pulling the surplus up and allowing it to fall over one shoulder. He kneels, facing the audience.

Arrange the pleats round your body and adjust the height of the kilt from a kneeling position so that it almost touches the floor. Almost but not quite. Otherwise you'll be known to all and sundry as Dreepie Drawers.

He rises, pulling the surplus over a shoulder.

If it's cold you can distribute the top end to keep you warm …

He does.

Or if you want to keep your arms free you can leave it like this ...

He drapes it loosely over one shoulder, round back, and over the other shoulder.

But if you get into a fight or want to charge in battle, it's a hell of a handicap to be lumbered with twelve square yards of heavy wool, so ...

He unbuckles the belt and it all collapses to the floor again. He steps out of the wool.

The sight of this, minus the underpants, with hairy bare hurdies gleaming in the sunlight, was enough to move the bowels of a sphinx.

He twangs the elastic in his briefs.

And here we stand – a nation emasculated by Marks and Spencer.

The extract is a cunning blend of familiarity and modification: the old music-hall joke about what Scotsmen wear under the kilt (namely, nothing) is fondly resurrected, as are military myths of the potency of Highland soldiers, the ancestors of the twentieth-century 'ladies from hell'. These conventional or 'default' elements of the tartanry script are woven into a text about corruption, both of the kilt and of the myths of Scottish soldiery. The kilt which Jock puts on is an 'authentic' one, before its corruption by commercialism, and Jock argues that the modern habit of wearing briefs under the kilt is symptomatic of a decline in Scottish manhood. The ambivalence to images of Scotland is well brought out by the play: it relies upon the familiarity of stereo-typical representations, but seeks to alter them, here by a nostalgic appeal to an idealised past, of which the modern images of Scots and Scotland are decadent, commercialised descendants. Jock's attitude here can be compared to those critics who argue against tartanry as a defor-mation of Scottish culture, and the play does end with a (failed) attempt to shrug off the legacy of the past: 'We know better than that now, don't we? ... We're our own masters now, aren't we?' asks Jock in none-too-convincing a manner. The immediate subject is the exploitation of the Scottish soldier, but the subtext could easily be the representations of Scots from outwith Scotland itself – from Ealing and Hollywood, for example.

A 'Scots myths' reading of *Jock* would partly miss the point, however. The play obviously revels in its stereotypical images – conjured by the jokes, anecdotes and shared cultural references – even when it might be construed as attacking them. As a one-man play, it owes part of its entertainment value to the music-hall tradition which Harry Lauder typified and MacDiarmid attacked. Its ambivalence is typical, as McCrone et al. point out in relation to the consumption of 'heritage' by the Scots (1995: 7):

> In asking who we are, the totems and icons of heritage are power-ful signifiers of our identity. We may find tartanry, Bonnie Prince Charlie, Mary Queen of Scots, Bannockburn and Burns false descriptors of who we are, but they provide a source of ready-made distinguishing characteristics from England, our bigger, southern neighbour.

In some eyes, perhaps, our adherence to romantic scripts of who the Scots are is an act of political self-betrayal. The scripts need to be purged or purified. The alternative sometimes offered is the Clydesider script, which permeates many modern novels and plays and finds ex-pression in, for example, Bill Bryden's *The Ship*, and in the opening of John and Willy Maley's community drama, *From the Calton to Catalonia* (Glasgow: Clydeside Press, n.d.). The play was conceived in 1989 and first performed by Lithgow Theatre, Govan, in 1990 when Glasgow was European City of Culture.

> CHORUS: Picture it. The Calton. Fair fortnight. 1937. Full of Eastern promise. Wimmen windaehingin. Weans greetin for pokey hats. Grown men, well intae their hungry thirties, slouchin at coarners, skint as a bairn's knees. The sweet smell of middens, full and flowing over in the sun. Quick! There's a scramble in Parnie Street! The wee yin there's away wae a hauf-croon.
>
> Back closes runnin wae dug pee and East End young team runnin wae the San Toy, the Kent Star, the Sally Boys, the Black Star, the Calton Entry Mob, the Cheeky Forty, the Romeo Boys, the Antique Mob, and the Stickit Boys. Then there wiz the Com-munist Party. Red rags tae John Bull. But if things wur bad in the Calton, they wur worse elsewhere. Franco in the middle. Musso-lini oan the right wing. Hitler waitin tae come oan. When they three goat thegither an came up against the Spanish workers, they didnae expect the Calton tae offer handers.
>
> The heirs a John MacLean, clutchin a quire a Daily Workers, staunin oan boaxes at the Green, shakin their fists at the crowds that gethered tae hear aboot the plight ae the Spanish Republic. Oot ae these getherins oan the Green came the heroes ae the International Brigade, formin the frontline against fascism.
>
> The Blackshirts, the Brownshirts, the Blueshirts, fascists of every colour an country came up against the men an women ae no

mean city, against grey simmets an bunnets an headscarfs, against troosers tied wae string an shoes that let the rain in, against guns that were auld enough tae remember Waterloo. Fae nae hair tae grey hair they answered the call. Many never came back. They wur internationalists. They wur Europeans. They wur Scots. Glasgow should be proud ae them!

Male orientation (despite some token references to women) and militarism apart, little could be further from the kilted Highlander, piping in a lonely glen. The Chorus here touches on nearly every imaginable con-stituent of a script of Clydeside Scots: the setting in Glasgow's East End, the Fair Holiday Fortnight celebrations, the gang violence, the poverty, the socialism, the pride. Implicitly there is also the football, in the way that the European conflict is represented as if it were a soccer commentary: 'Franco in the middle. Mussolini on the right wing. Hitler waiting to come oan.' When I have discussed this passage with students from different countries, the football allusion is often missed, even when comprehension of the Glasgow vernacular is otherwise very high. Female Scottish students sometimes miss it too, but in my experience the phrasing of the three sentences immediately triggers a 'football script' for most male Scottish students.

The question is whether this play is more 'authentic' than, say, *Jock*, which triggers and prompts the re-examination of scripts associated more with tartanry. The proliferation of Clydeside icons in the open-ing of *From the Calton to Catalonia* almost suggests parody, although the rest of the play, which fictionalises the experiences of the authors' fa-ther in a Spanish POW camp, would not confirm such a reading. The key to the raising of the Clydeside script in this play is probably again the question of identity: this is an example of community drama, for a very specific audience, about their own fathers and mothers. It is also designed to validate the experiences of a group – working-class Glaswegians – who have perhaps been neglected in some 'official' histories of the twentieth century. The extent to which *From the Calton to Catalonia* succeeds or fails in validating the community's experience is beside the point here. The point is that the raising of shared schemata in the opening passages immediately locates the play and brings on stage the collective mythology of a particular group. People know where they are, and more crucially they know what they are. Where *Jock* trades on the familiarity of some Scottish stereotypes, in order to question them, *From the Calton to Catalonia* invites unironic celebration of others.

Both *Jock* and *From the Calton to Catalonia*, by using such features as shared cultural references, schematic assumptions and (in *Jock*) direct address, position the audience as Scots – although, as we have seen in Chapters 8 and 9, this need not limit the audience to Scots. The final extract, on the other hand, was written for an audience as much outside Scotland as within it.

Sir Harry Lauder's autobiography, *Harry Lauder – At Home and On Tour* (London: Greening and Co., n.d.), was first published by Blackwood in 1907. The frontispiece to the Greening and Co. edition tells us that by April 1914, it had sold 45,000 copies. A second autobiography, *Roamin' in the Gloamin'*, was later published by Hutchinson in London, and also sold well. Many of these will have been sold in Scotland, but certainly, given the London imprint, many will have been sold in England and presumably America, where Lauder's tours were phenomenally popular. The opening paragraphs of *At Home and On Tour* locate the narrator by raising familiar details from the Kailyard/tartanry Script:

Extract A

How other chaps feel when they sit down to take their lives – I mean write them – I don't know, but at this moment I feel just about the most unhappy man on the face o' the earth. In fact I feel so queer that I would welcome anything or anybody – even suppose he came to borrow money – so long as I could find the slightest excuse for delaying once more my first attempt at authorship.

P.S. – Since writing the above I have eagerly waited a full hour listening for a knock at the door and have smoked six pipefuls of thick black to soothe my nerves. But nobody has come to cheer me up! Perhaps my friends have got to know that I am writing a book and have decided to leave me to my awful fate.

Extract B

My first appearance on any stage – this is absolutely original! – took place in a wee house in Portobello before an admiring audience of two, both of whom were paid for their presence. The stage, I need scarcely add, was the stage of life, and the audience consisted of a nurse and the village doctor. For reasons which I think will be fairly obvious, I have not included my mother amongst those 'in front'. Later the 'house' was augmented by the arrival of my father, who, I have been informed, expressed great satisfaction with the last 'turn'. The date of this appearance I am quite unable to vouch for personally, but I have my mother's word for it that it happened on 4th August 1870, somewhere about half-past five in the morning. The wag-at-the-wa' may have been a few minutes wrong either way, but in any case I was always an early riser.

Extract C

John Lauder, my father, was a native of Edinburgh, and my
mother was a MacLennan of the Black Isle, Ross-shire. So that I
am Scotch to the back-bone, as the phrase has it, a true native of
the land whose chief characteristics are generally supposed to be
mountain and flood, 'parritch' and kail, whisky and 'soor-dook'. I
have even heard it whispered that my paternal ancestors were direct descendants of Lauder o' the Bass Rock, home of the solan
goose and silver gull.

The opening paragraphs (extract A) establish the image of the canny Scot,
here displaced by the modest, or self-effacing, Scot – one to whom the
prospect of writing an autobiography so strongly suggests self-impor-
tance that he would even prefer to lend money than to embark upon it.
The narrative proper begins with the infant Lauder's birth (extract B),
presented to us in the appropriate extended metaphor of a music-hall
turn – giving a pleasing twist to the claim that someone is a 'born per-
former'. Thus the music-hall script is presumably triggered in the
reader, who, having purchased the autobiography on the strength of
Lauder's music-hall act, will presumably be gratified by the early reference. The extracts conclude with a return to the Kailyard/Tartanry
script, with Lauder establishing his family credentials (extract C).
Through his mother, he is distantly related to the Highland nobility, a
nobility associated with the romantic landscapes of mountain, flood,
sea, island and wildlife. Despite the noble connections, his family is also
associated with the Kailyard virtues of domesticity and homely fare.

It is perhaps fitting to end this chapter with a consideration of Sir
Harry Lauder, whose construction of a trademark identity from the
post-Walter Scott elements of Kailyard and tartanry was a massive success in the early twentieth century overseas and at home, and for many
formed (and still forms) the basis for a Scotsman script. Given the stake
that each Scot has in the process of creating an individual and group
identity, it is far from surprising that alternative representations are
vigorously presented and defended. The relationship of schematic
knowledge to history, to fact, is a difficult one: kilted Highlanders do
exist, and there is extreme urban poverty in parts of the major cities. But
the facts of our everyday existence become the raw materials of our self-
imagining by a dynamic process of selection, simplification and transformation.

11

———— • ————

BEYOND THE TEXT (2):
PROCESSING DISCOURSE

The study of literature from the perspective of linguistics has gone through various transformations, as the discipline of linguistics has itself evolved. For much of the time, as we have seen, our attention has been fixed on the text as the basis for statements about how a poem, play, story or even a single utterance should be interpreted. The assumption has been that, in order to understand the meaning potential of a text, it is both necessary and sufficient to account for the selections made at the levels of phonology, lexis, grammar and discourse. With the exception of the previous and present chapters, this book has largely followed that assumption: we have looked at sound patterning, grammatical patterning (transitivity and modality in particular), lexical patterning and various approaches to discourse patterning, including speech act theory and the identification of discourse units. These approaches to stylistic analysis all fall under the heading of discourse stylistics: we understand a text by paying close attention to its complex linguistic structure. We analyse the product. In periods when English Studies seemed to be characterised by subjective literary appraisals, stylistics promised a scientific approach: it borrowed the methodology of linguistics and appealed to hard and available evidence, namely the words on the page. The (apparent) scientific rigour of stylistics compared to traditional literary analysis seemed sufficient justification to move it into the mainstream: some believed that it would become English Studies. But any visit to a university Scottish or English Literature Department will quickly reveal that the revolution did not happen. What went wrong?

Although for much of this book we too have focused on textual organisation, there have been times when we have had to look up from the page and speculate a little about what people are doing with the texts under consideration, in other words the processes involved in making the textual product. Such speculation does not apply so much to speech act theory, perhaps, although speech act theory does attempt to classify utterances as behavioural acts. To some extent, the utterance is assumed to embody the act: a warning, for example, is a warning often because it has the formal characteristics of a warning. These characteristics can be described and utterances arranged in a classificatory system.

We are closer to the consideration of process when we consider conceptual metaphors (Chapter 5), or Grice's maxims of conversational interaction, which are attempts to formalise what people presuppose if they are to make sense of utterances (Chapter 6): they presuppose, for example, that other people are going to be cooperative, truthful and relevant. Such presuppositions continue even in the face of evidence to the contrary. And we are closer to process when, in the previous chapter, we speculated about the nature of stereotyped or schematic mental structures which might account for the content and organisation of discourse. At these points, we have moved away from a consideration of language *per se* and moved towards a consideration of how language comes to be. Our focus has moved away from text and towards text production.

Even in Chapter 10 we were concerned with process only insofar as we could extrapolate from texts. We asked: 'If this sequence of individual sentences makes up a coherent text, what can we say about how the reader makes sense of it?' This question has largely been answered by introspection, even if our individual insights have been structured by concepts derived from linguistics, psychology and artificial intelligence. So far, we have not looked at the people themselves as they produce or process discourse. This chapter will attempt to redress the balance by looking at a technique for investigating the on-line processing of text by others.

PRACTICAL CRITICISM REVISITED

The basic technique is simple: the researcher sits the subject down and the subject records as much as possible of what is happening as he or she reads or writes a piece of text. Since our concern here is with interpretation of text, we shall focus on reading. Nowadays, the subject usually 'thinks aloud' while reading (an activity which is actually quite difficult to do, and usually requires some practice) and the researcher tapes the records or protocols. The protocols are transcribed and the data analysed with a view to investigating what the subject is doing when he/she is actually reading the text.

This methodology will be familiar to those who are acquainted with I. A. Richards' *Practical Criticism*, first published in 1929 and never out of print since. In the days before widespread tape-recording, Richards presented a group of Cambridge undergraduates with a number of poems (thirteen are discussed in the book) – some by canonical writers, such as Gerard Manley Hopkins, D. H. Lawrence, John Donne; others by minor figures such as Phillip James Bailey and the Rev. G. A. Studdert Kennedy. Richards distributed these poems, omitting the title and poet's name, and asked his subjects to note down their comments on them. After a week, he would gather these 'protocols', and his book is devoted to picking out interesting comments and analysing them. Richards perceptively, and with typical eloquence, states the major methodological limitation of the technique (1929: 10; original emphasis):

> The indispensable instrument for this inquiry is psychology. I am anxious to meet as far as may be the objection that may be brought by some psychologists, and these the best, that the protocols do not supply enough evidence for us really to be able to make out the motives of the writers and that therefore the whole investigation is superficial. But the *beginning* of every research ought to be superficial, and to find something to investigate that is accessible and detachable is one of the chief difficulties of psychology. I believe the chief merit of the experiment here made is that it gives us this. Had I wished to plumb the depths of these writers' Unconscious, where I am quite willing to agree the real motives of their likings and dislikings would be found, I should have devised something like a branch of psychoanalytic technique for the purpose. But it was clear that little progress would be made if we attempted to drag too deep a plough. However, even as it is, enough strange material is turned up.

Richards' caution is well justified: we should beware of making an easy equation between what readers say they are doing and the actual cognitive processes which are occurring as they read. Even so, by substituting a tape-recorder and spontaneous on-line processing, for a week with a notepad and pencil, sufficient 'accessible and detachable material' might be gathered, which (chronologically at least) is as close to the inaccessible cognitive processes as possible. The question then arises about the researcher's stance: what does he or she do with the protocols? The final comment about 'strange material' rather gives away Richards' position.

Like his British contemporaries, Richards was interested in the formation of critical taste. His interest in students' protocols is not just in what goes into their process of interpretation; his interest is in where their processes of interpretation go wrong. Again, he writes (ibid.: 11):

That the one and only goal of all critical endeavours, of all interpretation, appreciation, exhortation, praise or abuse, is improvement in communication may seem an exaggeration. But in practice it is so. The whole apparatus of critical rules and principles is a means to the attainment of a finer, more precise, more discriminating communication.

Once communication has become 'finer ... more discriminating', Richards claims, the process of evaluation 'settles itself' (ibid.). This concern with the formation of critical taste might well explain this remarkable book's ambiguous status in the UK: on the one hand it has never been out of print; on the other it seems not to have opened up any sustained direct research route (although some follow-up work has been attempted, mainly in the USA; see, for example, Loban 1954, Squire 1964 and Wilson 1966; and there is an established line of empirical research in Europe; see, for example, Ibsch et al. 1991; and Steen 1994). *Practical Criticism*, nevertheless, serves mainly as a constant warning to British academics of the strange ideas that students would have if they were left to their own devices. The notion that such responses might merit detailed attention is usually brushed aside, even by those who have developed Richards' work. For example, Rosenblatt (1968: 97), quoting Richards, summarises his position so:

> The impact of the literary work is dulled when the reader brings to the text a fund of ready-made, sharply-crystallized ideas and habits of response. These responses are so easily touched off that they sometimes interfere with interpretation.

If we accept the premiss of Chapter 10 – that all discourse interpretation depends on the accessing of some kind of mental schemata – then Rosenblatt's argument looks a little different. Perhaps it is not the existence of 'ready-made ... habits of response' which are really at stake, but the kind of habits of response. 'Interpretation', as such, is not 'interfered with' by the reader's schemata, but the right interpretation might well be. And of course the right interpretation is the one validated by those critics who are in turn validated by the academic community. If we know that students tend to get it wrong – and Richards demonstrates this fact about students whom he emphasises are among the best in the country – then we can devote our energies and output to training them better. It may be significant that few researchers have attempted a similar experiment with a group of practising academics (though see Short and van Peer, 1989 and Steen 1994 for interesting exceptions to this rule).

SECOND-LANGUAGE READING

To see where Richards' work has, in fact, directly influenced a considerable body of research, we have to leave literary criticism for the realm of studies in psychology and second-language acquisition, particularly in North America. There, think-aloud protocol analysis has been used with some success to investigate the general reading and writing strategies of second-language learners, mainly students learning English as a Second or Other Language. Think-aloud protocols are used alongside other techniques (e.g. retrospection and learner diaries) to attempt to gain access to the strategies which learners use when they are attempting to acquire skills in another language. Protocol analysis has been used to compare the comprehension strategies of good and poor readers (see Davies 1995 for a brief overview). General comprehension strategies of good readers would include, for example, anticipation of content, recognition of a particular text structure, the integration of new information with previously-given content, inferencing (i.e. 'reading between the lines') and linking textual content to general knowledge (cf. Block 1986: 472–4).

PLANNING A READING PROJECT

A literature project for native speakers can be closely modelled on second-language reading projects. The following plan closely follows the guidance found in Rankin (1988):

1. *Choose your subjects*
   How many subjects should you select?
   What characteristics should they have (e.g. single or mixed nationality/region; same or different age groups; same or different educational background)?
   Do you have back-up subjects if something goes wrong?

2. *Select reading materials*
   What is the subject matter?
   How long is each text?
   What is the level of difficulty (in vocabulary choice, syntax, content etc.)?
   Is the ·text complete or is it an extract? Is it coherent out of context?

3. *Method*
   (a) Model the technique with subjects, for example by reading a text and saying aloud every thought that comes to mind.

(b) Point out to subjects that they should report their own thoughts, and not what they imagine someone else's might be.

(c) The subjects should try out the technique on one or more practice texts.

(d) The researcher should decide whether or not to remain in the room while the subjects are thinking aloud. If the researcher decides to stay, he/she should decide whether or not to interrupt to ask for clarification. Questions should be non-threatening, and leading questions should be avoided. For example, the researcher should ask questions like 'What were you thinking when you stopped here?' rather than questions like 'What do you think will happen next?' or even 'What is the significance that MacDiarmid is giving to 'the laverock's hoose' in this line?'

(e) Subjects should be made comfortable and familiar with the recording equipment. Some good protocols have been lost because someone didn't press the pause button to begin recording!

4. *Transcribing*

It might be a good idea to make back-up copies of tapes before transcribing – keep the original copies safe and in good condition. A good format for description is two columns: readings from the original text go on one side and comments go on the other. Glosses by the researcher should be clearly marked off (e.g. by brackets).

5. *Analysis*

Protocol analysis will depend on the specific questions being asked by the researcher. For example, you might be interested in how familiar subjects are with certain types of vocabulary, if or how they guess the meanings of unknown words, whether they anticipate content in advance, or whether they call upon preconceived ideas and/or general knowledge to help them interpret the text. To answer the questions, the subject's comments on the text might be assigned to certain reading strategies (e.g. the strategy 'comprehension check' might be signalled by the subject saying 'OK'). Lists of reading strategies can be found in various books and articles on language learning, and in studies of reading in particular (e.g. Davies 1995). Such lists might require modification in the light of your own findings.

Once strategies have been established, you might wish to compare different groups of subjects (e.g. people of different age groups/nationalities/

backgrounds etc.). Such comparisons may be of different groups read-ing the same texts, or the same group reading different texts.

As suggested above, there are few examples of the reading strategies of academics being put under the spotlight in the same way as those of undergraduates in Richards' experiment, or those of second-language learners in recent decades. In Short (1989), however, there are two examples of two stylisticians, Mick Short and Willie van Peer, conduct-ing an experiment on themselves to investigate their own reading processes. One deals with a Somerset Maugham short story. In the other, they asked a colleague to select a poem with which they were unfamiliar – it turned out, surprisingly, to be Gerard Manley Hopkins's 'Inversnaid'. Each subject was then presented with the poem (begin-ning with the title but without being told the poet), line by line, and they wrote down their thoughts as they read each line. Their general findings were:

1. Our interpretations and strategies for arriving at [our] interpre-tations were very similar;
2. we had made very explicit and very similar evaluative remarks on the text;
3. these evaluative statements centred on practically identical text locations. (Short and van Peer 1989: 22)

The emphasis on evaluation strategies is unsurprising given the two writers' interest in the processes of literary criticism. The similarity of their approaches is in contrast to the diversity found among Richards' undergraduates, and might point towards a uniform set of strategies developed by 'expert readers' in academia – a kind of 'literary com-petence' (cf. Culler 1975).

On the other hand, we should not generalise too much from this case study, interesting though it is. It is conducted on a sample of two, and is possibly compromised by the researchers analysing their own protocols – although there are advantages in allying think-aloud analysis with personal introspection, there must always be the danger of *post hoc* rationalisation, of effectively 'cooking the books'. Also, the written form of the protocols removes the experience a little from the spontan-eity of taped responses, and the fact that the subjects were presented with the poem line by line significantly distorts the authentic reading process. Studies of reading show that it is not a linear process: good readers skip forwards and back to form judgements, check hypotheses and integrate information. To be fair, Short and van Peer do stress that the study is a preliminary one, and call for further such experiments.

SCOTS READING SCOTS

An appropriate follow-up to Short and van Peer's work would be an investigation of the reading strategies employed by readers of literature in Scots. The project would combine various aspects of previous research: how do people process modern Scottish poetry, to what extent do they actually understand it at first sight (or is it effectively a 'second language' to them?) and how do they evaluate it?

A preliminary comparison of Short and van Peer with two readers of a poem in Urban Scots yields some interesting findings. Short and van Peer wrote down their protocols as the poem 'Inversnaid' was revealed to them, title first, then line by line. Their protocols of the first four lines are here reproduced:

'Inversnaid'
This darksome burn, horseback brown
His rollrock highroad roaring down,
In coop and in comb the fleece of his foam
Flutes and low to the lake falls home.

The protocol is numbered by title [0], then by line numbers [1–4]. The comments are assigned to Short [MHS] and van Peer [WVP]:

[0] *Inversnaid*
MHS   Name of Scottish town (cf. Inverness)? Meaning of *inver*?
WVP   Proper name (cf. Inverness)? Not in atlas. A real place? In*verse*?

[1] *This darksome burn, horseback brown*
MHS   Inversnaid = *this*? Poet is next to it, possibly addressing reader. Darksome is a neologism – 'made up of dark'. *Horseback brown* = metaphor, 'Brown as a horse's back'. Why bring in the horse and its back? Brown and dark = death? The burn is certainly dark coloured. So far only the subject NP (Noun Phrase).
WVP   Narrator is pointing to *this*. *Burn* is pre- and post-modified by *dark* and *brown*. *Burn* – Scots river. Possibly ambiguous: (a) something burnt; (b) a wound; (c) a stream. (c) is most likely, given the title of the poem. So the narrator points to a stream somewhere – Scotland (but does it exist?) and says it has a dark colour and compares it to a horse's back. Why is it compared to a horse? Is the water fast (cf. *horse*) or streaming gently (cf. smoothness of a horse's back)? The comma at the end of the line = a strong caesura. More qualities of the stream to come. Suggestion of something heroic (cf. the horse and dark colours, possibly associated with the past).

[2] *His rollrock highroad roaring down,*

MHS   i.e. roaring down his rollrock highroad. *Roaring* = fast flowing (cf. high road = large road). Hence a big river? *His* – capital letter but at the beginning of a line – God (from my general knowledge that Hopkins is a religious poet)? Possibly refers anthropomorphically to the river – or the horse? *Rollrock* = neologism. A high road down which rocks can be rolled. *High* + *rollrock* + *rolling* = river coming down the side of a mountain or steep hill. (Is the mountain God's high road?) A problem with reviewing the poem line by line is that we do not get it in sense units.

WVP   Does *his* refer to the burn? The first verb is *roaring down*: the burn is roaring down from a great height. Could explain the horse comparison in the first line. 'Gentle' possibly cancelled. *Rollrock* = neologism – rolling down from the rocks? Rolling down and rocking (fierceness)? *Highroad*: stream can't be running down a public road. So *road* = river's course, and *high* is opposed to *low*. The river comes straight down. Highwayman associations (cf. the horse)? The expectation about more information was confirmed. More to come? The rhythm is quite regular.

[3] *In coop and in comb the fleece of his foam*

MHS   Still more of the clause to come. *His* must now mean the river's – no capital; *foam* is also found in rivers. *Coop* = place of confinement/basket – for catching/holding fish? *Comb* – for hair? cockerel? crest of a hill? wave? Is the foam caused by going over and in between the rocks? *Fleece* = white and woolly. Sheep as well as horses? *Fleece of his foam, coop* and *comb* are all metaphors and all have possible animal connotations.

WVP   *Foam* seems to settle the ambiguity of *burn. Fleece* – animal (cf. horse!) *Coop* – ambiguous – chicken basket or fishing gear. Latter seems most likely in context. *Comb* = crest of a wave or comb of a bird. Former most likely. If the latter, *coop* might mean chicken basket after all. No verb – deleted or still to come? Is the river running down in the shape of a coop? Explains the foam and the roaring. Another description of energy – stream is running fast and gets trapped. Hence the waves, the crests (*comb*) of which form into a thick fleece. *His* = burn? Most likely (internal *comb/foam* rhyme strengthens this interpretation). Where is the river going next? What has the narrator to do with it? Will the description go on for ever? No rhyme with previous lines.

[4]   *Flutes and low to the lake falls home*

MHS   The verb! Metaphorical – so it makes a musical (high

pitched?) sound and then falls straight down into the lake (cf. the sound patterning and positioning of *low*). *Home* = end; but also anthropomorphic meaning (cf. *his*)?

WVP   A verb. Subject = *the fleece of his foam*? *Falls home* is deviant (but cf. *to plunge home*). Makes a musical sound? And grooves? Note vowel parallelism in *coop – comb/ flutes – low*; also the rhyme (*home/foam*). Hence this stanza 'describes' a stream thundering down from a height and dropping into the lake. In this dive, the water seems to come to a standstill: connotations of rest and peace – *home, flute, low*.

(Short and van Peer 1989: 28–9)

This is a fascinating and rich record of two stylisticians at work. Although they sometimes reach alternative readings, particularly about line [3], Short and van Peer are remarkably consistent in their explicit reading strategies: they begin by trying to construct the situation in which the communication is taking place: who is the poet/narrator, who is being spoken to and why? They are alert to possible plays on words ('verse'/ 'inverse'/'in verse/ 'Inversnaid'), ambiguities ('burn'/'comb') , connotations ('home'/'flute'/'low' = 'rest' and 'peace') and metaphors (the various animal references; the anthropomorphism of the burn). They pay attention to the syntax and its possible ambiguities, and they look to the sound patterning to support certain readings and deny others.

In brief, Short and van Peer milk this text for all that it is worth, investing in it more creative interpretation than would be expected in, say, the instructions for constructing a kitchen cabinet. Their behaviour as readers of the poem is consistent with Steen's characterisation of literary reception (Steen 1994: 34; discussed in Chapter 5). The communicative situation, the lexical, grammatical and semantic options in the poem are there to be negotiated at length rather than closed down: the 'richness' of the text lies partly in how open it is to varying readings. The poetical nature of the reading – and the literary competence of the readers – lies largely in their being alert to different possibilities and their ability to express them. They are also able to differentiate between the plausible reading (e.g. the reference to the horse conveying an impression of colour, but also of speed and power and majesty) and the just plain silly one (e.g. the references to 'comb' and 'coop' conveying the impression of a chicken's head falling into a basket).

Compare the strategies used by Short and van Peer with those employed by two undergraduate students reading a Tom Leonard poem, 'Paroakial'. There are some differences in methodology: the two undergraduate subjects were taped 'thinking aloud'; they did not have the time to note down their observations in written form – or to consult reference books such as dictionaries or atlases. The dialect poem also offers different problems to the Hopkins poem – it is in an unfamiliar spelling system which even Glaswegian students have confessed to finding difficult at first, simply because of its unfamiliarity. And, given the stage in their careers, the undergraduates are not as highly 'trained' readers of literature as Short and van Peer can claim to be. Still, the similarities in the protocols are as striking as the differences.

In this protocol, the poem is recorded on the left-hand side of the page, and the student's spoken observations are transcribed on the right-hand side:

Subject 1

Paroakial	paroakial
thahts no whurrits aht	thahts no whurrits aht
thahts no cool man	thahts no cool man
jiss paroakial	jiss paroakial
aw theez sporran head	saw theez sporran heads
tahty scone vibes	th thahty tahty scone vibes
thi haggis trip	thi haggis trip
	tahty scone vibes
	oh potato right
	mmm
bad buzz man	bad buzz man
dead seen	dead seen
goahty learna new langwij	goaty learna new langwij
sumhm ihnturnashnl	sum ihnturnashnl sum sumun
	sumhm sumhm ihnturnashnl
	something somethang [incompre-
	hensible] sumhm
	ihnturnashnl
Noah Glasgow hangup	no glasgow hangup
bunnit husslin	
gitinty elektroniks man	git iny elektroniks man
really blow yir mine	really blow yir mine
real good blast	real good blast
no whuhtu mean	no whu no whuhtu mean no
	whuhtu is that a 't' I can't decide
	whether I should say that 't' on the
	no whuhtu mean no whuhtu mean
mawn	mawn
turn yirsel awn	turn yirsel awn

oh well [incomprehensible] the
last bit's quite funny
the mawn turn yirsel on bit
emm
paroakial
quite quite fun again
like the practice one
it's fun reading stuff in eh in the
sort of eh vernacular or whatever
it's called the way it's spoken the
way you speak it and stuff
emm
[whispers] aw theez sporran heads
I find this one a wee bit difficult I
think because I think it's probably
quite Glasgow like I'm not quite
sure where to say the 't's
and stuff where there's 'h'
in front of it in tahty or whu
whuhtu or whuhtu I don't know
whether they use a glottal stop or
[incomprehensible]
emm [whispers: incomprehensible]
emm
god what else
feels quite modern
cause the electronics and stuff
obviously as
well but
emm
and just looks quite an urban
accent as well
I think
though the feel of it probably maybe
because it mentions glasgow I
think that I'm not quite sure
but the way it talks like the bad
buzz man
and all sort of stuff seems quite
urban
situation
mmm

I can't think too much else to say
about that one
don't have it's actually quite hard
to understand completely what
what's [incomprehensible] like
bunnit husslin
I don't know what that means and
(with emphasis) dead seen I sort of
get the feel of it from the first bit
before that but I don't know what
it means either

Subject 2

Paroakial

para-kial that's weird I wonder
what that means well never mind
I'll come back to that

thahts no whurrits aht   thahts no whurrits aht
thahts no cool man   thahts no cool man
jiss paroakial   just pa-kora paro ha wait jiss
                                paroakial par parochial?
                                again
                                thahts no whurrits at there's no
                                worries that must be it no that's
                                not what that's not where it's at
                                that's not cool man jiss purr
                                parakial still don't know that
                                parakial bit
                                that's no whurrits that's not where
                                it's at
                                that's not cool man yeah

aw theez sporran heads   aw theez sporran heads
tahty scone vibes   tahty scone vibes
thi haggis trip   the haggis trip
                                well I know haggis (laughs)
                                theez sporran heads
                                I'd say that's a bit of an insult really
                                tahty scone vibes
                                they've got vibes like potato scones?
                                I know tahty's the glaswe glaswegian
                                word for potato
                                potato scone vibes
                                strange

bad buzz man	bad buzz man
dead seen	dead seen
	bad buzz man
	well is he talking about
	hmm
	that sounds like someone from
	jamaica
	really (exaggerated accent) that's
	no where
	it's at
	that's not cool man
	but in the second stanza
	goes onto sporran head and tahty
	scone
	vibes (laughs)
goahty learna new langwij	well gotty learn new langwij
sumhm ihnturnashnl	sumh ihturnashnl
Noah Glasgow hangup	no glasgow hangup
bunnit husslin	bunnit husslin
	got to I've got to learn a new
	language
	some international no Glasgow
	hangup
	so international not at Glasgow
	hangup
	right I think I'll leave that bit for a
	minute
gitinty elektroniks man	gitinty elektroniks man get into your
	electronics man
really blow yir mine	really blow yir mind yeh that'll
	really blow your mind
real good blast	real good blast
no whuhtu mean	know what you mean
mawn	mawn
turn yirsel awn	turn yirsel awn
	right okay
	sounds like someone's trying to tell
	someone to try drugs
	yeh yeh that makes sense that
	makes sense
	that's not where it's at that's not
	cool man

jiss just jiss paroakial para-kial jiss
paroakial
hmm
theez sporran heads tahty scone
vibes
haggis trip bad buzz man dead
seen to learn a new language
international
no glasgow hangup bunnit husslin
get into your electronics man
hmm yeh it sounds like trying to get
someone to try a new drug
there's there's something of music
in it too
get into your electronics
hmm no I think I'll stick with the
drugs
yeh

There is greater diversity in the protocols of these students than in the remarkably similar protocols of the university lecturers, suggesting that (in the field of stylistics at least) readers develop an increasingly consensual approach to the interpretation of texts. Subject 1 does not express any global interpretation of the text at all, concentrating on purely local features ('tahty scone vibes' is glossed as 'potato'. This gloss is followed by the comprehension check 'right', without any indication of what a 'potato scone vibe' might be. Subject 2 puzzles over this problem at greater length, acknowledging that the collocation is 'strange'.) Both students spend much of their protocols glossing items, particularly at first. This is understandable given the unfamiliarity of the spelling system, even to Scots. It is interesting to note that the diversity of accents causes some problems for both students. Subject 1 is mostly concerned about the sound–symbol relationship, particularly with reference to the glottal stop: is it represented by the <ht> in words like <thaht>? Subject 2 initially glosses 'thahts no whurrits aht' as 'there's no worries' – the Scots 'wh' being read as an English 'w'. Another interesting feature of Subject 2's protocol is the multicultural range of references: the Australian idiom 'no worries' existing beside the misreading of 'paroakial' as 'pakora'. Glossing is evident also in the lecturers' protocols of 'Inversnaid', but only where Hopkins coins a neologism, like 'rollrock'. It is understandably more in evidence in the dialect poem. Glossing is about as far as Subject 1 goes, finding the poem as a whole 'quite difficult to understand'.

Being mainly concerned with glossing, Subject 1 hardly considers the communicative situation, that is, the relationship of the narrator to the reader – who is addressing whom and why – beyond noting that it 'seems quite [an] urban situation'. The question of the speaker's relationship with the listener is immediately addressed in the protocols of each of the lecturers – even though this line of enquiry is arguably less fruitful in the Hopkins poem, which is not a dramatic monologue. 'Paroakial' is, and the 'speaker–listener' relationship is crucial. Subject 2 eventually considers the question, coming to the conclusion that the speaker is trying to sell drugs to the listener. A more considered reading might well dismiss this interpretation as way off target, but it is interesting that as a first reading of the poem – even as a second – it 'makes sense' to Subject 2. Why does it do so? The protocol suggests that Subject 2 is making connections between certain elements which would support such a reading: talk of 'vibes', 'buzz', 'seen (= scene?)', 'blowing one's mind', 'real good blast', and possibly even the association of the phonetic representation of the Glasgow accent with a Jamaican accent. All these items have connotations of the drugs scene.

Having made these connections and come to an interpretation, Subject 2 quickly reviews the poem to see if the other parts fit. He/she still has trouble with the title ('para-kial jiss paroakial hmm') but the rest, it seems, could be fitted into such an interpretation ('yeh it sounds like trying to get someone to try a new drug'). For this interpretation to work, 'electronics' would have to be interpreted as a euphemism for some kind of 'new drug'. Towards the end of the protocol, an alternative suggests itself: 'electronics' and much of the 'drug slang' could equally be applied to the music scene. However, the alternative reading is quickly dismissed in favour of the 'drugs' reading.

We might here be tempted to argue, in the terms of Richards and Rosenblatt, that Student 2's interpretation is an instance of 'the impact of the literary work' being 'dulled' or 'interfered with' by the student's 'fund of ready-made, sharply-crystallized ideas and habits of response'. Yet, on the evidence of the protocols, this reader is doing what Short and van Peer are also doing: using the textual data to construct plausible scenarios which might then be modified in the light of further data. Short and van Peer toy with various possible readings – the Inversnaid burn is linked variously to horses, sheep, chickens, God and highwaymen as they come to a reading that satisfies them. Similarly Subject 2 considers the ideas of drugs and music as possible topics of the Glaswegian narrator's monologue.

If there is a difference in approach, it seems to lie in the lecturers' unwillingness to close poetic possibilities down, whereas the students seem to be seeking a 'correct' reading. This is perhaps best illustrated by van Peer's consideration of the ambiguities of 'burn', 'fleece', 'foam' and 'comb' and 'coop' – 'coop' is interpreted in two possible ways depending on possible collocates in two lexical sets: it might mean 'fishing gear' if it falls into the lexical set of 'burn' (= stream) and 'foam'; or 'chicken basket' if it falls into the lexical set of 'fleece' and 'comb' (as in 'head of a chicken'). Interpretations are seen in terms of likelihood, and the reader expects to work to create meaning. The students either give up on a global meaning (Subject 1: 'it's actually quite hard to understand') or they decide upon a particular interpretation too early, based on insufficient information ('I'll stick with the drugs, yeh').

This kind of project would have to be greatly expanded to gauge whether the responses described above could be generalised beyond these four individuals. But a wider study would presumably cast light upon the expectations about poetry which govern those who regard themselves as 'competent' at reading literature – at least in the academic arena. This is not to say that academics have necessarily a better interpretation of texts than a lay person – but they are trained to read literature in specialised ways, they evolve certain schemata governing how literature should be read, and they pass on these schemata, often indirectly, to their students. The strength of think-aloud protocols is that they help to make explicit various unvoiced expectations.

Chapters 10 and 11, together, have developed an aspect of the study of language and Scottish literature which is rather different from those described in the preceding chapters. The main claim in the last two chapters is that it is not the language itself which determines the literary nature of texts, but how readers respond to that language. The readers' response is, in turn, determined by both the individual schemata brought to bear on any text, and the value accorded to literary texts by society. Literary texts are those which people expect to work at in order to construct meaning – and the meanings will not necessarily be unambiguous or arrived at easily. Literary texts might also be more likely to upset or subvert existing schemata and prompt the reader to revise his or her expectations of how the world is, or indeed how literature functions. In short, the 'competent' reader of literature is one who is willing to work hard at constructing a reading when texts seem to be obscure, to hold multiple possible interpretations in mind, and to evaluate their likelihood on a variety of criteria. Not all texts demand this kind of response – the sports pages of a newspaper, for example, would not necessarily demand this level of reading competence. But with the hard work comes enjoyment and the creative satisfaction which comes from engagement with, rather than passive absorption of, a literary text.

12

THE LANGUAGE OF
OLDER SCOTTISH LITERATURE

RECONSTRUCTING THE PAST

In the last few chapters, we have seen a slight change of focus in the subject of this book. The shift to discourse processing raises particular problems in the study of language and Older Scots literature. Older Scots texts can, of course, be studied using all the stylistic tools discussed in the earlier part of this book. For example, Macafee (1981) does a thorough stylistic analysis of one of William Dunbar's poems, 'In Winter', using many of the techniques covered here. But it is worth considering Older Scots texts separately because they do raise some specific problems. The first is to do with shared expectations.

Quite simply, we do not share the context of Older Scots texts. Some texts, such as Robert Henryson's reworking of Aesop's *Fables*, of course, do have modern as well as ancient counterparts and therefore are more accessible than, say, William Dunbar's 'The Goldyn Targe'. But the 500-year gap between the Scots Renaissance and the present day has robbed us of the kind of common expectations and shared mental categories that we unconsciously and readily bring to bear upon modern texts. Much work in literary studies, then, goes into trying to recover contexts in which the texts make sense: using at times very little evidence, scholars construct possible biographies of writers, speculate on their relationships with audiences, and debate the reasons why the texts were produced. It's a fascinating endeavour, using scraps of historical data and, of course, the often ambiguous evidence of the texts themselves.

This is not to say that present-day readers unversed in medieval Scots scholarship cannot sit down with a copy of the poems of Henryson and Dunbar and not appreciate a text such as 'The Testament of Cresseid'. The reader might have to refer frequently to the glossaries, and he or she might have to work hard at understanding the reason for episodes like the extended vision of the gods and goddesses. The modern reader might relate this to one of the more surreal moments in an avant-garde television soap opera. One eminent scholar of literary Scots described Henryson's Fables, in a lecture to a general audience, as a series of 'Roadrunner' cartoons rewritten by Muriel Spark (Lyall 1994). To make sense of texts, we naturally and usefully reach out for and adapt existing knowledge. But this knowledge is quite radically different from the everyday assumptions of the original audiences.

A similar problem is that not just the fund of common knowledge but also the language of lowland Scotland has radically changed over five centuries. We are largely deaf to the more subtle nuances of the language of the makars because we cannot relate it, as they themselves could, to the language of everyday life. Our best source of information about language use of the older period is the *Dictionary of the Older Scottish Tongue*; and, as Macafee (1981: 359–60) cautions:

> The dictionary record is, of course, only of the written mode of the language, a fact which C. S. Lewis apparently forgets when he equates the plain style with the language of the court. This is possible but hardly testable. However it is fortunate that the corpus is large enough to allow valid generalisations in the dictionaries about the types of writing with which particular items are associated. Nevertheless, there remains an irresolvable element of doubt about how items which one might like to claim are foregrounded relate to Middle Scots in the abstract or, if you like, how the linguistic performance of the writer relates to his linguistic competence and that of his original audience.

In other words, we do not know how the contemporaries of Henryson and Dunbar actually spoke, and we will never know for certain if a particular linguistic feature which surprises us would have surprised them. We do not know if we respond to the language in a way that the original audience would have recognised at all. But we can make informed guesses and enjoy the inevitable discussions. Finally, it is important to add that I am not arguing that an interpretation of an Older Scots text, which is sensitive to scholarly reconstructions of author, audience, language and original purpose, is necessarily better or more 'real' than the interpretation constructed by a general reader encountering such a text for the first time. But it will be different in certain respects. And as students of literature and language, we should be aware of the different possible interpretations of texts and the foundations on which they are built. Our understanding of these texts – always provisional – thus becomes broader and deeper.

In this chapter, we shall consider the types of linguistic variation evident in Older Scots texts – taking the poetry of William Dunbar, usually acknowledged as the most accomplished of the earlier Scots stylists, as representative of the range of options available to poets. Dunbar's poems have long been subdivided into three categories: high, low and plain style. What does this variation suggest about the cultural context in which he was writing and how we might understand his poetry?

THE HIGH STYLE

This style of writing is associated with celebratory poetry: hymns to the Virgin Mary, poems marking royal occasions such as marriage, and sophisticated allegorical tales. To modern readers, it is often a cultivated taste. Linguistically, the high style is marked by a special kind of vocabulary, and to a lesser extent a special kind of grammar – both modelled on the most prestigious language of the Middle Ages, namely Latin.

Aureation

The 'high' style of medieval writing is marked by a high frequency of lexical items which are derived directly from Latin, or from Latin through French. The Latinate items are said to 'gild' the language, and the style is therefore sometimes called 'aureate' or 'golden'. The style is not particularly Scottish – much of the poetry of the English poets, such as Lydgate, is also obviously aureate – but it does feature in much early Scots poetry, and is important in Dunbar's work in particular. It is interesting to note that when Dunbar praises earlier exemplars, such as Chaucer, it is his 'rhetoric' that is specifically mentioned. This emphasis on 'rhetoric' suggests that high-style poetry held pride of place in the late medieval Scottish sensibility.

There are no less than fifteen items in the first stanza of 'Ane Ballat of Our Lady' which can be regarded as aureate terms (italicised):

> Hale, sterne *superne*, hale in *eterne*,
> 	In Godis sicht to schyne,
> *Lucerne* in derne for to *discerne*,		Lamp to see in darkness
> 	Be glory and grace devyne,
> *Hodiern, modern, sempitern,*			For this day, now, and forever
> 	*Angelicall regyne,*
> Our tern *inferne* for to *dispern*		To ward off our pain in hell
> 	Help, rialest *rosyne*.
> *Ave Maria gracia plena.*
> 	Haile, fresche floure *femynyne,*
> Yerne us *guberne*, virgin *matern,*		Govern us well, maternal virgin
> 	Of reuth baith rute and ryne.

The list of Latinate terms is based on studies by Ellenberger (1977) and Zettersten (1979) of the Latinate and aureate diction of Dunbar's poetry. Both regard the use of Latinate terms as a powerful stylistic strategy: the vernacular poet is making a claim to prestige by borrowing into Scots lexical items derived from the hallowed classical language of learning, and also from already-established continental vernacular languages. The medieval poets used Latin and Latinate words for effect in much the same way as Japanese advertisers, selling Japanese products to Japanese consumers in Japan, use English (or near-English) slogans today. They are borrowing the prestige of American and British popular culture along with the English linguistic items. It is interesting, in passing, to reflect upon the artificiality of Dunbar's high style and to compare it with its modern counterpart, Lallans, another self-consciously 'literary' medium which relies on borrowings, calques and translations to extend its functional range and raise its prestige (see Chapters 1 and 4).

Dunbar, in praising the queen of heaven, borrows high cultural prestige along with the Latinate lexical items. In a thorough statistical investigation into Dunbar's diction, Ellenberger discovered, for example, that the average frequency of Latinisms in Dunbar's corpus as a whole is 12.9 per cent. 'Ane Ballat of Our Lady', however, contains no less than 31.1 per cent Latinisms, almost every third word. However, it is evident from both Ellenberger and Zettersten that there is no simple correspondence between aureation and Latinate terms. Ellenberger distinguishes between those items which 'increase semantic density' and those which 'increase semantic range'. The former items are decorative, and the vernacular might already have synonymous terms which express the concept adequately. An example might be 'regyne' in 'Ane Ballat of Our Lady', a synonym for 'quene' (l. 37).

Other Latinate terms introduced into Scots concepts for which there were no native equivalents: he cites, from 'Dunbar at Oxinfurde', the phrase 'curious probation logicall' (for which a vernacular synonym would be difficult to find) and contrasts it with 'goldyn candill matutyne'. The latter phrase is less Latinate but arguably more aureate. The Latinate phrase 'curious probation logicall' extends the semantic range of the language: the terms are philosophical, or argumentative, or scientific, rather than purely decorative (Ellenberger 1977: 82–9). The greater degree of aureation of the not-so-Latinate phrase 'goldyn candill matutyne' derives from its expression of the positive values of *wealth* and *light*. Similarly, in 'Ane Ballat of Our Lady' (l. 1), the item 'sterne' (star) might be associated with aureate vocabulary because of its association with the positive value of *light*, even though it is of Norse etymology (Old Norse 'stjarna'). Therefore, the aureate style is associated with Latinate vocabulary so long as that vocabulary is principally decorative. Ellenberger comments that the Latinate vocabulary should also be polysyllabic, novel and of learned formation (1977: 82–9). It is also likely to have certain positive semantic associations (e.g. *wealth*, *light*, *purity*, *holiness*), and here it might be accompanied by native terms which have similar associations.

'Ane Ballat of Our Lady' is an extreme example of aureate diction: it is consistent throughout the poem. Other poems, such as 'The Goldyn Targe', have aureate 'purple patches' which mark the poem out as being of a high style; and others, such as the *Tretis of the Twa Mariit Wemen and the Wedo*, switch back and forth from high to low style for satirical effect. The following stanza, from Robert Henryson's 'The Testament of Cresseid', shows a shift from a more Latinate vocabulary in the verse introducing the procession of gods, to a more native vocabulary to describe 'crabbit' Saturn (ll. 148–61):

> [The seven planets, or gods] hes power of all things generabill
> To reull and steir be thair greit Influence,
> Wedder and wind, and coursis variabill:
> And first of all Saturne gave his sentence,
> Quhilk gave to Cupide litill reverence,
> Bot, as ane busteous Churle on his maneir,
> Come crabitlie with auster luik and cheir.

> His face [fronsit], his lyre was lyke the Leid,
> His teith chatterit, and cheverit with the Chin,
> His Ene drowpit, how sonkin in his heid,
> Out of his Nois the Meldrop fast can rin,
> With lippis bla and cheikis leine and thin,
> The Iceshoklis that fra his hair doun hang
> Was wondir greit, and as ane speir als lang.

Henryson's borrowings here tend to increase semantic range rather than depth, and as a result his verse has an air of authority rather than decoration. The lexical shift towards native vocabulary in the second stanza domesticates the character of Saturn: this is no awe-inspiring god, but a pitiable old man, whose only startling quality is the spear-long icicles which hang from his hair.

Henryson's Latinate terms here, then, are less decorative than those which Dunbar uses in 'Ane Ballat of our Lady' – Henryson's verse is therefore more authoritative than strictly aureate, a fact that links it to the 'plain style' of verse, to be discussed shortly. The Older Scots poets selected their vocabulary carefully, to achieve a range of stylistic effects, and we should be sensitive to the origins, meanings and associations of the words which they chose.

High-style Grammar

High-style grammar has generally been assumed to be marked by a syntactic complexity which also derives from Latin models. For example, A. J. Aitken (1983: 31) argues:

> No variety of Older Scots verse compares for average syntactic complexity with the most syntactically elaborate kinds of prose – the sustained orations in Bellenden's and the Mar Lodge translations of Boece and similar works. But though of course no kind of poetry has a monopoly of either syntactically complex or syntactically simple sentences, it is a reasonable generalisation that a much higher frequency of complex structures displaying much hypotaxis (i.e. in which the noun-phrase and verb-phrase elements of sentences are modified by words, phrases and clauses) is a normal concomitant of the less vernacular styles, and so is often found in courtly verse ... and didactic or discursive verse.

In short, there is a range of grammatical complexity in Older Scots: at one end of the continuum there are simple structures, linked by punctuation or by coordinating conjunctions, such as 'and' or 'but'. At the other end there are complex structures, with phrases and clauses embedded one within the other, perhaps linked by a subordinating conjunction such as 'for' or 'gif' (if). High-style poems tend to cluster around the 'complex' end of the continuum. The argument, indeed, does seem reasonable. Just as Latinate vocabulary is a feature of the aureate or high style, so a mimicry of highly-subordinated Latin syntax should also mark this style. To support his argument, Aitken cites the first two stanzas of Dunbar's 'The Thrissil and the Rois':

> Quhen Merche wes with variand windis past,
> And Appryll had with hir silver schouris
> Tane leif at Nature with ane orient blast,
> And lusty May, that muddir is of flouris,
> Had maid the birdis to begyn thair houris   5
> Amang the tendir odouris reid and quhyt,
> Quhois armony to heir it wes delyt:
>
> In bed at morrow, sleiping as I lay,
> Me thocht Aurora with hir cristall ene
> In at the window lukit by the day10

And halsit me, with visage paill and grene,
On quhois hand a lark sang fro the splene,
'Awalk, luvaris, out of your slomering!
Se how the lusty morow dois up spring.'

The first stanza is an extended subordinate clause of time, the subject
and main verb ('Me thocht') is delayed until line 9, and the rest of the
second stanza is a nominal clause telling us what the narrator perceived.
The placement of the highly-subordinated clause at the beginning of a
poem might well be part of a strategy (alongside the springtime setting
and the Latinate diction) to mark out the poem as high-style.

However, Aitken is right to be cautious when making generalisations
about grammar and style. No systematic study of the grammar of Older
Scots poetry has yet been undertaken. Macafee's (1994) short descrip-
tion of Older Scots grammar is based on the Dictionary of the *Older
Scots Tongue*, and, although the Helsinki University Corpus of Older
Scots is yielding fascinating insights into the evolution of written Scots,
it is a general survey of Older Scots prose, and excludes poetry (see
Meurman-Solin 1993, discussed later in this chapter). Moreover,
Aitken's characterisation of high-style verse is apparently contradicted
by Agutter's description of high-style syntax (1988: 20):

> A characteristic of high style was the use of parallelism – the
> repetition of a grammatical structure especially within a stanza,
> for example
>
> '(Quhone) sabill all the hewin arrayis
> With mystie vapouris, cluddis and skyis,
> Nature all curage me denyis
> Off sangs, ballatis, and of playis.'
> (Dunbar's 'Meditatioun in Wyntir')
>
> In this example, the syntactic structure: (conjunction) subject,
> object, verb, followed by a triple prepositional phrase, is followed
> by the structure: subject, direct and indirect objects, verb and a
> triple prepositional phrase. Although the effect is offset in this
> case by the use of grammatical patterns which are unfamiliar in
> present day English, the use of this device often gives high style
> verse an apparent grammatical simplicity not found in low style
> verse, which uses a wider range of grammatical constructions
> some of which may be colloquial in origin.

Agutter agrees with Aitken that low-style verse often omits conjunctions which would probably be present in high-style verse; however,
there seems to be a contradiction here between the notion of syntactic

complexity as a high-style marker, and apparent syntactic simplicity resulting from the parallelisms found in high-style poetry. Many of the lines found in the high-style celebration 'The Thrissil and the Rois' exhibit just the kind of parallelism that Agutter describes. There is obvious parallelism, for example, in the list of attributes given to the Lion in stanza 14:

> This awfull beist full terrible wes of cheir,
> Persing of luke and stout of countenance,
> Rycht strong of corpis, of fassoun fair but feir,
> Lusty of schaip, lycht of deliverance,
> Reid of his cullour as is the ruby glance.   95
> On feild of gold he stude full mychtely,
> With flour delycis sirculit lustely

Most of this stanza is taken up with an extended complement made up largely of parallel constructions (i.e. 'This awful beast was A of B, C of D, E of F' and so on). Syntactically, the stanza is not very complex: parallel structures give, however, an ornate effect. A similar technique is employed in the lines quoted earlier from Henryson's 'Testament of Cresseid'.

Parallel structures, however, are not confined to high-style verse. Dunbar's low-style poem, 'The Flyting', contains long lists of vocative noun phrases which are, according to Aitken (1983: 32), 'a natural feature of passages of personal abuse'. Name-calling is undoubtedly a natural feature of insults; but then again, similar long lists of vocative noun phrases are also found in Dunbar's 'Ane Ballat of Our Lady' and in the parodic love poem, 'In secreit plais this hyndir nicht' – hardly poems of personal abuse, but of religious adoration and parodic seduction respectively.

Where does this leave us? It leaves us very probably with grammatical simplicity and complexity being very weak markers of stylistic level in themselves. However, it is fair to say that no marker of different styles, whether diction, grammar or topic, exists in isolation. The construction of the high, low or plain style depends on a blend of some or all of the various linguistic ingredients. It is also unwise to set up stylistic categories which are too mechanistic: the diction and the subject matter work against 'The Flyting' as a high-style poem, but it could well be seen as a negative image of 'Ane Ballat of Our Lady', employing some similar stylistic strategies to oddly similar effect.

Other Markers of High-Style Verse

Diction is the most obvious marker, and syntactic complexity perhaps the weakest marker of stylistic categories in Older Scots verse. Other markers of the high style are worth mentioning briefly (cf. Aitken 1983; Agutter 1988).

Many Scots high-style poems exhibit occasional southern English spellings or word-forms. For example, the substitution of English <o> for <a> appears in the use of 'fro' and 'both' in 'The Thrissill and the Rois' (lines 56 and 171). The use of <o> for <a> might also explain the odd substitution of 'lork' for 'lark' in line 24: Aitken (1983: 29–30) suggests that this is an example of hypercorrection. The use of anglicisms in the high style is even more marked when it is compared with their absence in low-style poetry.

High-style poems tend to be marked by complicated rhyme schemes, for example, units of up to seven or nine lines, following a prescribed rhyming convention such as 'rhyme royal' (see 'Common Stanzas in Scots Poetry', following this chapter). Such complicated rhymes are used, for example, by James I in *The Kingis Quair*, and the shift from one rhyme scheme to another marks an elevation in tone for the 'Complaint' sequence in Henryson's 'Orpheus and Eurydice'.

Last but certainly not least, the rules of decorum dictate that the subject matter of the poem is usually appropriate to the style: 'high'-style poetry will normally celebrate a patron, a dignitary, a special event, a religious figure or a scriptural episode. Alternatively, an allegorical tale, full of classical allusions, with a moral or romantic theme, might be appropriate to the high style.

Although we normally link high-style poetry with courtly or allegorical or religious verse, we should be alert to the possibility of subverting expectations and modulating effects, such as the comic earthiness of diction displayed by the goddess May in 'The Thrissil and the Rois' when she wakes the sleeping poet with the less-than-flattering words: '"Slugird," scho said, "awalk anone for schame."'

THE LOW STYLE

The high style and the low style can be seen as existing in diametrical relation to each other: as the high style has a celebratory function, the low style deals in comedy and satire, with peasants and vices, and with immorality and vulgarity. Furthermore, as the high style is marked by anglicisation, the low style is marked by its virtual absence. The rhyme schemes of low-style poetry are usually quite simple, a favourite form being the couplet. Dunbar's 'The Dance of the Sevin Deidly Sins'

varies the couplet form a little, by utilising a stanza with the structure
aabccb. This stanza form allows for the possibility of three-line discourse
units (*aab* + *ccb*), with a barbed comment or witticism on the third and/
or sixth line, for example:

> Full mony a waistless wallydrag
> With wamis unweildable did furth wag
>   In creische that did incres:
> Drynk! ay thay cryit, with mony a gaip –
> The feyndis gaif thame hait leid to laip –
>   Their lovery wes na les.

(ll. 97–102)

The extent of the relationship of opposites between high-style and
low-style poetry is such that low-style counterparts can often be found
for Dunbar's high-style poems: I have already mentioned the
similarities between 'Ane Ballat of Our Lady' and 'The Flyting'.
Courtly love lyrics such as 'Sweit Rois of Vertue' are parodied in 'In
secreit plais', and 'The Dance of the Sevin Deidly Sins' does have some
passing similarity to 'The Thrissil and the Rois'. Possibly written to
commemorate the religious holiday of Fastern's Eve, or Shrove
Tuesday, 'The Dance of the Sevin Deidly Sins' is a parodic inversion of
a celebratory poem in the high style. Like 'The Thrissil and the Rois',
it is couched in a dream vision, and as 'The Thrissil and the Rois'
chronicles events linked by adverbs and conjunctions such as 'quhen',
'than' and 'syne', so too does 'The Dance of the Sevin Deidly Sins'
portray a progression of characters linked by adverbs such as 'than',
'nixt' and 'syne'.

Low-style Diction

Where the high style is marked by the presence of Latinisms, the low
style is marked by vernacular diction, or 'northernisms' (that is, those
words deriving from Old Norse and Gaelic, found more often in Scotland and northern England at the time) and comparatively few
Latinisms. For example, Ellenberger (1977: 68) calculates that only 6.3
per cent of the vocabulary of Dunbar's 'The Dance of the Sevin Deidly
Sins' is Latinate in origin. This is less than half of the average frequency
found in Dunbar, and a fifth of the frequency found in 'Ane Ballat of
Our Lady'. Those Latinisms which are found in 'The Dance of the
Sevin Deidly Sins' tend also to be the converse in meaning, or semantic
association, from those Latinisms which appear in the high style: for
example, we find 'yre', 'malyce', 'dissymlit', 'fals', 'vice', 'monstir',

'unsasiable'. Some of these Latinisms may have been part of the common Scots word-stock by Dunbar's time; 'monstir', for example, is first recorded in Middle English c. 1325, and 'fals' even earlier, c. 1000. They may be classed therefore as unexotic Latinisms, or at least Latinisms which extend semantic range rather than density.

Northernisms in 'The Dance of the Sevin Deidly Sins' include 'graith' (prepare, from ON greða), 'rumpillis' (tails, from ME 'rump', Scand. origin), 'ockeraris' (usurers, from ME, cf. Scand. 'okr', usury), and 'midding' (midden, ME from ON mykidlyngja). These are typical of low-style poems: everyday vocabulary, often Norse in origin, sometimes vulgar or even obscene in meaning or association. We do not find the same propensity for neologisms in the low style.

Low-style Grammar

Features widely associated with low-style grammar can also be illustrated by Dunbar's 'The Dance of the Sevin Deidly Sins': for example, there is ellipsis of the main verb and the reflexive pronoun in lines 79–81:

> Than Lichery that lathly cors [entered]
> Berand [himself] lyk a bagit hors –
>   And Lythness did him leid.

If high-style grammar leans towards written Latin models, then low-style grammar leans towards the syntax of spoken Scots. However, once again we have to beware of clear-cut oppositions: there are more complex constructions in this poem, such as the single sentence which runs from lines 103 to 108:

> Na menstrallis playit to thame but dowt
> For glemen they were halden owt
>   Be day and eik by nycht –
> Except a menstrall that slew a man,
> Swa till his heritage he wan
>   And enterit be breif of richt.

The connectives here ('for', 'except' and 'swa') do indicate complex relations between propositions (although these syntactic units seem simpler than those of 'The Thrissil and the Rois' partly because they coincide with line units). The complexities of such constructions again serve to remind us to avoid simple generalisations about Older Scots syntax as a style-marker. Differences are of degree rather than of kind.

To summarise thus far, we find in Older Scots poetry two apparently distinct styles: a high style, used in courtly and allegorical poetry, and in poetry of religious celebration, and a low style used in comic and grotesque poems, burlesques and parodies. High-style poetry looks outside Scotland for models, and brings into Older Scots a learned and ornate vocabulary, complex rhyme schemes and possibly a tendency towards syntactic complexity. Low-style poetry uses the native word-stock and simpler rhyme schemes, and may be more likely to use less complex sentence structures.

When we consider these two rather idealised styles in the context of a poet like Dunbar, we can see one style as the reverse of the other: a high-style poem of courtly love can be mirrored by two peasants copulating in a barn; a high-style celebration of a court event can be mirrored by allegorical vices having an orgy in hell. The two styles are not so much distinct as mutually dependent. We read poems in one style with the knowledge that another, oppositional, reading is possible. This may be why some critics see irony in high-style poems where others do not, and why some critics see morality in the low-style poems, where others do not (cf. Scott 1966).

THE PLAIN STYLE

All this brings us, briefly, to the plain style, which, as Macafee (1981: 368) notes, has served too often as a 'dustbin for the residue from other more clearly definable styles'. As far as Dunbar is concerned, Ellenberger (1977: 71–15) subdivides this category into 'petitionary poems', 'moralising poems' and 'personal poems'. In fact, reading through Dunbar's works, it becomes clear that petitions figure largely in his canon: Dorsch (1968: 286) calculates that no fewer than a quarter of Dunbar's surviving poems are directly or indirectly petitionary in nature. When we add to the petitionary poems 'personal' poems such as the 'Lament for the Makaris', then we see that the 'dustbin' of the plain style is an important and intriguing one.

The plain style has often been described by what it is not: it is a style which shuns aureate Latinisms, it avoids slang and obscene northern-isms, it is not marked by elaborate stanza forms or markedly colloquial patterns of speech. In short, it is a style defined by absences.

If we turn our attention to what is actually there in plain-style poetry, we can see that the construction of directness and authority are the key.

Plain-style Vocabulary

Dunbar's plain style utilises native, everyday terms alongside the kind of specialised, Latinate vocabulary which increases semantic range rather than depth. In other words, the Latinate vocabulary found in the plain style is primarily learned rather than decorative. Its function is not so much to celebrate beauty as to impress with learned authority. The common items construct a sense of forthrightness which is approprate to this sense of authority.

Take, for example, the poem 'Of Discretioun in Geving', which Ellenberger calculates as having 26.1 per cent Latinisms – higher than Dunbar's average (12.9 per cent), and 10 per cent higher than the frequency of Latinisms in 'The Goldyn Targe' (16.1 per cent). The plain-style poem also has a high frequency of polysyllabic Latinisms. However, on closer inspection, the Latinisms are not decorative neologisms but established technical items such as 'discretioun', 'caus', 'service', 'convenient', 'cure', 'honour', 'suppois', 'remedy' and 'fortoun'. The semantic associations are diverse, but the register is largely legal and ecclesiastical. Many of the terms are still in common use today. Northernisms in the poem include 'bot', 'bouth' and 'tynes' – again, the words are common enough and seem, as far as we can guess, to form part of the linguistic background of Older Scots. Anglicisms and obscure or slang items are fairly rare: of the latter, 'dronis' and 'drene' seem to be onomatopoeic. Learned Latinisms and blunt northernisms combined, then, give an air of authority and directness to plain-style poems.

Plain-style Grammar

The syntax of plain-style poetry is as difficult to characterise precisely as that of the high and low styles. Dunbar varies the type and complexity of his syntactical structures according to his immediate purpose. He might employ quite complex constructions, usually when presenting a detailed argument, or he might issue forth a series of simple constructions (for example, direct imperatives), the cumulative effect of which elicits a more emotional reaction.

In 'Of Discretioun in Asking', we see again Dunbar's favoured technique of building up a series of parallel constructions: stanzas 2, 3, 9 and 11 largely consist of a sequence of phrases beginning 'Sum gevis ...'. The technique is comparable to that found in stanzas 13 and 14 of 'The Goldyn Targe', which are built around parallel constructions beginning 'Thare saw I ...' and 'Thare was ...' This predilection for parallel constructions is evident in all Dunbar's styles. The extent to which parallelism is used may be a particular feature of Dunbar's work; however, the technique is certainly found in other poets' work, as the following passage from Gavin Douglas' *Eneados* illustrates (Prologue, Bk IV 43–9):

Thou makist febill wight and lawyst the hie,
Thou knyttis frendschyp qhuar thar beyn na parage,
Thou Jonathas confederat with Davy,
Thou dantyt Alexander for al his vassalage,
Thou festnyt Jacob fourteyn yheir in bondage,
Thou techit Hercules go lern to spyn
Reke Dyomeir hys mays and lyoun skyn.

Once more, we see that cumulative repetition is a favourite strategy of Older Scots poets, a strategy that cuts across stylistic boundaries.

Dunbar's plain-style poems exhibit a small degree of anglicisation, but not nearly to the same degree as high-style poetry. The rhyme schemes are quite simple, and short tetrameter lines are preferred to showier pentameter lines.

The construction of a forthright, authoritative persona is appropriate to the plain-style poems, particularly if we regard the 'personal' poems as being closely related to the 'moralising' poems. Poems in which the narrator takes an unironic moral stance demand a degree of moral authority. Similarly, petitionary poems, in which the poet's problematic task is to lecture a patron who is in a far superior social position, demand the construction of a persona whose learning and wisdom act as a counterbalance to his inferiority in rank.

ANALYSING OLDER SCOTS POETRY

The three 'styles' of verse described in this chapter, largely in relation to Dunbar's poetry, are to an extent an abstraction, and we have seen the dangers of making the styles seem too separate. Certainly, different styles can coexist in a single poem to interesting effect (the changes in tone of different sections of the *Tretis of the Twa Mariit Wemen and the Wedo* are Dunbar's most obvious example of this style-switching) however, arguments based on the switching of styles presuppose some expectation or knowledge about the cluster of features which together characterise any one style. Therefore, when reading any Older Scots poet, then, it is useful to pay attention to the following features:

1. *Vocabulary* What is the origin of the words? Pay particular attention to the presence of Latinisms, northernisms and words whose origins are obscure (i.e. slang items such as 'wallidrag'). What semantic areas do the words fall into? Are the areas largely positive (e.g. *holiness, purity, light*) or negative (e.g. *vice, darkness* etc.)? Do the words increase the semantic density of the language (i.e. are they decorative?) or do they increase its

semantic range (i.e. are they learned, technical)? As far as we
can gather from reference books such as dictionaries, were the
words new and surprising, or common and everyday?

2. *Grammar*   For reasons discussed, it is problematic to consider
syntax as a primary style-indicator. However, it is still useful to
consider the features of grammar in combination with other
style-markers. Are the sentences long and complex or short and
simple – that is, are they more or less likely to be imitative of
everyday speech? To what extent are parallel constructions
used? To what extent do they imitate the complex Latinate
constructions found in the prose of the period (discussed later
in this chapter)?

3. *Sound structure*   Are complex rhyme schemes used or is the
verse in simple couplets? Is the stanza form associated with an
illustrious predecessor? It is also worth considering the use of
the types of sound effect discussed in Chapter 6: is alliteration,
for example, used extensively, and, if so, why – for emphasis on
words within a line, or to bind related lines together?

4. *Anglicisation*   Is there evidence of English spelling of words
common to Scots and English (or even 'hypercorrection' of
some items)? To what extent does the poem fit into a Scottish
and/or European tradition? Does the poet acknowledge
models outwith Scotland? (Note that in some cases English
spelling might be due to scribal corruption rather than
authorial intention.)

5. *Topic*   Do the subject matter and the language 'fit' in an
appropriate way? If there is some inappropriateness, try to
account for it (i.e. is it the diction, the complexity of syntax, the
rhyme scheme or the degree of anglicisation)? Can you use the
presence or absence of such a 'disjunction' to indicate the
'sincerity' of the narrator in any particular poem?

By paying attention to these features of Older Scots poems, we can
go some of the way towards reconstructing the conditions in which the
texts were produced and understood. The 'foreign' element (Latin and
English) in the valued high-style poetry suggests a mind-set that
privileges a non-native tradition for the 'serious' matters of divine and
secular celebration. The nativeness of the low-style poems – and the
occasional intrusions of low-style language into high-style poems –
suggests an association between familiar language and the intimacy
demanded of comic and parodic genres. Comedy and parody both trade in
stock situations and stereotypes, and shared laughter, like a common
language, bonds and differentiates communities. The plain style, with

its mix of learned Latinisms and (possibly) everyday northernisms, suggests an authoritative persona, perhaps conscious of social inferiority and compensating by appealing to wisdom and morality.

There will always be a tantalising degree of uncertainty about our reading of older literature. Assuming that schemata and stereotypes have altered somehow over the past five centuries, we can never be entirely sure how our ancestors understood the poetry which survives from the period. All we can do is be aware that their assumptions are likely to have been different, pay close attention to what does survive, and, using our knowledge of language in association with our knowledge of history, try to reconstruct plausible interpretations.

INVESTIGATING PROSE

So far in this chapter, we have considered the difficulties of conducting stylistic analyses of texts whose contexts have been lost in the mists of time. When considering texts written now, at the end of the twentieth century, we have an intuitive grasp of the norms of language, and we know (or can guess) when these norms are being departed from for stylistic effect.

But imagine if, in the early years of the twenty-first century, there were a series of revolutions which all but wiped out large numbers of earlier texts. Civilisation enters a new dark age, from which it emerges in 200 years. Stylistics as a discipline is reborn in the twenty-fourth century, and in the year 2525 a student is settling down to write an essay on newspaper language in Scotland in the late twentieth century. However, all that has survived is a few copies of the *Sunday Post* and the sports pages of an edition of the *Scotsman*. The chances are that our future student will come to very different conclusions from us about the norms governing twentieth-century language use and the cultural expectations which informed it. We are in a roughly similar position as we look back five centuries and try to reconstruct Older Scots. A range of Older Scots prose texts and text-types does exist, of course: there are, for example, histories, religious and political pamphlets, legal documents, trial records, diaries and letters. An example of a text written around seventy years after Dunbar's time, probably in the 1570s, is Robert Lindsay of Pitscottie's The *Historie and Cronikles of Scotland*, in which the following story about Siamese twins appears (reprinted in Jack 1971: 91–2):

> In the meane tyme thair was ane great marvell sene in Scottland.
> Ane bairne was borne, raknit to be ane man chyld bot frome the

waist upe was two fair, fair persouns witht all memberis and protratouris pertainand to twa bodyis, to wit twa heidis, weill eyit, weill eirit and weill handit be twa bodyis. The on bak was to the utheris, bot frome the waist done they war bot on personage and could not weill knaw be the ingyne of man quhilk of the twa bodyis the legis and previe memberis proceidit. Notwithstanding, the kingis majestie gart tak great cure and deliegence upoun the upbringing of thir two bodyis in ane personage, gart nurische them and leir them to pley and singe upoun the instrumentis of musick, quho war become in schort tyme verie ingeneous and cunning in the art of musick, quhairby they could pleay and singe two pairtis, the on the tribill, the uther the tennour, quhilk was very dulse and melodious to heir be the commoun pepill, quho treatit thame wondrous weill. Allso they could speik sindrie and dyviers langagis, that is to say Latine, Frinche, Italeans, Spanis, Dutch, Dens and Inglische and Earische.

We can, of course, consider this text on its own terms, and compare it with a small body of other texts, as, similarly, we can look at the work of, say, a poet like Dunbar, and compare it to that of Henryson, Douglas or Lindsay. We can consider variation within that small corpus of texts. The kind of observations we could make would perhaps be, again, to do with vocabulary choice (the Latinate 'protratouris', or 'limb', coexisting with the Norse-derived verb 'gar', meaning 'to cause to'). We could also draw attention to the complexity of the structure of the sentences, particularly the one beginning 'Notwithstanding'. Such observations can lead us to certain limited claims about the appropriacy of particular forms of language to certain genres of text.

However, the larger questions are still intriguing: how close an understanding can we achieve of the way in which language in general was used in medieval and Renaissance Scotland? Obviously, we have lost all direct record of the spoken language (although some clues to older spoken Scots might be gleaned from such written texts as trial records, parts of which may be written verbatim), but we do have a range of written texts, prose and poetry. If we could gather together these texts and analyse aspects of variation within them, then perhaps patterns would emerge that might indicate more precisely the meanings of linguistic variation in earlier Scottish culture.

We have, for example, suggested that anglicisation is a marked stylistic feature in Older Scots poetry: Dunbar, for example, uses anglicisms (words and spellings) apparently only in high-style passages of religious and courtly celebration. It has been suggested that this choice means that Dunbar accorded literary prestige to English forms – that the selection of an anglicised word or spelling is an appeal to the established literary prestige of such as Chaucer. And there is other evidence in the poetry to support such a reading.

But what of the written language more generally – the letters, the histories, the pamphlets, the legal and administrative texts? Do we find conscious anglicisation there; and, if so, what might its function be? We have made much of the Latin and vernacular elements in Older Scots poetry – what, then, are their function in Older Scots prose? How might this be investigated more generally?

ENTER COMPUTERISED CORPORA

One way of investigating such questions is by utilising the technology of the late twentieth century, specifically, computerised corpora of texts, to investigate a large sample of Older Scots texts and to consider the function of anglicisation within the sample. The present discussion is based very much on Anneli Meurman-Solin's work, published in *Variation and Change in Early Scottish Prose* (1993), which in turn is based on the Helsinki Corpus of Older Scots. Questions have been raised about how representative the texts used in the Corpus are, as well as the accuracy of the editions of the texts used – as Meurman-Solin herself acknowledges – but while her results may still be provisional, her methodology is extremely interesting and serves as a useful model for similar studies.

WHAT IS A COMPUTERISED CORPUS?

A computerised corpus of texts is simply a large collection of texts (or samples of texts) in electronic or machine-readable form. If you write documents on a word-processor, then the diskette or hard disk contains them in electronic form, which the computer can read. Advances in technology have meant that many printed texts can now be scanned into a corpus, rather than laboriously typed in. The saving in time means that the assembly of a sizeable corpus is now relatively quick and easy.

The advantage of having a computerised corpus is that searching it for certain linguistic features becomes incredibly fast and easy. Imagine if – fifteen years ago – someone had wanted to compare the variant past-tense suffixes '-ed' (English) and '-it' (Scots) in a range of Scots texts. That person would have had to gather together a range of texts and read through them, noting each occurrence of the Scots and English variants. Such an operation now takes seconds, no matter how large the number of texts investigated. The researcher now instructs the computer, and the computer searches the texts.

CORPORA AND STYLISTICS

Meurman-Solin was interested in investigating the use of anglicisation in Older Scots texts: to what extent was it a marked stylistic feature? To answer this general question, she had to consider certain specific ones: for example when was anglicisation used, who used it, and in what types of text?

The study that Meurman-Solin conducted is a preliminary one in many ways. Her initial corpus is quite small, and, as already mentioned, its accuracy is often compromised by the nature of the editions used (although a larger and more accurate one is in preparation). It is a small corpus by present-day standards, the original version amounting to about 600,000 words, made up of shorter texts and samples of longer ones. In order to investigate the question of anglicisation, these texts needed to be classified in a variety of ways. The texts were classified according to eight constraints, as follows:

Text-type

Texts were classified according to their purpose or function: they were drawn from a range of non-literary genres, including burgh records, trials, diaries, letters and treatises. It is important to note here that text-types are problematic categories: they are constructed in one way here and might well be constructed in other ways elsewhere. 'Religious writing', for example, might include certain educational treatises, sermons and pamphlets, not to mention the Bible. Some diaries are difficult to distinguish from autobiographies and travelogues. Educational and scientific writing may overlap with handbooks to some extent. Some categories might have more internal variation than others. Some text-types are better represented than others in certain periods. However, some preliminary sorting has to be attempted if we are to give an account of how language variation works.

Period

The texts were classified according to four subperiods: 1450–1500, 1500–70, 1570–1640 and 1640–1700. The period 1450–1700 corresponds to Aitken's category of Middle Scots (Early Middle Scots being 1450–1550, Late Middle Scots 1550–1700). The specific subperiods of the Scots corpus are to allow for comparisons with the separate Helsinki Corpus of Early Modern English.

Dialect

The texts were classified regionally into two categories: Central Scots being the south-sastern part of present-day Scotland, based in Edinburgh, and Northern Scots being the north-eastern part, based in Aberdeen.

Print or Manuscript

Printing has been seen as a major anglicising influence on Scots. It is therefore important to note whether texts were in manuscript or print form.

Author Variables

The texts were classified according to three author-related variables: sex, social rank and age. Obviously, the distribution of texts varies according to each category. Women's writing is represented only by letters, both private and official. Male writers' rank is represented largely by the professional classes and gentry. (Women are automatically classed as non-professional gentry.)

When known, the language of younger writers can be compared with that of writers of older generations; however, the age of a writer is sometimes difficult to ascertain. Meurman-Solin notes that Melville of Halhill's memoirs cover the period 1549–93. The dates suggest that he started writing them when he was 14 years old. However, they were not published until around 1610, and the extent to which the early memoirs were rewritten is simply unknown.

Audience Variables

The question of the relationship between author and audience is a crucial one when considering the extent of anglicisation. The more local or indeed domestic the audience – as one might expect – the more Scottish the language. Meurman-Solin classifies her texts into the following audience-related categories: professional, official, royal court and nobility, administration, general public, family, unspecified.

Again, it may not be easy to slot texts neatly into one or another category: for example, a memoir written initially for one's own family might be published more generally later. As the centuries progress, the audience for different text-types might become more or less institutionalised. Memoirs might come to be written for general audiences if an audience was established. (Compare today's situation – it would be a naive politician who did not write a diary with a view to future publication.) However, there is sometimes evidence in prefatory material, dedications, etc., which enables us to assign texts to the given categories.

Participant Relationship

The Helsinki Corpus codes the social relationship between writer and reader in private letters as follows: intimate down (letter to child or wife); intimate up (letter to parent or husband); intimate equal (letter to sibling). The coding of letters from husbands and wives to each other obviously reflects medieval assumptions rather than modern ones. Official letters (and other types of text) have been left unclassified because the variation in social position is hard to gauge.

Degrees of Interaction

Texts can be classified according to the degree of interaction or 'involvement' between author and audience explicitly acknowledged. Among the least interactive of texts would be legal texts, which serve mainly as documentary records of decisions made. More interactive would be letters and polemical pamphlets, as well as handbooks which guide readers so that they can perform certain activities.

The eight sections above show the ways in which a corpus might be structured before any analysis of its linguistic features is undertaken. The texts are selected, sampled, keyed in or scanned, and then tagged according to a set of stated extralinguistic variables. This is not an entirely objective process: obviously we have some notion before we start that the period of the text, its function, its geographical origin, the sex, age and rank of its author, and his/her relationship with an audience are going to be important. So we construct likely categories and code the texts accordingly. Then we look at them to see what the language is doing.

CHOOSING THE LINGUISTIC VARIABLES

Again we have to be selective: even with a computer, it is difficult to look at everything that the language is doing. We have to have some idea of what we are looking for. From what we know of Older Scots texts, we can think of various avenues of approach.

Lexical Analysis

We could take a look at the incidence of certain types of lexical item (e.g. Latinisms or northernisms) in the categories constructed above. This is simply a larger-scale version of the kind of analysis discussed in the first half of this chapter. The movement of a particular loanword (and its derivatives) can be charted from its initial arrival in one particular text-type to its diffusion throughout others (or perhaps disappearance). The proportion of a set of lexical items of a particular type (e.g. anglicisms) can be followed through time. This kind of search means that the electronic text has to be 'tagged'; that is, the words in the text have to be labelled. These 'tags' would differentiate between different words which have the same form, for example, whether 'flour' in a text would mean 'flower', 'flour' or even 'floor'. They might also give information about the grammatical function of the word, for example, whether the occurrence of 'grudge' in a text is a noun or a verb.

In addition to the information about individual lexical items, collocation patterns can also be observed, that is, the tendency of items to appear together. Frequently-appearing pairs of items might be considered formulaic or unmarked, rare ones might be stylistically important.

Grammatical Analysis

Grammatical analysis can be morphological or syntactic. In the former category, we might consider whether texts use the Scots '-it' past-tense suffix or the English '-ed'. Scots and English forms of the present participle and gerunds might also be investigated. In earlier Scots texts, the present participle ends in the inflexion '-and', later reduced to '-in'. Only the gerund or verbal noun end in '-ing', so there was a difference in Scots between the participle form in 'Scho wes singand', and the gerund in 'The singing wes sweit'. Later, Scots, like English, adopted the '-ing' inflexion for the participle, too. Texts can be quickly scanned to see what the proportion of '-and' and anglicised '-ing' inflexions are.

On the syntactic side, Meurman-Solin investigates the use of the so-called do-periphrasis (e.g. 'he did, within the House and Kitchin of New-milns, call for Ale to drink some Healths'). She argues that this feature, while originally influenced by anglicisation, develops in Scots in such a way that in time it is distinguished as a northernism. In brief, it is introduced into Scots from English and proliferates in the north while it declines in the south.

Orthographic Analysis

Scots spellings can be compared with English spellings to gauge the degree of anglicisation. Meurman-Solin investigates the 'i-digraph' (i.e. the Scots spellings found in words such as 'befoir', 'heid', 'buik', 'cair') and Scots 'quh', '-ch' and 'sch-' spellings, among others.

Phonological Analysis

Certain spellings which are recognised as reflecting distinctively Scots pronunciations can be searched. For example, the <ai> and <a> spellings in 'aith', 'baith', 'maist', 'ga', 'quham', 'sa' etc. reflect early Scots / a:/ as opposed to early Modern English /o:/ in 'oath', 'both', 'most', 'go', 'whom', 'so' etc. For a detailed reconstruction of the Older Scots sound system, see Aitken (1977).

RESULTS

As mentioned earlier, Meurman-Solin's results are compromised by two main factors: first of all, the Helsinki Corpus of Older Scots is relatively small. This is not a great problem when considering spellings or certain grammatical or phonological analyses, but it is a problem when considering lexical analyses. Crudely put, the incidence of certain spellings (e.g. i-digraphs) is likely to be much more frequent in a 600,000-word corpus than the occurrence of certain words. With a small corpus, we tend to find ourselves making generalisations about lexis from very little data (cf. Sinclair 1991).

Second, and more problematically, the editions used to compile the Helsinki Corpus are not always reliable – some are nineteenth-century editions of earlier texts. Sometimes there is no guarantee that at some stage along the way the language (whether at spelling, word or grammatical level) has not been 'normalised', by which would be meant 'anglicised' by scribe, printer or editor. Meurman-Solin acknowledges that in future her results might have to be modified in the light of an expanded corpus and more accurate editions of early texts. In the meantime, we must view her findings as preliminary.

With this proviso, many of these findings are useful and interesting. Anglicisation seems, not surprisingly, to have been a patchy phenomenon, moving at a faster pace in some areas than others. Central Scots seems to have anglicised at a faster pace than Northern Scots. The date of a text and its type alone do not seem to account for anglicising spelling practices – author, audience and participant relation do seem to play an important part. Women's language seems to be more conservatively Scottish than men's in the periods analysed. Men also resist anglicisation when writing to women and children, even up to the end of the seventeenth century. When texts are written for a local audience (e.g. burgh records), they tend to be Scots until quite late, whereas texts written with a southern audience equally in mind (e.g. reformers' texts) tend towards early anglicisation. And it is important to note that certain items (e.g. do-periphrasis) might begin life as anglicisms and then, as the two varieties north and south diverge, might end up as a northernism.

If nothing else, Meurman-Solin's results show us that the linguistic situation in Scotland was complex. Simple generalisations should be avoided. This is apparent even more when her statistical analyses are considered: while her mean frequencies for the occurrence of various diagnostic features point to certain possible trends as the 250 years progress, the standard deviation scores are quite high. Simply put, a high standard deviation score means that variation from the mean or average is considerable: so at any one period there will be a great deal of variation in any of the established categories. For example, not all women's letters will be conservative, some men might anglicise when writing to children, some reformers will use Scots forms, and so on. The texts are heterogeneous rather than homogeneous. To confirm trends, we really do need to consider a corpus which is as large as possible, and which contains reliable editions. And, as Meurman-Solin demonstrates, we need to consider a range of factors in our analysis.

CONCLUSION

The birth in the 1980s of large-scale corpus linguistics in machine-readable form means that this generation of language specialists has access to a tool denied those before us. The computer is still a tool; it is still people who have to decide how it is to be used and how best to use it. The computer will not come up with a set of definite answers to any given problem. But it can search for data in a number of ways which were previously impracticable, and so provide evidence for and against certain claims, linguistic and stylistic. So, for example, if we were arguing that a certain writer were anglicising for a certain stylistic effect, we might look at the general pattern in similar text-types in similar contexts, and see if anglicisation was common in that text-type. We would then know how strong our claim was. This kind of comparative study is now easier, faster and increasingly more accessible. More Scottish texts are becoming available in machine-readable form, and, as part of Glasgow University's STARN and COMET projects, many hitherto inaccessible Scottish texts are becoming widely available in the Internet via the World Wide Web. As Kirk (1992/3) suggests, in an overview of the potential of computing for Scottish linguistic studies, future re-search in Scots – whether prose or poetry, literary or non-literary, older or modern -will increasingly depend on it.

COMMON STANZAS
IN SCOTS POETRY

The following are examples of rhyme schemes which have been particularly popular in Scottish poetry, although, of course, most are not unique to Scottish literature. (See also Malof 1970, Appendix 1; Wittig 1958: 114–17).

Ballad stanza

A four-line stanza, in which the second and fourth lines rhyme (*abcb*). In the folk tradition, the metre is pure stress: four beats alternating with three beats plus a pause. As the ballad moves into the literary tradition, the lines become alternating iambic tetrameter and trimeter. Not to be confused with the ballade.
Example: Anon., 'The Battle of Otterbourne' and hundreds of others.

Ballade

Not to be confused with the ballad stanza, the ballade usually consists of three stanzas of eight lines each, each one often rhyming *ababbcbc*. The final line of each stanza is identical. The metre is either four-beat pure stress or iambic pentameter. If the three stanzas have eight lines each, they are then followed by an 'envoy' of four lines; if not, the envoy contains half the number of lines found in each stanza. The envoy might or might not maintain the rhyme scheme of the stanzas, or it might introduce some new rhymes. It will, however, keep the recurring final line found in the three stanzas.
Example: Alexander Scott, 'Ballade of Beauties'.

Bob-wheel stanza

This stanza has no fixed length or defined metre, but is in three parts: the 'frons', the 'bob'-verses and the 'tail'. The main part of the stanza is the frons; it is followed by one or two very short lines (the bob-verses); and finally the tail consists of one slightly longer line which rhymes with the bob but not the frons.

If the words of the bob and tail are repeated from stanza to stanza, then they are referred to as the 'refrain'. If the words are changed but the metrical pattern remains, then bob and tail are referred to as the 'bob-wheel'. Example: Anon., 'Christ's Kirk on the Grene'.

Bob-wheel stanza (modified)

Allan Ramsay modified 'Christ's Kirk on the Grene', omitting the bob-wheel and in its place substituting a short final line, ending 'that day'. This stanza was taken up particularly as a vehicle for the description of popular festivals and entertainments, as in Burns' 'Hallowe'en', below. Alternatively, a short line near the end could be linked by rhyme to another short line, which concludes the stanza – this form is popular in mock-elegies, as in Burns' 'Poor Mailie's Elegy'. These variations on the bob-wheel are sometimes known as 'tail-rhyme' stanzas (see also 'Standard Habbie' below):

> 'Hallowe'en'
> Some merry, friendly, countra folks
>   Together did convene,
> To burn their nits, and pou their stocks,
>   An' haud their Hallowe'en,
>   Fu' blythe that night.

> 'Poor Mailie's Elegy'
> Lament in rhyme, lament in prose,
> Wi' saut tears tricklin' down your nose;
> Our Bardie's fate is at a close,
>   Past a' remead!
> The last, sad cape-stane of his woes;
>   Poor Mailie's dead!

Burns stanza

See 'Standard Habbie'.

Ottava rima

The rhyme is *ababababcc*; the metre is iambic pentameter.
Example: Sir William Alexander, 'An Exhortation to Prince Henry'.

Rhyme royal

The rhyme is *ababbcc*; the metre is iambic pentameter. In some cases, the syntax divides the stanza into three parts: *ab* + *ab* + *cdd* – the first two parts are called the 'pedes' and the final part is the 'cauda'.
Example: James I, *The Kingis Quair*.

Scottis metre

The rhyme is *ababbcbc* with a turn after the fourth line, often beginning a counter-argument. The metre can be iambic trimeter, tetrameter or pentameter. Example: William Dunbar, 'Of Christ's Resurrection'.

Sestina

For poets who wish to demonstrate their formal ingenuity, the sestina and villanelle (see below) offer a considerable challenge. The sestina usually has the following form:

Rhyme	*Metre*
no rhyme; six stanzas of six lines each, plus an envoi of three lines. The final words in each line of the first stanza are repeated in subsequent stanzas in the following order:	varies, if any

1 ABCDEF
2 FAEBDC
3 CFDABE
4 ECBFAD
5 DEACFB
6 BDFECA
envoi BDF or ACE

Example: Tom Scott's 'Sestina: Aberfan', in *Chapman* 47–8, 1987.

Sonnet

The sonnet consists of fourteen lines of iambic pentameter. The two main types of sonnet are the Italian or Petrarchan, which divides the poem into an eight-line 'octave' and a six-line 'sestet'. A possible rhyme scheme is *abba abba cde cde*. Other variations are possible. The English or Shakespearean sonnet is divided into three four-line 'quatrains' plus a two-line 'couplet'. One possible version is *abab cdcd efef gg*. The rhyme scheme might well affect the discourse organisation of the sonnet: the Petrarchan sonnet might pose a complication in the octave, which after the turn is solved by a resolution in the sestet. A complication in a Shakespearean sonnet might be prolonged until it is suddenly and surprisingly resolved in the concluding couplet.

The sonnet is probably the most popular and enduring of stanza forms – it has therefore been subject to considerable innovation and experimentation over the years. Robert Garioch's 'Edinburgh Sonnets' and Edwin Morgan's 'Glasgow Sonnets' are fairly recent examples; again there are hundreds from the time of James VI onwards.

Spenserian stanza

The rhyme is *ababbcbcc*; eight lines of iambic pentameter are followed by a single iambic hexameter line (i.e. an alexandrine).
Example: Robert Burns, 'The Cottar's Saturday Night', itself based on Fergusson's modified use of the Spenserian stanza in 'The Farmer's Ingle'.

Standard Habbie

A variant on the modified bob-wheel stanza (above). The rhyme is *aaabab*; and the metre is usually two lines of iambic tetrameter plus a line of iambic dimeter, repeated once. The first dimeter line is called 'the waist' and the final dimeter line is 'the tail'.
Examples: Robert Sempill of Beltrees, 'The Life and Death of Habbie Simson, the Piper of Kilbarchan'; Robert Burns, 'Holy Willie's Prayer'.

Tail-rhyme stanza

See 'Bob-wheel stanza (modified)'.

Villanelle

For poets who wish to demonstrate their formal ingenuity, the sestina (see above) and villanelle offer a considerable challenge. The villanelle usually has the following form:

Rhyme	Metre
five tercets, all rhyming *aba* plus a final quatrain *abab*. Lines 1 and 3 are alternately the final lines of each of the remaining tercets, and together are the final lines of the poem.	varies, if any

Example: Margaret Winefride Simpson, 'Villanelle'.

GLOSSARY OF LINGUISTIC TERMS

The definitions in this glossary are necessarily brief. For a more detailed explanation, see a dictionary of linguistic or stylistic terms (e.g. T. McArthur 1992; or Wales 1989).

accent   The pronunciation associated with a particular language variety.

address, direct and indirect   Direct address occurs when the text calls the reader by name, or gives the reader explicit instructions. Indirect address occurs when the text assumes that the reader holds a particular set of beliefs and values.

adjective   A part of speech used to modify a **noun**; for example, 'black' in 'black widow'.

adverb   A part of speech which is used to modify the meaning of an **adjective** or another adverb (e.g. 'gey' and 'very' in 'gey dreich' and 'very quickly'). Adverbs also modify the meaning of **verbs** (e.g. 'quickly' in 'She spoke quickly').

adverbial   (see **clause**)

allegory   A narrative that can be read on different 'levels'; for example, a medieval poem which literally tells of a battle between angels and demons might be read, on other 'levels', as a battle between virtue and sin, or between rationality and sensuality.

alliteration   The repetition of the initial consonant of words in a line, or adjacent lines, of poetry; for example, the /b/ sound is repeated in the following line:

> Tae the lochan's bosom the burnie goes.

anglicisation   The use of a southern English pronunciation, word or expression, particularly when a Scots equivalent is available.

anglicism   A southern English pronunciation, word or expression, used in preference to a Scots equivalent.

archaism   A vocabulary item from an older speech variety, now obsolete.

aureation   The use of (a) decorative loanwords from Latin, and (b) words which have meanings associated with value, wealth, light and power, in order to create a highly ornate, 'golden' style.

auxiliary verb   A class of verbs which are used to modify other verbs: for example, 'primary' auxiliaries ('be' and 'do') are used in question forms ('Do you come here often?'), while 'modal' auxiliaries add certain types of meaning (possibility, permission, obligation etc.) to the main verb ('Can I go?'). The use of modal auxiliaries differs between southern Standard English and Scots.

axes of selection and combination   (see **paradigmatic** and **syntagmatic**)

calque   A word formed by translation from another language: for example, the use of the word 'makar' to mean 'poet' is based on the literal translation of the Greek term 'poietes', a maker.

canon (adj. **canonical**)   A body of texts, institutionally regarded as the 'best' or 'most valuable' works in a literary tradition. Those texts which are not so valued are termed 'non-canonical'.

clause (S, P, O, C, A)   The construction of various phrases in relation to a verb phrase, or **predicator**, for example 'tastes'. A phrase which has a relationship of 'agreement' with the predicator is the **subject** (e.g. 'I' and 'it' in 'I made' and 'it tastes'). An **object** is a phrase which has the potential to become subject, but is not (e.g. 'the sauce' in 'I made the sauce'; this phrase could become subject: 'The sauce was made by me'). A **complement** is a phrase which cannot become subject, but which expresses an attribute or gives the identity of the subject or object: for example, 'good' in 'The sauce tastes good'. The **adverbial** is a phrase which gives additional information in the clause: for example, information about time, place or the speaker's attitude; for example, 'fortunately' in 'Fortunately, the sauce tasted good'.

clause relations (**matching relations** and **logical sequences**)   The relationship between **clauses** often falls into a limited set of patterns. Some clauses are related because they express similar or contrasting meanings (**matching relations**); other clauses are related because they are patterned as generalisations followed by examples; conditions followed by consequences; causes followed by consequences; or problems followed by solutions (**logical sequences**). A similar framework of description is **cohesion**.

Clydesideism   A particular **stereotype** of Scottish identity, which emphasises lowland, urban, working-class experience in preference to the images associated with **Kailyard** and **tartanry**.

code-switching   The movement, within a stretch of text, between two or more varieties of language: for example, 'The inordinate amount of effort involved in the activity gart me pech lik an auld, ricketty cairt-horse'.

coherence   The underlying relationship of meaning between clauses which allows them to make sense.

cohesion   The use of grammatical and lexical features to indicate the relationship of meaning , or **coherence**, between different clauses. Features of cohesion include the omission of repeated elements in a complex **clause**: for example, the omission of the second **subject** in 'Liz ran the marathon and then (Liz) competed in the long jump'. A similar framework of description is that of **clause relations**.

collocation   The appearance of words or phrases in close proximity in a text.

commissive   (see **speech act theory**)

complement   (see **clause**)

conative function of language   The use of language principally to persuade or direct the person to whom it is addressed. See **emotive**, **metalingual**, **phatic**, **poetic** and **referential** functions of language.

conceptual metaphor   (see **metaphor**)

conjunction (coordinating and **subordinating)**   Two main ways of linking **clauses**. Coordination refers to the linking of clauses by coordinating conjunctions such as 'and' and 'but'; subordination refers to the embedding of one clause inside another, as signalled by the use of a subordinating conjunction such as 'if', 'because', 'although' etc.

connotation   The meanings that are associated with a word or expression, but which are not part of its 'basic' meaning or **denotation**. For example, the colour 'green' might have associations of fertility, youth, envy or, in the context of traditional ballads, the supernatural.

consonant   A **phoneme**, or unit of sound, which is pronounced by making an obstruction to the air-flow at some position in the vocal tract. For example, the consonants /b/ and /p/ are realised by closing the lips and then 'exploding' the suppressed air through them. See **phoneme** and **vowel**.

constative   (see **speech act theory**)

conversational implicature   The study of those rules of conversation which allow participants to understand what people are saying, even when they are not saying what they mean. For instance, the utterance 'Can you help me with this box?' is technically a question, but it will usually be interpreted as a request for help.

cooperative principle   A formula which tries to account for our knowledge, or at least our assumption, that people normally work together to achieve communication in mutually helpful ways. Specifically, we interpret other people's utterances by assuming that they are conforming to **Grice's maxims**, a series of 'rules' that state that contributions to conversation should be taken to be truthful, relevant and sufficient for successful under-standing to achieved. See **politeness principle**.

corpus (pl. **corpora**)   A collection or 'body' of texts. Such a collection may be structured, for example to represent a particular speech variety, genre or period, and it may be stored in computerised form, for ease of access and interrogation.

couplet   A pair of lines of verse, usually linked by **rhyme**; for example:

> The grey bird cries at evenin's fa'
> 'My luve, my fair one, come awa'.

defamiliarisation   The breaking of an established pattern of language (which may be metrical, grammatical or lexical) in order to **foreground** a particular part of a text.

deixis (person, place and **time)**   Those words whose expression of person and spatio-temporal location depends on who is speaking. Such items include 'I'; 'here/there'; and 'now/then'.

demonstrative   A type of **determiner** which expresses the literal or metaphorical proximity or distance of a noun: in Scots, for example, 'thir buiks' (near); 'thae buiks' (distant); 'yon buiks' (remote).

denotation   The basic or 'core' meaning of a word or phrase. For example, the denotation of 'green' is the colour green, although that colour may have, in addition, various associative meanings or **connotations**.

determiner   A part of speech which specifies the noun, for example by indicating whether or not it is definite ('a/the buik'); by indicating its location (see **demonstrative**); or by indicating its quantity or extent ('every book'; 'aa the buiks').

dialect   A variety of speech, distinguished from other varieties by particular features of vocabulary and grammar. See **accent, standard language**.

digraph   Two letters which represent one sound: for example, <ui> in 'luik' ('look'); <ai> in 'cair' ('care'); and <ei> in 'heir' ('here'). Each of these Scots examples can be classed as an 'i-digraph'. See **grapheme**.

diphthong   A single vowel sound which 'glides' from one quality to another, as the tongue moves slightly while it is being pronounced. Examples include /ɔe/ in 'boy', and /ʌɪ/ in 'bite'. See **vowel**.

direct speech, bound and free   The representation of what a character in a narrative actually said. If there is an explicit signal of this in the narrative (e.g. 'he/she said'), then the direct speech is 'bound'; if there is no indication, then the direct speech is 'free'.

direct thought, bound and free   The representation of the actual thoughts of a character in a narrative. If there is an explicit signal of this in the narrative (e.g. 'he/she thought'), then the direct thought is 'bound'; if there is no indication, then the direct thought is 'free'.

directive   (see **speech act theory**)

discourse   Structured sequences of language which are longer than a sentence. 'Discourse' sometimes refers only to spoken sequences of language; elsewhere, as in this book, 'discourse' and '**text**' are used synonymously.

domain   (see **register; metaphor**)

Doric   (see **Scots**)

ellipsis   The omission of a piece of text, usually because it appears previously in the text and is therefore 'understood'. See **cohesion**.

emotive function of language   The use of language principally to express the beliefs, feelings or attitude of the person who is speaking. See **conative, metalingual, phatic, poetic** and **referential** functions of language.

etymology   The study of the origins and history of a word.

field   (see **register**)

focalisation   Whether the **narrative point of view** is that of an 'independent' third-person narrator or that of one of the characters participating in a narrative. Focalisation is obviously related to the type of **narrator**, but even a 'third-person' **narrative** can privilege the perceptions and viewpoint of one of the participating characters in a story. See **perspective**.

foreground   To highlight a particular part of a text for some special reason, for example by **defamiliarisation**, or by using it in an unexpected context.

free verse   Poetry that is unconstrained by the regulations governing **metre** and **rhyme**.

gloss   To define or paraphrase a word or longer expression.

goal   (see **schema**)

grammar   The study of the organisation of words and phrases in sentences. Traditionally, grammar includes the study of word-formation ('morphology') and the sequencing of words and phrases in **clauses** ('syntax').

grammatical items   The finite or 'closed' set of words in the vocabulary of a language which serve mainly to give grammatical information or to indicate grammatical relationships, namely **prepositions, conjunctions, determiners** etc. See **lexis, lexical items**.

grapheme   The smallest unit in a writing system, consisting of one or more characters which represent a sound or **phoneme**. For example, the grapheme <wh> represents the sound /w/ in English and /ʍ/ in Scots.

Grice's maxims   (see **cooperative principle**)

grounds   (see **metaphor**)

high style   Particularly in older Scottish literature, a style of writing that associates elevated topics (e.g. religious or secular celebration) with a decorous language, marked by **aureation**. See **low style, plain style**.

hypercorrection   In Scots, usually an attempt to approximate some feature of **received pronunciation** (RP) which fails because it goes too far. See **Kelvinside**.

ideational function of language   In Hallidayan linguistics, the use of language to represent some state or event in a real or fictional universe. Similar to Jakobson's **referential** function of language.

ideology   A system of beliefs and values which may be linguistically encoded either implicitly or explicitly.

illocution/illocutionary act   (see **speech act theory**)

indirect speech, bound and free   The representation of what a character in a narrative said, mediated by a narrator. If there is an explicit signal of this mediation in the narrative (e.g. 'he/she said that …'), then the indirect speech is 'bound'; if there is no indication, then the indirect speech is 'free'.

indirect thought, bound and free   The representation of what a character in a narrative was thinking, slightly mediated by a narrator. If there is an explicit signal of this mediation in the narrative (e.g. 'he/she thought that …'), then the indirect thought is 'bound'; if there is no indication, then the indirect thought is 'free'.

inflexion   The change in the form of a word to signify its grammatical status (for example, whether a noun is singular or plural, or whether a verb is present or past tense). Inflexions may involve the addition of suffixes (e.g. '-s' in 'dog'/'dogs'), or the change of a vowel (e.g. 'u'/'a' in 'run'/'ran').

Insular Scots   The variety of Scots which is indigenous to the island groups of Shetland and Orkney. See **Norn**.

Kailyard   Literally 'cabbage-patch', this refers (1) to a literary genre of the nineteenth and twentieth centuries which deals with small-town life and values, and (2) to a **stereotype** of Scottish identity which is informed by these values – the couthy, rustic Scot whose humility is matched only by his homespun wisdom. See **Clydesideism** and **tartanry**.

Kelvinside   An **accent** associated with but not confined to the Glasgow district of Kelvinside, it is often mocked for its social pretensions and, in particular, its tendency towards **hypercorrection**. The Edinburgh equivalent is 'Morningside'.

Lallans   (see **Scots**)

Latinism   A word borrowed from Latin into Scots, sometimes to express a new concept in the language, and sometimes for decorative effect (see **aureation**, **high style**).

lexical items   Those words in the vocabulary of a variety of language which express most meaning: that is, the **nouns**, **verbs**, **adjectives**, etc. Unlike **grammatical items**, this is an open set of words, and can be added to by **neologisms**.

lexis   A term used for the vocabulary of a variety of language, in particular the **lexical items** as opposed to the **grammatical items**.

literary linguistics   (see **poetics**)

locutionary act   (see **speech act theory**)

logical sequences   (see **clause relations**)

low style   Particularly in older Scottish literature, a style of writing that associates 'low' topics (e.g. comedy, parochial life) with a 'rude' language, marked by slang, and northern vocabulary (often of Norse or Gaelic origin). See **high style**, **plain style**.

matching relations   (see **clause relations**)

metalingual function of language   Language used to describe linguistic features; usually technical in origin. This glossary, for example, is a case of language used metalingually. See **conative**, **emotive**, **phatic**, **poetic** and **referential** functions of language.

metaphor   Traditionally regarded as a figure of speech which promotes the comparison of two things by saying that one (**tenor**) is equivalent to the other (**vehicle**) owing to a certain similarity (**grounds**): for example, 'language is a tree'. More recently, **conceptual metaphors** have been considered to be the mental 'mapping' of one domain of experience onto another. A particular kind of metaphor, **reification**, involves representing an action as a 'thing', often by a grammatical means called **nominalisation**.

metre The arrangement of words in a line of poetry, usually so that the stressed and unstressed syllables fall into a conventional pattern.

modality Refers to the ways in which a certain set of meanings – mainly about possibility, obligation, desires, beliefs and attitudes – are expressed in language, mainly through **auxiliary verbs** such as 'can', 'should' etc. and **adverbs** such as 'hopefully', 'certainly' and 'sadly'.

mode (see **register**)

narrative In general terms, either a story, whether true or fictional, or the process of telling one.

narrative report of a speech act The representation of what a character in a narrative said, but almost totally paraphrased by the narrator. For example, a character's words, 'Yes, that's right', might be presented as 'She absolutely agreed'.

narrative report of a thought act The representation of what a character in a narrative was thinking, but almost totally paraphrased by the narrator.

narrator, types of The person telling a story might be presented as a character who to a greater or lesser degree is participating in the narrative (a 'first-person narrator'); or the narrator might be external to all the events ('a third-person narrator'). 'Third-person' narrators can present the events in the story from an 'omniscient' **point of view**, or from that of one of the characters (see **focalisation**). Rarely, a 'second-person' narrator is used to give the **point of view** of a general or particular 'you', who may even be identified with the reader of the narrative.

neologism The coinage of a new word, often to express a concept for which no other word exists in the language variety.

nominalisation The grammatical process whereby events are expressed as nouns: for example, the process 'to demonstrate' can be expressed as 'demonstration'. See **metaphor**, **reification**.

Norn A Scandinavian language variety, spoken in Orkney and Shetland up until the beginning of the twentieth century, and a strong influence on present-day **Insular Scots**.

northernisms Those words in **Scots** which derive from Norse and Gaelic rather than, say, Old English, French, Latin or Dutch. They are often a marker of the **low style** in Older Scots literature.

noun A part of speech, traditionally thought of as naming 'things'. Nouns combine with **determiners** and **adjectives** to make up phrases which, in turn, can act as **subject** or **object** in **clauses**. Examples would be 'dog', 'buik', 'indignation'.

object (see **clause**)

orthography The study of the spelling system of a language, and its connection with the sound system. See **phonology, grapheme, digraph**.

paradigmatic The relationship which holds between items of language which can be substituted for each other. For example, the word 'sings' in the sentence 'The boy sings' could be replaced by various other words, for example 'sighs', 'laughs', 'groans', 'greets', 'girns' etc. Another way of putting this is to say that the items exist on the same **axis of selection**. See **syntagmatic**.

parody An imitation of a particular style with the intent to mock or amuse. A parody often exaggerates characteristic linguistic features of the original style.

partitive construction A grammatical construction, usually realised by the **preposition** 'of', which (1) relates a part to a whole, for example 'the branch of a tree'; (2) states the quantity of an item, for example 'a loaf of bread', 'a pint of milk'; or (3) expresses the quality of something, for example 'fair of countenance'; 'stern of demeanour'.

passive (see **voice**)

performative (see **speech act theory**)

perlocutionary act (see **speech act theory**)

perspective, internal and external Whether a **narrative point of view** allows the reader access to the thoughts or emotions of the characters described. 'Internal perspective' gives the reader access to these 'private' thoughts and emotions; 'external perspective' retains the privacy of these mental events.

phatic function of language Language used to initiate and maintain social relations: for example, 'small talk', 'gossip' etc. See **conative, emotive, metalingual, poetic** and **referential** functions of language.

phoneme The technical term for a basic unit of sound. See **consonant, phonology** and **vowel**.

phonology The general term for the study of the sound system of a language; that is, its system of **phonemes** as well as its patterns of rhythm and intonation. See **consonant, phoneme** and **vowel**.

plain style Particularly in older Scottish literature, a style of writing associated with those topics where the **narrator** assumes a learned, authoritative persona (e.g. conventional moralities and petitionary poems). This style is marked by the use of learned vocabulary (e.g. **Latinisms** of a technical nature) alongside everyday **Northernisms**. See **high style, low style**.

plan (see **schema**)

poetic function of language In Jakobson's terms, language used 'playfully', for its own sake. Such language would tend to be highly patterned and decorative; for example, it would tend to be rhythmical and rhymed, and employ word-play and repetition. See **conative, emotive, metalingual, phatic** and **referential** functions of language.

poetics The study of the principles and techniques of literary language. The term has been revived in the twentieth century by literary theorists and linguists who attempt to find a 'scientific' framework for the description of literary language. Some theorists, however, prefer the term **literary linguistics**. See also **stylistics**.

point of view The general term for the set of ways in which a narrative constructs a particular representation of a real or fictional world. **Point of view** will depend on factors such as the type of **narrator**, the **focalisation**, and whether the **perspective** is internal or external.

politeness principle A formula which tries to account for our knowledge, or at least our assumption, that the structure and realisation of people's communication is partly governed by their adherence to social conventions generally accepted as 'polite'. See **cooperative principle**.

pragmatics The study of 'language in use', focusing on issues such as how participants in conversation manage to understand a speaker's intended meaning, even when this intended meaning is not literally expressed. Sometimes considered a branch of **semantics**. See also **speech act theory**, **conversational implicature**, **cooperative** and **politeness principles**.

predicator (see **clause**)

preposition Grammatical words which are placed in a position before (i.e. 'pre-positioned' beside) a **noun** or noun phrase. Prepositions, such as 'in', 'to', 'over', 'by' etc., express the grammatical relationship between the preceding phrases and the following noun phrase. Together, the preposition and the noun phrase are termed a 'prepositional phrase'.

process types (see **transitivity**)

pronoun A set of grammatical words which may be substituted for **nouns**. 'Personal pronouns' such as 'I', 'he/she', 'we', etc. substitute for people's full names. Other types of pronoun include 'possessive pronouns' ('his/ hers', 'mine/yours', etc.); reflexive pronouns ('myself', 'yourself', 'him/ herself', etc.); and relative pronouns ('who', 'which', 'that').

prose Coherent stretches of written **discourse**, usually lacking the stylised characteristics of poetry.

protocols (see **think-aloud investigations**)

quatrain A four-line verse unit, usually determined by its **rhyme**.

reader, actual, implied and resisting The 'implied reader' is one who conforms to the 'roles' for him/her implied or stated in a text; the 'actual reader' is the person actually processing the text; and the 'resisting reader' is an actual reader who challenges the roles created for him or her by the text.

received pronunciation (RP) The most prestigious **accent** of English, originating in the region around london, but spread to other areas of the United Kingdom (including Scotland) by institutions such as the public school system. It is associated (sometimes derisively) with the middle classes and, even today, with established institutions such as the monarchy and the BBC.

referential function of language Language used to communicate information, and to express states or actions. Similar to the **ideational** function of language in Hallidayan linguistics. See **conative**, **emotive**, **metalingual**, **phatic** and **poetic** functions of language.

register The variation in features of language according to 'the context of situation'. 'Context of situation' is conceived of as having three variables: **field** or **domain**, which specifies the topic of the text; **mode**, which specifies the text-type and whether the text is written or spoken; and **tenor**, which specifies the social relationship between the producer and processor of the text. As field, tenor and mode change, so the language changes in systematic ways.

reification   (see **metaphor**)

resisting reader   (see **reader**)

rhetoric   A general term for the craft of speaking, particularly the techniques employed in speaking and, later, writing effectively and persuasively.

rhotic   An **accent** in which the **phoneme** /r/ is pronounced before a **consonant**, and before a pause. All **Scots** accents are rhotic, and the /r/ is pronounced in words like 'bird' and 'car'. **Received pronunciation** is not.

rhyme   The relationship in sound between words which end with the same sound or sounds; in particular, the same stressed **vowel** and any following unstressed vowels and consonants. For example, in traditional **Scots**, 'arm' would rhyme with 'warm' and 'arming' with 'warming'. However, 'arming' would not rhyme with 'forming', since the stressed vowels are different.

RP   (see **received pronunciation**)

schema (pl. **schemata**) **theory**   A model of knowledge which assumes that it is structured as a series of linked concepts and routines. Linked concepts would be **scripts**, or **stereotypes**; **plans** are routines which help us to create **scripts** in unfamiliar situations; and **plans** in turn serve personal **goals**, those specific purposes which help to fulfil **themes**, or more general desires. Together, these elements of schema theory help to explain certain aspects of (1) why texts are structured as they are by writers, and (2) different meanings and responses constructed from texts by different readers.

Scots (Lallans, Doric, Older, Modern, rural, urban)   The language varieties spoken in Scotland; specifically, those varieties related historically to Old English, which were originally spoken in Lowland Scotland, and which have now spread throughout most of the country. Older Scots is conventionally subdivided into Early Scots (1100–1450) and Middle Scots (1450–1700). Modern Scots dates from 1700 to the present day. The most conservative Modern Scots varieties are rural, sometimes referred to as **Doric**, although this has latterly become associated with the variety of rural areas around Aberdeen. **Urban Scots** varieties retain some traditional features, alongside a number of innovations that have caused them to be considered 'corrupt'.

The lack of a non-regional, 'classless' variety of Scots has prompted some 'Scots language activists' to promote **Lallans**, a 'synthetic' or 'plastic' variety which incorporates current features of traditional Scots alongside **archaisms, neologisms** and **calques**.

The **standard language** spoken in Scotland (Standard Scottish English) is superficially different from its southern counterpart in a number of surface features (for example, in its use and distribution of certain lexical items, in its prepositional constraints, aspectual features and use of modal auxiliary verbs). 'Inclusive' definitions of Scots would include Standard Scottish English; 'exclusive' definitions would simply regard it as a bastardised English or hopelessly corrupted Scots.

Scotticisms, overt and covert Those expressions which are peculiar to **Scots**, and which are not part of the 'common core' of expressions shared with varieties of English. An 'overt' Scotticism is an expression that a speaker would recognise as Scots; for example, 'wee dram'. A 'covert' Scotticism is an expression which a speaker would not necessarily recognise as Scots; for example, 'stay' in 'where do you stay?' (= 'where do you live?').

script (see **schema**)

semantic density The extent to which borrowings, particularly **Latinisms**, increase the number of synonyms in a language variety. Expressions from other languages which are borrowed to increase the semantic density of a variety usually have an ornate, decorative or aesthetic quality. See **semantic range**.

semantic range The extent to which borrowings, particularly **Latinisms**, increase the number of concepts which can be expressed by a language variety. Expressions from other languages which are borrowed to increase the semantic range of a variety usually have no near-synonym in that variety. See **semantic density**.

semantics The study of the ways in which meaning is structured and expressed in a language variety. Semantics may focus on relations such as synonymy and antonymy, or it may be concerned with the ways in which people construct meanings from texts. (Compare **pragmatics**.)

semiotics The study of the systems of 'signs' in a culture. Semiotics includes the study of language, as one of the most complex and sophisticated sign-systems, but its range extends to any other cultural artefact or mode of behaviour which can carry meaning: for example, dress, body language, hair-style, musical preference etc.

slang Colloquial expressions, often of obscure origin, often short-lived, and usually socially stigmatised.

speech act theory A theory of language which focuses on aspects of its use rather than on its formal organisation. Specifically, speech act theory classifies utterances according to the types of behaviour which they accomplish. The basic act of uttering is a **locution** or a **locutionary act**, the act of uttering something that can be recognised as fitting into the conventional communicative system (say, a statement or a question) is an **illocutionary act** and the act of uttering something that elicits a response from a hearer is a **perlocutionary act**. Speech acts which aim to be perlocutionary might be explicit commands or requests, that is, direct **directives**, such as 'Open the window'; or they might be indirect **directives**, such as 'It's cold in here'. Both utterances would be intended to elicit the same response. Those speech acts which commit the speaker to certain types of action are called **commissives**, for example, 'I promise to pay the bearer five pounds'. Special types of speech acts are **performatives**, that is, acts which are accomplished through language; for example, a judge in a court dismisses a case by saying 'I dismiss this case'.

standard language   A variety of language which has become associated with certain prestigious social and institutional functions (for example, it will be used in mass-media communication, and it will be the medium in which official documents are written). **Scots** has never evolved a distinct, widely-accepted standard language, although some propose that **Lallans** should serve that role. See **dialect** and **Scots**.

stanza   A group of poetic lines, linked by a particular pattern of **rhyme**. Also, more generally, known as a 'verse'.

stereotype   (see **schema**)

stylistics   The study of style in language, usually but not exclusively literary style. In this, it is distinct from **literary linguistics** or **poetics**.

subclause   (see **clause**)

subject   (see **clause**)

suffix   (see **inflexion**)

syllable   A unit of speech, consisting of either one **vowel** or **consonant**, or a combination of a single vowel plus one or more consonants. Words may be single syllables or monosyllables, for example 'sang'; or they may be 'polysyllabic', for example 'hydroelectricity', which has seven syllables.

synonym   Expressions which are equivalent, or nearly equivalent in meaning. Few if any total synonyms exist; synonymous expressions usually differ in **register** or in **collocation**. For example, 'sofa' and 'couch' may be near-synonyms, but we would not speak of 'sofa potatoes' or 'casting sofa'.

syntax   The sequencing of words and phrases into larger grammatical units, such as **clauses** and sentences.

syntagmatic   The relationship which holds between items of language which combine with each other. For example, the phrases 'The boy' and 'is singing' in the sentence 'The boy is singing' are syntagmatically related: if one phrase changes (for example, if 'boy' is changed to 'boys'), then the other is affected ('is' must be changed to 'are'). Another way of putting this is to say that the items exist on the same **axis of combination**. See **paradigmatic**.

syntax   The sequencing of words and phrases into larger grammatical units, such as **clauses** and sentences.

tartanry   A **stereotype** of Scottish identity which privileges the romantic image of the highlander, usually in a kilt, and in a setting of mountain, loch and rugged glen.

tenor (see **register; metaphor**)

text A continuous, structured and coherent piece of language; the term often refers specifically to written language, although some theorists use 'text' and '**discourse**' synonymously.

theme (see **schema**)

think-aloud investigations A way of researching the strategies that readers use when they are constructing meaning from written texts: the readers are trained to 'think aloud' as they are processing the texts. The records of their reading (that is, the **protocols**) are then analysed to see, for example, how the readers use inferencing skills, presuppositions and background knowledge.

transitivity In traditional grammar, transitive **verbs** are those which are necessarily followed by **objects** (see **clause**). In Hallidayan linguistics, 'transitivity' is extended to include a discussion of the types of **process** which the verb phrase expresses (whether 'material', 'mental' or 'existential' etc.) and the kinds of participant which might be associated with each process-type. Transitivity analysis is a sensitive indicator of **ideology** and **point of view**.

variety of language (see **dialect**)

vehicle (see **metaphor**)

verb A part of speech which serves to express the occurrence of actions, or states. Main or 'lexical' verbs combine with 'auxiliary verbs' to form phrases which, in turn, function as **predicators** in the **clause**.

vernacular The language which is regarded as native or natural to a particular place. Can be used to distinguish **Scots** from Latin, the language of learning in medieval times; to distinguish spoken Scots from the **standard language** used in the present day.

vocative The form of language used to address someone directly.

voice (**active** and **passive**) A grammatical term, used to distinguish those **clauses** where the **subject** of the sentence coincides with the agent ('active' clauses such as 'The thief stole a valuable document') and those in which the subject coincides with the affected participant ('passive' clauses such as 'A valuable document has been stolen').

GLOSSARY OF SCOTS TERMS

ablaich	(= ablich)
ablich	worthless person; dwarf
abune	above
ackually	(= ackwallie)
ackwallie	actually
a-gley	awry
aiblins	perhaps
anerlie	only
antrin	(1) chance; (2) strange
ashet	oval serving-plate
assay	test
atweel	assuredly
ava	at all
awbodie	everybody
aye	(1) yes; (2) always
back of, the	just after (time)
baill	remorse
bairn	child
barrie	slang term of praise
big	build
blinterin	glimmering
booed	bowed
boudin	grievous
bourding	jesting
brae	hill; slope
bramble	blackberry, blackberry bush
breengin	rushing carelessly
brig	bridge
bubbly-jock	turkey-cock

bukkill	grasp
bunnet; bunnit	cap; lit. 'bonnet'
bunnit husslin	presenting a stereotypically working-class image
burn; burnie	stream
byrse	bristles (of beard)
canny	careful (usually with money)
certie	certainly
chiel	fellow
close	enclosure; entry to a tenement
coft	bought
convoy	companion
creische	grease; fat
cry	call, give a name to
culpable homicide	manslaughter
daill	distribute
dauner	stroll
delitabill	delightful
derne	darkness
devaul	stop
disjaskit	dejected
dispern	ward off
docken, scarcely worth a	hardly worth a thing
dolor	misery
dominie	teacher

douce	(1) gentle; (2) respectable	halsit	hailed
		handers	help
dram	a small alcoholic drink	haveril	chatterbox
		heildin	tilting
dree	suffer	hodge	twitch
dreich	miserable	hurdies	buttocks
drookit	drenched		
dwaibelt	enfeebled	ilka	each
dyoob	deep	ingle	hearth
		ithergates	elsewhere
ettle	attempt		
		kail	kale; cabbage
fash	bother	kecklin	cackling
fassoun	fashion	ken	know
fause-bounder	'gerrymander'; lit. 'false-boundary'	kittlin	(1) kitten; (2) brat
		ken	know
feart	afraid, frightened	kye	cattle
feint foondit	'damn all'		
feir, but	without equal	laldie, to gie it	to do something vigorously
fettelt	attended to the needs	lane, thy	alone
forbye	(adverb) addition ally; (prep.) except	lave	remainder
		leet	list
		leid	(1) language; (2) lead ('hate leid' = hot lead)
forfeuchan	exhausted		
fremmit	distant		
frimple-frample	random	limmer	rascal
fusion	energy	linty	linnet
		loon	boy
gait	(1) way; (2) street	lucerne	lamp
gallus	rascally; slang term of praise	lugs	ears
		lum	chimney
gang	go		
gar	cause (to)	makar	poet
get	offspring; brat	man (= maun)	
get aff with, to	seduce	maun	must
gigot chop	lamb chop	messages, to go the	to do the shopping
gin	if		
gloamin	twilight	midden	rubbish heap
glowmyng	scowling	mirl	tremble
gree, bear the	win the prize	mishanter	disaster
greet	weep	mowse	grimace; joke
		muckle	(1) much; (2) great
haar	sea mist		
hairst	harvest	nefelling	fisticuffs

neffis	fists	sassenachs	(1) lowlanders;
neuk	corner		(2) English
nickum	scamp	sauter	shrew
		scart	(1) scratch; (2) scrape
onding	downpour		together
orra	nondescript;	scaud	scald
	worthless	schoris	threatens
oxter	(n.) armpit; (v.)	sclent	slither
	embrace	sclenter	(1) loose stones;
			(2) stony hillside;
painch	entrails		(3) movement
paroakial	parochial	scoukin	scowling
parritch	porridge	scramble	the throwing of coins
patter	(1) fluency (of		to children at a
	speech); (2)		wedding
	Glaswegian Scots	scrievar	writer
pech	gasp	scrieve	write
piner	labourer, porter	scunner	(n.) loathing; some
pokey hat	ice-cream cone		thing disgusting;
polis	police		(v.) disgust
pow count	opinion poll	seiver	drain
preclair	illustrious	sensyne	
procurator	legal position,	(= sin syne)	
fiscal	similar to district	sharged	stunted
	attorney in the USA	sharn	dung; excrement
promp	assist	sheuch	ditch
puggie, fu as a	very drunk	shoodir	shoulder
puirtith	poverty	sic	such
		siccar	sure
quernstane	millstone	sich (= sic)	
quhilk	which	siller	money (= 'silver')
quine (also		simmet	vest, undershirt
quean)	girl; young woman	sin syne	ago
qweir	choir	skailt	spilt; emptied
		skint	(1) skinned;
rebiggin	rebuilding		(2) penniless
reek	(1) smoke; (2) smell	skyrie	bright, gaudy
reft	stole	smeddum	(1) fine powder;
rocket	rochet; a bishop's		(2) spirit, energy
	surplice	smoorichan	kissing; cuddling
rone pipes	drain pipes	smout	an insignificant
rowin	(1) rolling; (2)		person
	rowing (a boat)	sonsie	(1) pleasant; (2)
ryne	rind; bark		plump; (3) lucky
		soor-dook	a kind of sweet

spicket	tap	trencher	wooden serving-plate
sporran	leather pouch worn in front of a man's kilt		
		unca; unco	(adj.) strange; (adv.) to a remarkable degree
sporran heads	people who flaunt their Scottish identity		
		undeemous	incalculable
sprikklin	wriggling	unthirldom	'independence', literally 'unyokedom'
stellit	placed in position		
sterne	star		
stew	dust		
stey	steep	wabbit	exhausted
stievemakkin	making firm	wag-at-the-wa'	an uncased pendulum-clock
stookit sheaves	bundled-up sheaves of corn		
		wainz (= weans)	
stoot	stout	waistles	worthless
stravaigin	wandering	walin	choice; election
superne	above; supreme	wallydrag	contemptible person
suthfast	true	wamis	stomachs
sweir	reluctant	warstle	wrestle
swick	cheat	wean	child
syne	then	wee	small
		weedie	widow
tatties	potatoes	weel-faur'd	handsome
tent, tak	pay heed		
tern	pain	yark	tug
thae; they	those	yird	(1) earth; (2) grave
thairm	intestine	yistrene	yesterday evening
thir	these	yon	that (remote)
thon (= yon)			

BIBLIOGRAPHY

Agutter, A. (1988) 'Middle Scots as a Literary Language', in R. D. S. Jack (ed.), *The History of Scottish Literature*, vol. I, Aberdeen: Aberdeen University Press, pp. 13–25.

Aitken, A. J. (ed.) (1973) *Lowland Scots: Papers Presented to an Edinburgh Conference*, Edinburgh: Association for Scottish Literary Studies.

Aitken, A. J. (1977) 'How to Pronounce Older Scots', in A. J. Aitken et al. (ed.), *Bards and Makars* Glasgow: Glasgow University Press pp. 1–21.

Aitken, A. J. (1979) 'Scottish Speech: A Historical View, with Special Reference to the Standard English of Scotland', in Aitken and McArthur, (eds), pp. 85–119.

Aitken, A. J. (1983) 'The Language of Older Scots Poetry', in J. D. McClure (ed.), *Scotland and the Lowland Tongue* Aberdeen: Aberdeen University Press, pp. 18–49.

Aitken, A. J. (1984) 'Scottish Accents and Dialects', in Trudgill (ed.).

Aitken, A. J. (1985) Introduction to M. Robinson (ed.), *The Concise Scots Dictionary* Aberdeen: Aberdeen University Press, pp. ix–xvi.

Aitken, A. J. (1991) 'Progress in Older Scots Philology', *Studies in Scottish Literature* vol. XXVI, pp. 19–37.

Aitken, A. J. and T. McArthur (eds) (1979) *Languages of Scotland* Edinburgh: Chambers.

Aitken, A. J., A. McIntosh and H. Palsson (eds) (1971) *Edinburgh Studies in English and Scots* London: Longman.

Anderson, B. (1983) *Imagined Communities* London: Verso.

Anon, (ed.) (1995) *Collins Gem Scots Dictionary* London: Harper Collins.

Apple Computer, Inc. (1992) *Macintosh User's Guide* Cupertino, CA: Apple Computer, Inc.

Ash, B. (ed.) (1977) *The Visual Encyclopedia of Science Fiction* London: Pan.

Attridge, D. (1982) *The Rhythms of English Poetry* London: Longman.

Austin, J. L. (1962) *How to Do Things with Words* Cambridge, MA: Harvard University Press.

Beveridge, C. and R. Turnbull (1989) *The Eclipse of Scottish Culture: Inferiorism and the Intellectuals* Edinburgh: Polygon.

Block, E. (1986) 'The Comprehension Strategies of Second Language

Readers', *TESOL Quarterly* 20: 3 pp. 462–93.

Booth, W. C. (1961) *The Rhetoric of Fiction* Chicago: University of Chicago Press.

Brown, G. and G. Yule (1983) *Discourse Analysis* Cambridge: Cambridge University Press.

Brown, P. and S. C. Levinson (1987) *Politeness: Some Universals in Language Usage* Cambridge: Cambridge University Press.

Burton, D. (1982) 'Through Dark Glasses, Through Glass Darkly', in R. Carter (ed.), *Language and Literature* London: Allen and Unwin, pp. 195–214.

Cameron, D. (ed.) (1990) *The Feminist Critique of Language* London: Routledge.

Cameron, D. (1992) *Feminism and Linguistic Theory* 2nd edn, London: Macmillan.

Cameron, D. (1995) *Verbal Hygiene* London: Routledge.

Caughie, J. (1990) 'Representing Scotland: New Questions for Scottish Cinema', in Dick (ed.), pp. 13–30.

Coates, J. (1986) *Women, Men and Language* Cambridge: Cambridge University Press.

Cook, G. (1994) *Discourse and Literature* Oxford: Oxford University Press.

Cooper, R. (1989) *Language Planning and Social Change* Cambridge: Cambridge University Press.

Corbett, J. (1996) 'COMET and *The House Among the Stars*: Scottish Texts on the Internet', *The Glasgow Review* vol. 4, pp. 89–103.

Craig, C. (1983) 'Visitors from the Stars: Scottish Film Culture', *Cencrastus* 11, pp 6–11.

Craigie, W. and A. J. Aitken (eds) (1929–) *The Dictionary of the Older Scottish Tongue.*

Culler, J. (1975) *Structuralist Poetics* London: Routledge & Kegan and Paul.

Davies, F. (1995) *Reading* Harmondsworth: Penguin.

Dick, E. (ed.) (1990) *From Limelight to Satellite: A Scottish Film Book* London: BFI/SFC.

Donaldson, W. (1986) *Popular Literature in Victorian Scotland* Aberdeen: Aberdeen University Press.

Donaldson, W. (1989) *The Language of the People* Aberdeen: Aberdeen University Press.

Dorsch, T. S. (1968) 'Of Discretioun in Asking: Dunbar's Petitionary Poems', in A. Esch (ed.), *Chaucer und seine Zeit* Tübingen: Max Niemeyer, pp. 285–92.

Ellenberger, B. (1977) *The Latin Element in the Vocabulary of the Earlier Makars Henryson and Dunbar* Lund: C. W. K. Gleerup.

Fabb, N., D. Attridge, A. Durant and C. McCabe (1987) *The Linguistics of Writing* Manchester: Manchester University Press.

Fairclough, N. (1989) *Language and Power* Harlow: Longman.

Fetterley, J. (1978) *The Resisting Reader* Bloomington: Indiana University Press.

Fish, S. (1980) *Is There a Text in This Class?* Cambridge, MA: Harvard University Press.

Fowler, R. (1977, rev. 1983) *Linguistics and the Novel* London: Methuen/New Accents.

Fowler, R. (1990) *Language in the News* London: Routledge.

Gifford, D. (ed.) (1988) *The History of Scottish Literature* vol. 3 Aberdeen: Aberdeen University Press.

Gorlach, M. (ed.) (1985) *Focus on: Scotland* Amsterdam: John Benjamins.

Graham, J. J. (1979) *The Shetland Dictionary* Stornoway: Thule.

Grant, W. and D. Murison (eds) (1929–76) *The Scottish National Dictionary*.

Grice, P. H. (1975) 'Logic and Conversation', in P. Cole and J. H. Morgan (eds), *Syntax and Semantics III* New York: Academic Press.

Halliday, M. A. K. (1971) 'Linguistic Function and Style: An Inquiry into the Language of William Golding's *The Inheritors*', in S. Chatman (ed.) *Literary Style: A Symposium* London and New York: Oxford University Press, pp. 330–68.

Halliday, M. A. K. (1985) *An Introduction to Functional Grammar* London: Edward Arnold.

Halliday, M. A. K. and R. Hasan (1976) *Cohesion in English* London: Longman.

Haugen, E., J. D. McClure and D. S. Thomson (eds) (1981) *Minority Languages Today* Edinburgh: Edinburgh University Press.

Hodge, B. and G. Kress (1988) *Social Semiotics* Oxford: Polity/Blackwell.

Hoey, M. (1983) *On the Surface of Discourse* London: George Allen and Unwin.

Hough, G. (1969) *Style and Stylistics* London: RKP.

Hurford, J. and B. Heasley (1983) *Semantics: A Coursebook* Cambridge: Cambridge University Press.

Ibsch, E, D. H. Schram and G. J. Steen, GJ (eds) (1991) *Empirical Studies in Literature: Proceedings of the Second International Conference, Amsterdam 1989* Amsterdam: Rodopi.

Jack, R. D. S. (1971) *Scottish Prose 1550–1700* London: Calder and Boyars.

Jack, R. D. S. (1972) *The Italian Influence on Scottish Literature* Edinburgh: Edinburgh University Press.

Jakobson, R. (1960) 'Closing Statement: Linguistics and Poetics', in Sebeok (ed.), pp. 350–77.

Jones, C. (1995) *A Language Suppressed: The Pronunciation of the Scots Language in the Eighteenth Century* Edinburgh: John Donald.

Kay, B. (1986) *The Mither Tongue* London: Grafton.

Kirk, J. (1992/3) 'Computing and Research on Scots', *Scottish Language* 11/12 pp. 75–131.

Lakoff, G. (1987) *Women, Fire and Dangerous Things* Chicago: University of Chicago Press.

Lakoff, G. and M. Johnson (1980) *Metaphors We Live By* Chicago: University of Chicago Press.

Lakoff, G. and M. Turner (1989) *More Than Cool Reason* Chicago: University of Chicago Press.

Lakoff, R. (1973) 'The Language of Politeness, or Minding your P's and Q's', in *Papers from the Ninth Regional Meeting of the Chicago Linguistic Society* Chicago: University of Chicago Linguistics Department.

Leech, G. (1983) *Principles of Pragmatics* London: Longman.

Leech, G. (1987) *Meaning and the English Verb* London: Longman.

Leech, G. (1992) 'Pragmatic Principles in Shaw's *You Never Can Tell*', in Toolan (ed.), pp. 259–78.

Leith, D. (1983) *A Social History of English* London: Routledge.

Leonard, T. (1984) 'The Locust Tree in Flower, and Why it had Difficulty Flowering in Britain', in *Intimate Voices* Newcastle upon Tyne: Galloping Dog Press.

Letley, E. (1988a) *From Galt to Douglas Brown: Nineteenth Century Fiction and Scots Language* Edinburgh: Edinburgh University Press.

Letley, E. (1988b) 'Language and Nineteenth Century Scottish Fiction', in Gifford (ed.), pp. 321–36.

Levinson, S. C. (1983) *Pragmatics* Cambridge: Cambridge University Press.

Lewis, M. (1986) *The English Verb* Hove: Language Teaching Publications.

Little, W., H. W. Fowler and J. Coulson (1973) *The Shorter Oxford English Dictionary on Historical Principles* 3rd edn, rev. and ed. C. T. Onions, Oxford: Clarendon Press.

Loban, W. D. (1954) *Literature and Social Sensitivity* Champaign, IL: National Council of Teachers of English.

Lyall, R. J. (1994) 'Address to the Henryson Society' Dunfermline: Robert Henryson Society (unpublished talk).

Lyall, R. J. and F. Riddy (eds) (1981) *Proceedings of the Third International Conference on Scottish Language and Literature* Universities of Stirling and Glasgow.

Macafee, C. (1981) 'A Stylistic Analysis of Dunbar's "In Winter"', in Lyall and Riddy (eds). pp. 359–69.

Macafee, C. (1983) *Glasgow* Amsterdam: John Benjamins.

Macafee, C. (c. 1988) *Modern Scots* Unit 3A of M.Phil. in Scottish Literature; Department of Scottish Literature, University of Glasgow.

Macafee, C. (c. 1989) *Origins and Development of Older Scots* Unit 1A of M.Phil. in Scottish Literature; Department of Scottish Literature, University of Glasgow.

Macafee, C. (1992–3) 'A Short Grammar of Older Scots', *Scottish Language* vols 11/12, pp. 10–36.

Macafee, C. (1994) *Traditional Dialect in the Modern World: A Glasgow Case-Study* Frankfurt am Main: Peter Lang.

Macafee, C. and I. Macleod (eds) (1987) *The Nuttis Schell* Aberdeen: Aberdeen University Press.

McArthur, C. (1981–2) 'Breaking the Signs: "Scotch Myths" as Cultural Struggle', *Cencrastus* 7, pp. 21–5.

McArthur, C. (ed.) (1983a) *Scotch Reels: Scotland in Cinema and Television* London: BFI.

McArthur, C. (1983b) 'Scotland: The Reel Image', *Cencrastus* 11, pp. 2–3.

McArthur, T. (ed.) (1992) *The Oxford Companion to the English Language* Oxford: Oxford University Press.

Macaulay, R. K. S. (1977) *Language, Social Class and Education* Edinburgh: Edinburgh University Press.

Macaulay, R. K. S. (1991) *Locating Dialect in Discourse* Oxford: Oxford University Press.

MacCallum, N. and D. Purves (eds) (1995) *Mak it New* Edinburgh: Mercat Press.

McClure, J. D. (1979) 'Scots: Its Range of Uses', in Aitken and McArthur (eds), pp. 26–49.

McClure, J. D. (1981a) 'The Language of *The Entail*' *Scottish Literary Journal* VIII, pp. 50–1.

McClure, J. D. (1981b) 'Scottis, Inglis, Suddroun: Language Labels and Language Attitudes', in Lyall and Riddy (eds), pp. 52–69.

McClure, J. D. (1981c) 'The Synthesisers of Scots', in Haugen et al. (eds), pp. 91–9.

McClure, J. D. (ed.) (1983) *Scotland and the Lowland Tongue* Aberdeen: Aberdeen University Press.

McClure, J. D. (1988) *Why Scots Matters* Edinburgh: Saltire Society/Scots Language Society.

McClure, J. D. (1995) *Scots and its Literature* Amsterdam: John Benjamins.

McClure, J. D., A. J. Aitken and J. T. Low (1980) *The Scots Language* Edinburgh: Ramsay Head.

McCrone, D. (1992) *Understanding Scotland: The Sociology of a Stateless Nation* London: Routledge.

McCrone, D., A. Morris and R. Keily (1995) *Scotland – The Brand: The Making of Scottish Heritage* Edinburgh: Edinburgh University Press.

MacDiarmid, H. (1987) *A Drunk Man Looks at the Thistle* ed. K. Buthlay, Edinburgh: Scottish Academic Press.

McFadyen, N. L. (1975) 'The Sytlistic Influence of the Alliterative Tradition on the Poetry of William Dunbar', unpublished Ph.D. thesis, University of Florida.

Mackay, M. A. (1973) 'The Scots of the Makars', in Aitken (ed.), pp. 20–37.

Macleod, I. (ed.) (1990) *The Scots Thesaurus* Aberdeen: Aberdeen University Press.

Macleod, I. and P. Cairns (eds) (1993) *The Concise English–Scots Dictionary* Edinburgh: Chambers Harrap.

Malof, J. (1978) *A Manual of English Meters* Westport, CT: Greenwood Press.

Meurman-Solin, A. (1993) *Variation and Change in Early Scottish Prose* Helsinki: Suomalainen Tiedeakatemia.

Mills, S. (1995) *Feminist Stylistics* London and New York: Routledge.

Milroy, J. (1981) *Regional Accents of English: Belfast* Belfast: Blackstaff.

Montgomery, M., A. Durant, N. Fabb, T. Furniss and S. Mills (1992) *Ways of Reading* London: Routledge.

Morgan, E. (1992) *Edmond Rostand's Cyrano de Bergerac* Manchester: Carcanet.

Munro, M. (1985) *The Patter: A Guide to Current Glasgow Usage* Glasgow: Glasgow District Libraries.

Murison, D. (1977) *The Guid Scots Tongue* Edinburgh: Blackwood.

Murison, D. (1979) 'The Historical Background', in Aitken and McArthur (eds), pp. 2–13.

Myers, G. (1989) 'The Pragmatics of Politeness in Scientific Articles', *Applied Linguistics* 10:1, pp.1–23.

Nicolaisen, W. F. H. (1977) 'Line and Sentence in Dunbar's Poetry', in A. J. Aitken et al. (eds), *Bards and Makars* Glasgow: Glasgow University Press.

Orwell, G. (1946) 'Politics and the English Language', rep. in S. Orwell and I. Angus (eds) (1968) *The Collected Essays of George Orwell*, vol. 4 Harmondsworth: Penguin.

Palmer, F. (1979) *Modality and the English Verb* London: Longman.

Pratt, M. L. (1977) *Towards a Speech Act Theory of Literary Discourse* Bloomington: Indiana University Press.

Purves, D. (1993) Editorial, *Lallans* 41 (Mairtinmas), p. 4.

Quirk, R. and S. Greenbaum (1973) *A University Grammar of English* London: Longman.

Rankin J. M. (1988) 'Designing Thinking-Aloud Studies in ESL Reading', *Reading in a Foreign Language* 4(2), pp. 119–32.

Reid, D. (ed.) (1982) *The Party-Coloured Mind* Edinburgh: Scottish Academic Press.

Richards, I. A. (1929) *Practical Criticism* London: Routledge & Kegan Paul.

Richards, I. A. (1936) *The Philosophy of Rhetoric* Oxford: Oxford University Press.

Rimmon-Kenan, S. (1983) *Narrative Fiction: Contemporary Poetics* London: Methuen.

Robinson, M. (ed.) (1985) *The Concise Scots Dictionary* Aberdeen: Aberdeen University Press.

Rosenblatt, L. M. (1968) *Literature as Exploration* London: Heinemann.

Saussure, F. de (1916; 1974) *Course in General Linguistics* London: Fontana.

Schank, R. C. and R. Abelson (1977) *Scripts, Plans, Goals and Understanding* Hillsdale, NJ: Lawrence Erlbaum.

Scott, T. (1966) *Dunbar: A Critical Exposition of the Poems* Edinburgh: Oliver and Boyd.

Searle, J. R. (1969) *Speech Acts* London: Cambridge University Press.

Sebeok, T. A. (ed.) (1960) *Style in Language* Cambridge MA: MIT Press.

Short, M. H. (ed.) (1989) *Reading, Analysing and Teaching Literature* London: Longman.

Short, M. H. and W. van Peer (1989) 'Accident! Stylisticians Evaluate: Aims and Methods of Stylistic Analysis', in M. H. Short (ed.), pp. 22–72.

Simpson, J. A. and E. S. C. Weiner (eds) (1989) *The Oxford English Dictionary* 2nd edn, Oxford Clarendon Press.

Simpson, P. (1992) 'The Pragmatics of Nonsense', in Toolan (ed.), pp. 281–305.

Simpson, P. (1993) *Language, Ideology and Point-of-View* London: Routledge.

Sinclair, J. (1991) *Corpus, Concordance, Collocation* Oxford: Oxford University Press.

Skirrow, G. (ed.) (1983) 'Women, Women and Scotland: "Scotch Reels" and Political Perspectives', *Cencrastus* 11, pp. 3–6.

Smith, A. (1937) *The Wealth of Nations* ed. E. Cannan, New York: Random House.

Smith, A. (1983) *Lectures on Rhetoric and Belles Lettres* ed. J. C. Bryce, Oxford: Clarendon Press.

Smith, J. J. (1994) 'Norse in Scotland', *Scottish Language* 13, pp. 18–35.

Smith, J. J. (1995) *An Introduction to Older Scots* Department of English Language, University of Glasgow (mimeo).

Smith, J. J. (1996) 'Ear-Rhyme, Eye-Rhyme and Traditional Rhyme: English and Scots in Robert Burns's *Brigs of Ayr*', in *The Glasgow Review* 4, pp. 76–87.

Squire, J. R. (1964) *The Responses of Adolescents While Reading Four Short Stories* Champaign, IL: NCTE Research Report No. 2.

Steen, G. (1994) *Understanding Metaphor in Literary Texts* Harlow: Longman.

Templeton, J. (1973) 'Scots: An Outline History', in Aitken (ed.), pp. 4–19.

Thompson, D. (ed.) (1995) *The Concise Oxford Dictionary of Current English* 9th edn, Oxford: Clarendon Press.

Toolan, M. (ed.) (1992) *Language, Text and Context: Essays in Stylistics* London: Routledge.

Traugott, E. C. and M. L. Pratt, (1980) *Linguistics for Students of Literature* New York: Harcourt Brace Jovanovich.

Trudgill, P. (ed.) (1984) *Language in the British Isles* Cambridge: Cambridge University Press.

Trudgill, P. (1994) *Dialects* London: Routledge.

Tulloch, G. (1989) *A History of the Scots Bible* Aberdeen: Aberdeen University Press.

Wales, K. (1989) *A Dictionary of Stylistics* London: Longman.

Wareing, S. (1990) 'Women in Fiction: Stylistic Modes of Reclamation', in *Parlance* 2:2, pp. 72–85.

Wareing, S. (1994) 'And then he kissed her: The Reclamation of Female Characters to Submissive Roles in Contemporary Fiction', in K. Wales (ed.), *Essays and Studies 1994: Feminist Linguistics in Literary Criticism* Woodbridge: Boydell and Brewer, pp. 117–36.

Wells, J. C. (1982) *Accents of English* vols 1–3, Cambridge: Cambridge University Press.

Widdowson, H. G. (1975) *Stylistics and the Teaching of Literature* London: Edward Arnold.

Widdowson H. G. (1992) *Practical Stylistics* Oxford: Oxford University Press.

Wilson, J. R. (1966) *Responses of College Freshmen to Three Novels* Champaign, IL: NCTE Research Report No. 7.

Winter, E. (1977) 'A Clause-Relational Approach to English Texts', *Instructional Science* 6, pp. 1–92.

Winter, E. (1982) *Towards a Contextual Grammar of English* London: George Allen and Unwin.

Withers, C. (1992) 'The Historical Creation of the Scottish Highlands', in I. Donnachie and C. Whately (eds), *The Manufacture of Scottish History* Edinburgh: Polygon, pp. 143–56.

Wittig, K. (1958) *The Scottish Tradition in Literature* Edinburgh: Oliver and Boyd.

Young, D. (1946) *'Plastic Scots' and the Scottish Literary Tradition* Glasgow: William MacLellan.

Young, D. (1958) *The Puddocks* 2nd edn, Tayport: Douglas Young.

Youngson, M. (1992) 'A Plea for Respite from the "Aiblins" School', in *Chapman* 69–70, pp. 91–2.

Zettersten, A. (1979) 'On the Aureate Diction of William Dunbar', M. Chesnutt et al. (eds), in *Essays Presented to Knud Schibsbye* Copenhagen: Akademisk Forlag, pp. 51–68.

INDEX